The Collector's Dictionary of QUILT NAMES & PATTERNS

DOGWOOD BLOSSOM   See page 64.

The Collector's Dictionary of QUILT NAMES & PATTERNS

Yvonne M. Khin

Drawings by the Author and color photographs by Glen San Lwin

ACROPOLIS BOOKS LTD.
Washington, D.C. 20009

ACROPOLIS BOOKS LTD.
Colortone Building, 2400 17th St., N.W.
Washington, D.C. 20009

Printed in the United States of America by
COLORTONE PRESS, Creative Graphics Inc.
Washington, D.C. 20009

Book design by Robert Hickey.

Library of Congress Cataloging in Publication Data

Khin, Yvonne M. 1916-
  The Collector's Dictionary of Quilt Names and Patterns.

  Includes index.
  1. Quilting—Patterns, I. Title. II. Title:
Quilt names and patterns.
TT835.K47   1980   746.9'7041   80-14246
ISBN 0-87491-408-6
ISBN 0-87491-409-4 (pbk.)

DOUBLE PAEONY See page 186.

I would like to dedicate this book to the old-time quilters whose work never fails to inspire and encourage all newcomers to the ageless art of quilt making.

I would also like to include in this dedication the members of my family:

(1) my dear husband, U Khin, whose enthusiasm for quilting and designing new patterns, constant help, and severe criticism made this work possible,

(2) my mother, Mrs. Mae C. Christoffelsz, whose needlework inspired me to perfection and who has now caught the "bug" of quilting, and

(3) my sister-in-law, Daw Khin Nyunt, whose memory for quilt names and patterns far surpasses my own and whose unfailing help allowed the completion of this book and also those long-promised quilts for family and friends.

To all, my grateful and heartfelt thanks.

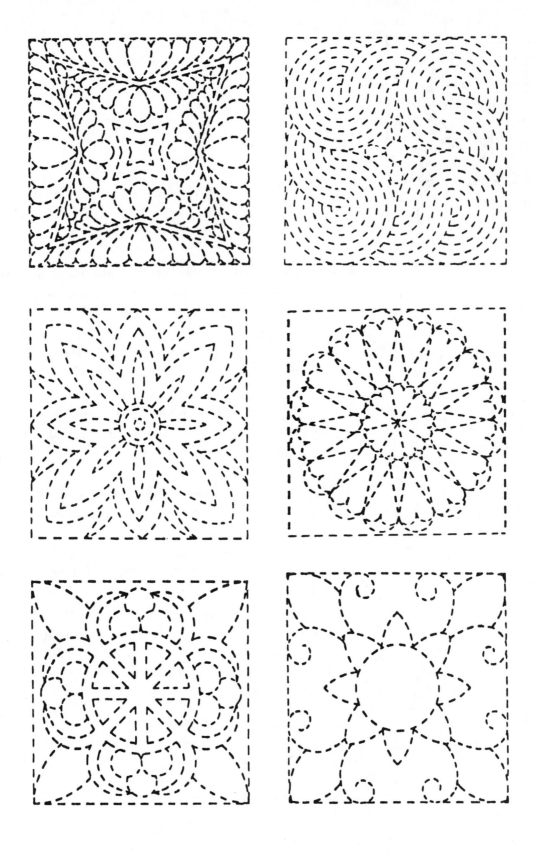

SWEET CLOVER See page 308.

Contents

POINTSETTIA   See page 347.

SUNBURST   See page 263.

TWIST PATCHWORK See page 392.

Acknowledgements

I would like to acknowledge the help and assistance of:

Mrs. Mabel Rea Wolf and Mrs. Mary Rea for allowing me to use their collection of "Laura Wheeler" quilt designs;

Mrs. Mollie Teter, a real quilt enthusiast, for her constant help in tracking down old or antique quilts and for suggestions on the patterns;

Mrs. Jo Denton Bryant for providing me with old pattern books and sources;

Mrs. Ma-Than-É Fend for help in editing the manuscript;

Mrs. Grace H. Coutant, ABAA, of Scotia, N.Y., for invaluable aid in searching for needlework books and magazines from which older quilt designs were obtained; and

Glen San Lwin, my brother and professional photographer, who has been responsible for taking photographs of quilts at quilt shows, exhibitions, museums, and private homes for my collection and study, and for the photographs of the quilts in my collection.

My thanks are also due to Mrs. Otto Grun for valuable suggestions and encouragement of quilt projects; and to Mrs. Mark O. Hatfield for searching and sending me an autographed first edition of Ruth E. Finley's *Old Patchwork Quilts and the Women Who Made Them*. This book solved many controversial questions on quilt names and patterns, as well as sources.

Mrs. Sandra Alpert, Editor of Acropolis Books Ltd., for her guidance in editing the manuscript and suggestions in the format of the book,

Mr. Robert Hickey, Art Department Director, Acropolis Books Ltd., for the excellent layout of the quilt diagrams and painstaking art work, and

Mr. Brett Ferrigan, Assistant Editor of Acropolis Books Ltd., for help in proofing the manuscript and his helpful suggestions.

INDIAN TRAIL   See page 417.

WILD ROSE See page 285.

ECCLESIASTICAL   See page 276.

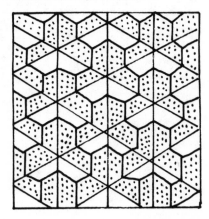

GOLDEN CORN See page 362.

Foreword

The recent resurgence of arts and handicrafts have been especially noticeable in quilt making, as more and more quilt groups and associations are springing up in various communities all over the United States. Quilting is one of the oldest American crafts—perhaps as old as America herself. When the early colonists came to the American continent, they brought with them the skills of their respective countries and put them to use when the occasion arose.

In the beginning the new country was cold, rugged, and hostile toward the colonists, whose first need was comfortable coverings to keep out the cold. The pioneer women brought out needle and thread and began making quilts by cutting painstakingly from bits and pieces of fabric they had brought with them, or salvaged from old clothes, and sewing the pieces into various designs. Hundreds of patterns were thus created as more and more quilts were made to keep the colonists warm.

It may perhaps be said that the history of America was unwittingly recorded in the quilt patterns and names. Many of these patterns do reflect the political, social, and religious thinking of the pioneer days.

Quilting, of course, is not a new form of art. Evidence of applique, pieced or patchwork, and quilted materials was found in the clothing of the people in the early civilizations of Babylonia,

China, Egypt, India, Palestine, and Syria dating several thousand years back.

Many museums and art galleries are now collecting old and famous quilts, while others are enlarging their exhibits to include contemporary quilts. Many famous quilts are still in private collections and appear only occasionally in private and public exhibitions. Nevertheless, it is a joy to look at a beautiful quilt and to admire the work that went into it, ranging on the average from 150 to 500 hours of painstaking labor on each quilt. Many times a needlewoman will come back from a show and feel the urge to make a quilt of her own; often she fails to remember the pattern or the name that fascinated her. (These days it is not surprising to find that men are quilting too.) "What's the name of this quilt?" "My grandmother made a similar quilt, but I've forgotten the name." These are some of the comments one often hears at quilts shows and exhibitions.

The need for *The Collector's Dictionary of Quilt Names and Patterns* is obvious. There may be many more American quilt patterns, but they have been lost or forgotten through the passage of time. I have included all of the quilt patterns that have written documentation. Thus, this work contains over 2,400 quilt patterns of traditional American quilts, a few of which have more than one name. I have excluded Hawaiian quilts from this collection, as they are comparatively contemporary and are in a class by themselves.

In order to identify quilt patterns, one has to consider the basic design of each single quilt. Quilt designs or patterns may be classified into patches that go into each basic design, such as the four-patch, the five-patch, the six-patch, the seven-patch, the sixteen-patch, etc., but quilts are not made from patches alone. Apart from patched quilts we have appliqued quilts, embroidered quilts, printed or stenciled quilts, etc. It would be cumbersome, therefore, to classify them into patches, which would not cover all the quilt patterns anyway. I have therefore rejected the patch

WHIRLING SWASTIKA   See page 354.

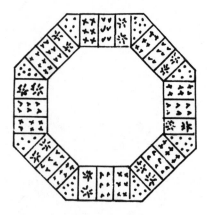

WEDDING RING TILE   See page 177.

SUNBURST   See page 150.

quilt idea and reverted to the age-old idea of identifying by the geometric designs method.

The three earliest basic designs in quilting are the square, the rectangle, and the diamond. The circle and the hexagon may be considered secondary designs, making a total of five basic designs. The various categories into which these designs may be divided form the entire range of quilting patterns. I have divided the quilting patterns into the following seven categories:

1. square   5. hexagon

2. rectangle   6. applique

3. diamond   7. miscellaneous.

4. circle

It is, of course, debatable whether certain designs should be listed in this or that category, but I have included in each category patterns that appear to me bested suited to that particular one. In my opinion, whatever design stands out as most striking should determine the category. For instance, a four-patch should obviously be in the square category. However, when a design contains may squares, rectangles or circles and it is hard to discern which one dominates, then I include it under "miscellaneous."

Square: Any pattern that obviously has a square or parts thereof will be considered a square. The original four-patch quilt is a square design.

Rectangle: Any pattern that contains a rectangle (a four-sided regular figure) or parts thereof, such as a log cabin quilt, will be shown under "rectangle."

Diamond: The diamond pattern looks like two isosceles triangles with a common base. Most star patterns are diamond patterns.

Circle: Circle patterns or parts thereof, such as arcs, will be considered circles. A Drunkard's Path quilt is obviously a circle pattern.

Hexagon: A six-sided pattern or parts thereof will be included in this category. The famous Grandmother's Flower Garden quilt or the Honeycomb quilts are typical examples.

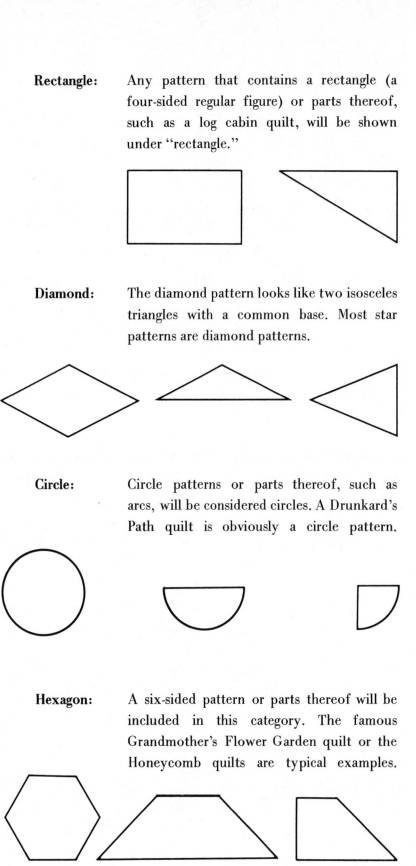

Applique: Applique quilts belong to a small group. No matter what particular design group an applique quilt may fall into, it is listed in this book in the applique section. Applique quilts deserve special treatment as many consider them to be the "cream of the quilts."

Miscellaneous: If you are not sure under which category a particular quilt design should fall, you will probably find it in the miscellaneous section.

Of course, many designs change their looks when different color arrangements are used. Patterns cut from the same design with different color arrangements—i.e., light and dark combinations achieved by setting the blocks diagonally, horizontally, and with sashes or strips—will appear as completely different designs. The basic design remains the same, and it is that basic design that one must look for in trying to determine under which particular category it might appear. If you do not find a design in one category, you will find it in another. Whereas one person may consider a design to be a geometric pattern, another may consider it otherwise. In any case, the quilt patterns in this book are so numerous and fascinating, you will want to look at each and every one.

This dictionary is also designed to be used with ease to find a particular pattern if you know its name. The names are listed in alphabetical order in the index.

I reduced all of the basic designs and drew them to approximately two-inch square blocks. Where quilts have more than one name, they are cross-referenced under each name, though not under each pattern. Remember that each pattern merely indicates the name of the quilt, that contains many blocks of that pattern. However, you may see quilts that contain many blocks with varying patterns, such as the Bridal quilt, Freedom quilt, Friendship quilt, Presentation quilt, Sampler quilt, etc. These may be a combination of various patterns.

This dictionary is not an instruction book. Many quilt books already on the market provide instructions. I hope that this venture will benefit quilters and that they will have as much fun out of it as I have had in compiling and preparing it.

DIADEM STAR See page 214.

ANGEL'S TRUMPET See page 341.

SQUARE DEAL See page 58.

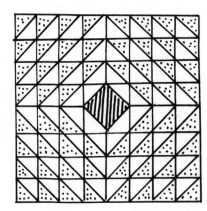

NOISY GEESE See page 364.

Some Helpful Publications

(In Chronological Order of Publication)

I am also grateful to the following for granting me permission to use patterns from their publications:

Quilt Patterns, Patchwork and Applique. St. Louis: Ladies Art Company, 1889.

Webster, Marie D. *Quilts: Their Story and How To Make Them.* New York: Doubleday, Page and Company, 1915.

Sexton, Carlie. *Early American Quilts.* Southampton, New York: Cracker Barrel Press, 1924.

Sexton, Carlie. *Old Fashioned Quilts.* Des Moines: (Publisher unknown), 1928.

Sexton, Carlie. *Yesterday's Quilts in Homes of Today.* Des Moines: (Publisher unknown), 1930.

Bannister, Barbara. *Grandmother Clark's Patchwork Quilt Designs, Books 20 and 21.* Alanson, Michigan: Needlecraft Books, 1973, (reprinted from 1930's).

McKim, Ruby Short. *One Hundred and One Patchwork Patterns.* Independence, Missouri: McKim Studios, 1931.

Hall, Carrie A. and Kretsinger, Rose G. *The Romance of the Patchwork Quilt in America.* Idaho: The Caxton Printers Limited, 1935.

Danner, Scioto Imhoff. *Mrs. Danner's Quilts, Books Nos. 1 and 2.* El Dorado, Kansas: (Publisher unknown), 1934.

Robertson, Elizabeth Wells. *American Quilts.* New York: The Studio Publications, Inc., 1948.

Ickis, Marguerite. *The Standard Book of Quilt Making and Collecting.* New York: Dover Publications, Inc., 1949.

Peto, Florence. *American Quilts and Coverlets.* New York: Chanticleer Press, 1949.

Danner, Scioto Imhoff. *Mrs. Danner's Quilts, Book No. 3.* Wichita, Kansas: McCormick-Armstrong Co., Ltd., 1954.

Danner, Scioto Imhoff. *Mrs. Danner's Quilts, Book No. 4.* Emporia, Kansas: (Publisher unknown), 1958.

Danner, Scioto Imhoff. *Mrs. Danner's Quilts, Book No. 5.* Emporia, Kansas: (Publisher unknown), 1970.

Martens, Rachel. *Modern Patchwork.* Philadelphia: Farm Journal, Inc., 1970.

Ericson, Helen. *Helen's Book of Basic Quiltmaking.* Emporia, Kansas: (Publisher unknown), 1973.

Gutcheon, Beth. *The Perfect Patchwork Primer.* New York: David McKay Company, Inc., 1973.

Household Magazines.

Needlecraft Magazines (later known as *Needlecraft—The Home Arts Magazines).*

Woman's World Magazines.

Note: These old magazines are too numerous to list but where a quilt pattern is shown, the publication date of the source magazine is shown.

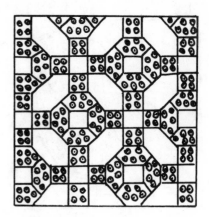

PUZZLE TILE   See page 59.

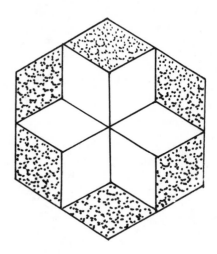

TEXAS STAR   See page 278.

LITTLE BEECH TREE   See page 117.

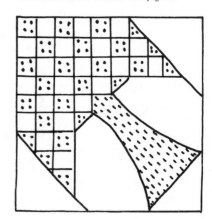

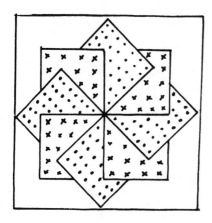

TWISTING STAR   See page 149.

Author's Note

I have recorded all of the available anecdotes about the patterns and sources in this book. There is no known history for many of the popular quilt designs, many have passed down through generations of quilters leaving only their visual imprint. However, if any of my readers discover additional anecdotes, please pass them along to me as I always wish to expand my collection.

Please note that the source beneath the pattern is always the first company which published the pattern. Additional listings indicate later sources. "Also" introduces alternate names for the pattern, and the comments below tell about its history, if any historical material is available. Where I have listed an individual's name, it refers to the quilt designer who designed the pattern.

CALIFORNIA STAR   See page 165.

THE LITTLE GIANT See page 221.

Introduction

Having been a needlewoman from early school days, I became fascinated with the art of quilting when I first came to the United States of America. I came from a warm Asian country—Burma—where quilts were not needed and consequently I was not exposed to quilting. When my favorite aunt settled down with her husband in Scotland, after the war, her need for a quilt became acute during one severe winter. Because there was only one fireplace in her home and no central heating I wanted to give her an American quilt as a present. I chose a "Tumbler" pattern for her quilt, but I could not find a suitable quilter to finish the quilting. Eventually I decided to do it myself. I found quilting relaxing, and I enjoyed watching quilts grow from start to finish.

That was in the late 1960's and I have been quilting ever since. As my knowledge of quilts and quilt patterns grew, I began to collect antique quilts for study. I then started a reference library with a few cards with patterns and quilt names and I carried my card-index box wherever I went—to quilt shows, exhibitions, auctions, garage sales, flea markets, etc. Very soon my card-index box overflowed and when I began getting inquiries regarding quilt names and patterns, I decided to edit my reference cards, put them into book form and to call the book *The Collector's Dictionary of Quilt Names and Patterns.*

Financial limitations and the difficulty I encountered finding an artist to draw the hundreds of patterns I had now collected, forced me to collect enough courage to draw all the patterns myself. I would not like to take all the credit, however, because my husband, U Khin, who is also an accomplished quilter, stood by me and helped me draw to scale those intricate patterns which I could not fathom.

It is my sincere hope that this collection of quilt names and patterns will benefit quilters who would like to look up names and patterns or to form ideas for the quilts they may attempt to make.

Yvonne M. Khin

Yvonne M. Khin

Bethesda, Maryland

DOGWOOD BLOSSOM　See page 64.

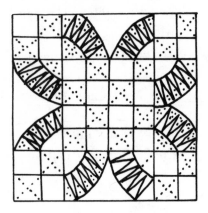

PICKLE DISH　See page 239.

ELECTRIC FANS　See page 57.

STAR AND PLANETS   See page 231.

Origin of Quilt Names

Mother Nature has always been a source of human inspiration for the forms used in all kinds of crafts. Animals, flowers, trees, butterflies, and colors from nature have been the source for creative expressions. Early American quilts reflect nature's inspiration. Feelings for religion, history, tradition, and the environment also creep into the artistic endeavors of the early Americans. The *Sunburst* (sun), *Ocean Waves* (ocean), *Bear's Paw* (animal), *Lincoln's Platform* (politics), *Coxcomb* (flower), *Cherries* (fruit), *Crown of Thorns* (religion), and *World Without End* (Bible) patterns are good examples.

Some popular quilt patterns have many names because names have been changed with the locale, tradition and events of the time. For instance, one quilt pattern when pieced in most color combinations is called *Shoo Fly* but when it is green and yellow pieced with white, it is renamed *Chinese Coin.*

The diamond pattern for stars called *Star of Lemoyne* was named for the Le Moyne brothers who settled in Louisiana in 1699 and founded the city of New Orleans. In the North, the name of the pattern was corrupted and shortened to *Lemon Star* due to the difficult pronunciation of the French name.

The manipulation of patterns is seen in the transformation of the *Jacob's Ladder* pattern which dates from the pre-Revolutionary days. This original design is made in only two tones— very dark and very light patches—since the fundamental idea is a dark ladder running up and down or diagonally across the quilt. The same block pattern using the reverse light and dark patches and adding a third intermediate color is called *Stepping Stones* in Virginia and New England; the *Tail of Benjamin's Kite* in Pennsylvania; the *Underground Railroad* in the West, and the *Trail of the Covered Wagon* or *Wagon Tracks* in the prairie states.

Economic conditions, climatic variations, and the mood of the people also contributed to changes in quilt making. When the pioneers first arrived in the Eastern region, they had to fight the cold by quickly making quilts from bits and pieces of material which was usually in short supply. As years went by and time and materials became increasingly available, the number of quilts became abundant and their quality improved. Applique quilts, which used greater varieties and quantities of material, were preferred over the traditional pieced quilts, and people had time to employ more sumptuous quilting stitches and designs.

American quilts are generally categorized into five distinct periods. First, the Colonial period when the quilts somewhat reflected the crafts of the lands from which these quilt makers had come; then the Revolutionary era reflecting French accents, flower sprays cut from *toile* and appliqued on the background, depicting tribute to gallant allies; then the Pioneer period depicting the winning of the West up to the time of the gold rush days of '49; then the Civil War era of the 1850's and 1860's; and finally the Centennial period.

AIRCRAFT QUILT   See page 109.

WHITE ROSE   See page 238.

PINEAPPLE   See page 179.

MONKEY WRENCH See page 387.

A Bit About Quilting

The many quilt patterns and names in this book may inspire you to create a quilt yourself. Piecing a quilt is not particularly difficult; it only requires accuracy, patience, and some sewing ability.

First select a design—either purchase a pattern, borrow one from a friend, or enlarge one from a magazine or book.

Wash all material before using, and be sure to cut all pieces accurately. From your quilt pattern cut a master pattern or template for each piece, using cardboard, pressboard, or even sandpaper. For patch or pieced patterns, lay this template on the wrong side of the material and mark around it with a pencil. When cutting, allow for all seams. You may like a three-eighth-inch or a one-quarter-inch seam allowance. The two pieces to be joined must be accurately placed and sewn together.

To estimate the amount of material required for each color in the pattern, count the pieces of that color in the patch and lay the templates for those pieces on a sample strip of paper the size of one-quarter of a yard of material. (If the material you plan to use is 36 inches wide, your sample strip would be 36″ x 9″.) Trace as many pieces on this sample strip as you can. Multiply the number of pieces of that particular color in each patch by the number of patches required for the quilt top. This will give you the number of pieces of that color in the finished quilt. Divide the number obtained by the number of pieces you could cut from the sample strip and then divide by 4, which gives you the yardage of that color you will need to purchase. Estimate each color separately.

For applique or "laid-on" quilts, cut the patterns and estimate in the same way as for a pieced quilt. When cutting the patches, lay the template on the right side of the material. This will serve as a guide for turning under the edges. Baste the color patches onto the design; then turn and hem the edges neatly with matching color thread. Keep the work flat while basting the applique.

To ensure that the pattern is correct, it is advisable to make up a sample square or block before attempting to cut out all the patches.

Quilts should be securely sewn because of the strain placed on them in the quilting process.

There are many ways of setting a quilt top together—the blocks may be all the same for an allover effect, or they may be alternated with squares of white or colored material or strips of one or more colors. Examine old quilts to give you an idea of what type of setting to choose for your top.

The backing is the bottommost layer of the quilt. It can be made of muslin or other firm material. Some backs are pieced from remnants. Muslin sheets can also be used. Choose a color that is compatible with the quilt top.

Between the top and the bottom is the filler of cotton or polyester batting. The quilting stitches hold the filler in place.

The quilting stitch is a fairly small running stitch through three layers of material: the pieced or appliqued top, the batting, and the backing.

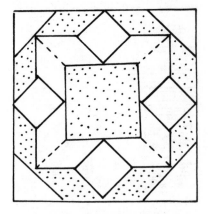

BATON ROUGE BLOCK   See page 66.

FULL BLOWN ROSE   See page 287.

WEAVING PATHS   See page 436.

THE BASKET   See page 46.

OKLAHOMA SUNBURST   See page 258.

RIGHT ANGLES PATCHWORK
See page 445.

The raw edges of the completed quilt must be bound. A narrow edge of backing can be turned over the top and hemmed down, or the edges of the back and top can be turned in and slip stitched together. Commercial bias binding or binding you make yourself in a contrasting color can also be used for this purpose.

Finally, embroider or quilt in your name and the date the quilt was completed.

There are already quilt books available that tell you how to enlarge a pattern for your own quilt. If you are interested, this book can be a "gold mine" from which you can enlarge as many patterns as you desire. If you are not too skilled at such work, you can find someone else to enlarge a pattern for you or you may order a particular pattern from a large quilt accessories store, asking for it by the right name. In addition, you may be able to order the required templates, if you so desire, from stores that specialize in templates. One such store is run by Roy Daniel, Tinsmith, 10 Union Street, Camden, Maine 04843. Better still, if you want a quilt made for you, you can have it done by those who are in the quilt business.

The following is a short bibliography of books and magazines giving instruction in quilting:

Gutcheon, Beth, *The Perfect Patchwork Primer.*

Ickis, Marguerite, *The Standard Book Of Quilt Making And Collecting.*

Lady's Circle Patchwork Quilts—published four times a year by Lopez Publications, Inc., 23 West 26th Street, New York, N.Y. 10010.

McKim, Ruby Short, *One Hundred And One Patchwork Patterns.*

Puckett, Marjorie, & Giberson, Gail, *Primarily Patchwork.*

Quilt—published four times a year; Harris Publications, Inc., 79
Madison Avenue, New York, N.Y. 10016.

Quilters Newsletter; Leman Publications, Box 394, Wheat Ridge,
Colorado 80033.

CHINESE FAN   See page 248.

SNOWFLAKE   See page 368.

MOTHER'S FANCY STAR   See page 87.

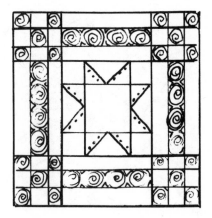

JONQUILS   See page 296.

Helpful Quilting Terms

The terms *quilt* and *counterpane* are used interchangeably to mean a bed cover. The counterpane has always been the spread used on the top of a bed, while the quilt could double as an extra blanket.

The **top** may be pieced work, applique or embroidered or just a single piece of cloth.

The **back** or **lining** and the **batting, wadding, filler,** or **interlining** are the necessary parts of a quilt.

To **piece** means to sew small patches of material together with narrow seams.

To **applique** is to lay smaller patches of cloth on blocks or on a single piece of cloth and to hem or button-hole these to secure them. Applique is also referred to as **laid-on work.** Some tops are entirely pieced or appliqued, while many combine both techniques.

A **block** is a pattern composed of patches, either pieced or appliqued.

To **set together** means to sew completed blocks together to form a top. This can be done by combining the blocks with plain squares, strips, or sashes.

To **mark** is to trace on the fabric top the design to be quilted.

Putting in is securing the edges of the back and top to the quilt frame between which the filler, batting, or wadding is evenly spread.

To **quilt** means to stitch or sew together at frequent intervals in order to hold in place the several layers of cloth and filler.

Rolling means turning the two end frames over and over in order to roll up the quilted portions so that the unquilted portions of the quilt can be reached for quilting.

Taking out means removing the completely stitched quilt from the frame.

A **template** is a piece of metal, wood, plastic, or cardboard made to the actual size of a pattern and used as a guide to cut accurate fabric patches for piecing or appliqueing.

Binding means finishing the raw edges of a completed quilt.

LEMON STAR   See page 159.

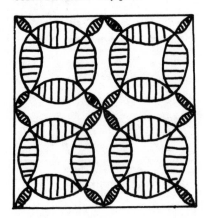

ORANGE PEEL   See page 233.

STAR TULIP   See page 142.

ALL TANGLED UP See page 433.

Types of Quilts

Album Quilt—composed of individual quilt blocks made by different people and then joined together to form a single quilt. The themes may be completely different from one another, the designs and colors being left to the individual contributors. This kind of quilt is often presented as a token of esteem to a deserving friend or distinguished person.

Autograph Quilt—usually made up of individual blocks, featuring signatures that are written in or embroidered over.

Begger Block—usually designed of scrap pieces of material begged from friends and neighbors.

Bride's Quilt—a quilt using heart designs. These designs were used exclusively in this quilt since it was considered unlucky for young girls to use the heart in any other quilt in order to avoid a broken engagement.

Crazy Quilt—irregular shaped bits and pieces of material joined together at random in a jigsaw puzzle fashion and then attached to a foundation block. The patches are usually satin, silk, or even velvet and are generally embellished with sumptuous embroidery work.

Freedom Quilt—created specially to commemorate the coming of legal age of a boy—his twenty-first birthday. As his special girlfriends came to congratulate him, they presented him with the Freedom Quilt made of scraps from their own prettiest gowns or specially made blocks. Eventually the girl he married would acquire it.

Friendship Quilt—similar to the Album Quilt and Presentation Quilt and usually presented as a going-away present or wedding gift or to commemorate a special occasion.

Medallion Quilt—may be either pieced or appliqued. Usually a large central theme or motif of printed chintz, applique, or embroidery is chosen, or a commemorative handkerchief or scarf may even be used. Strips of pieced or appliqued material are added around the central motif to form concentric rings. The strips could have corner blocks of various patterns depending on the choice of the quilt maker. Skill and coordination of colors are needed to make the result a work of artistic beauty.

Presentation Quilt—similar to the Album Quilt and usually presented to a local dignitary or minister and his wife.

Scrap Quilt—as the name suggests, usually made of leftover scraps of fabric joined together in random fashion.

Scripture Quilt—made of blocks containing quotations from the Bible, a verse, or even admonitions written in indelible ink or embroidered.

LILY POOL   See page 158.

GOLDEN WEDDING RING   See page 240.

MAYFLOWER   See page 56.

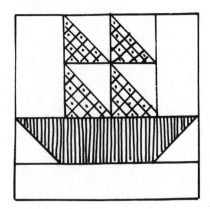

PLATE 1 **BARBARA FRITCHIE STAR**

Courtesy of Mr. & Mrs. G.F. Meakes

Pieced and quilted by Yvonne M. Khin. When the Confederate troops occupied Frederick, Maryland during the Civil War, they received a cool welcome by the citizens who minded their own affairs but tried not to offend the Rebels. To display a Union flag was to court trouble as also to speak sympathetically of the Union cause. This did not disturb the 95-year old Barbara Fritchie, who did not conceal her sympathies nor the flag — both were for the Union! When the Southern troops began to leave the city westward along Patrick Street directly past her house she stood waving the Union flag at them. Neither threats nor persuasions could move Barbara Fritchie to yield her flag to the Confederates. Finally an officer ordered that she be permitted to wave her flag as long as she pleased without further molestation. This design was dedicated to Barbara Fritchie for her heroism and patriotism to the Union.

PLATE 2 **STATE BIRDS OF AMERICA**

Embroidered and quilted by U Khin. Colors of the birds researched from Audubon bird books.

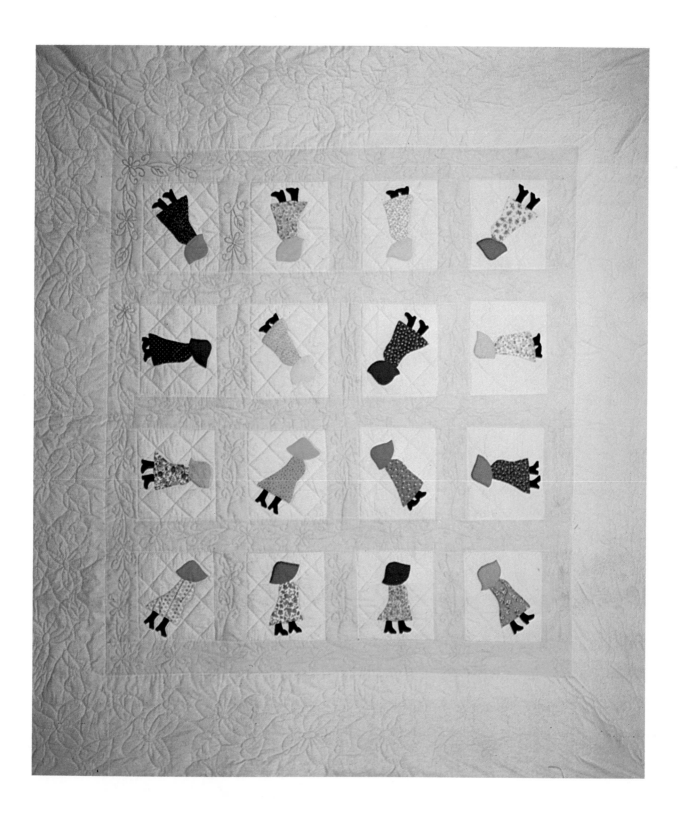

PLATE 3 **LITTLE LADIES**

Appliqued by Yvonne M. Khin and quilted by Daw Khin Nyunt.

PLATE 4 **LOG CABIN — LIGHT AND DARK**

Collection of the Khins

Pieced and quilted by U Khin in 1975.

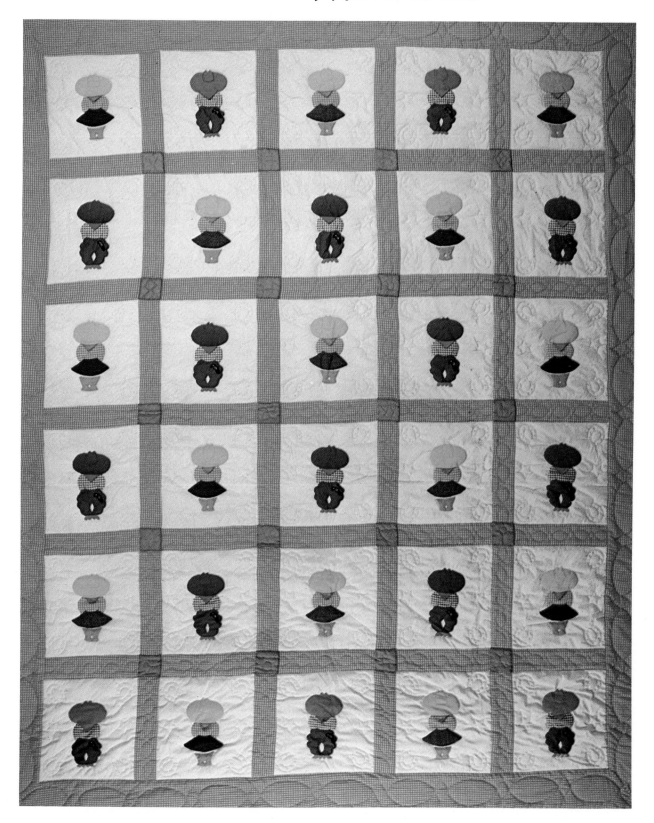

PLATE 5 **COWBOY AND COWGIRL**

Courtesy of Miss DeeDee Dalgarn

Appliqued and quilted by Yvonne M. Khin. The various cattlebrands were used as the quilting motifs.

PLATE 6 **PANDAS**

Designed, appliqued and quilted by U Khin. Each panda has a different expression.

PLATE 7   **CHIMNEY SWEEP**

Reproduced from an antique quilt made in New England in the 1860's. Pieced by Yvonne M. Khin and quilted by U Khin.

BUTTERFLY AT THE CROSSROADS
See page 73.

Quilt Collecting Today

Many people have been collecting quilts for ages. If you are a late comer, don't despair. Better late than never.

Old quilts are still available in the United States. They are not easily and conveniently available in urban areas, however, and you might have to travel into the country to make your "find."

Old quilts are still being discovered in odd places and circumstances. Search the countryside; visit wayside stalls, flea markets, country stores, and auctions. If you don't see any quilts, ask whether there are any addresses you can look up. If you are driving around in the country, look at clotheslines; you may find a freshly laundered quilt drying in the breeze—especially during late spring and summer.

It may also be possible for you to find unfinished tops and blocks sewed together but not quilted, or even batches of cut pieces ready to be pieced, appliqued or quilted into a master piece.

If you decide not to attempt the quilting yourself, ask at a church sewing group or a country store for the name of an old-time quilter who might finish the quilt for you.

Whether you are looking for a pieced quilt, an applique quilt, an embroidered quilt, or whatever, you should first be attracted to it visually. It should have the kind of appeal that makes you turn around and look at it again as you are walking away from it. Does it show a feeling for color, form, or line? You may then approach it and look at the fabric. If you know fabric, you should be able to guess its age, condition and how long it will last. When you are satisfied with the condition of the material, you should examine the way the quilt is put together and especially how well the stitches were executed. A quilt must not only be visually pleasing; it must be elegant and sophisticated and show taste and ingenuity.

Some contemporary quilts also are extremely beautiful and they should not be overlooked for your collection. After all, in time they may also find honored places among the antiques.

Quilts—any kind of quilts—are expressive of their time, and each is created for a purpose. A collection of quilts is therefore like a history book that reveals much more information than meets the eye. A "gold mine" for researchers, such collections should occasionally be displayed or exhibited for the benefit of all quilt lovers.

When such materials as calico from India, silks from Europe, and finer cottons from England reached the New World, quilts reflected this lavish abundance. There were silk comforters, quilted satin coverlets, and velvet pillows. Even the discarded cutting from dresses and clothing became Crazy Quilts in which the pieces of valuable fabrics were not cut to standard sizes to make regular pieced quilts but were joined together as they were with elaborate embroidery stitches.

Regionally, New England produced somewhat subdued and modest quilts, perhaps because it was colder and salvageable materials were scarcer. The Amish settlers showed more somber tastes, while the less orthodox Dutch often produced quilts in gay and sometimes bold unconventional colors. The South produced elegant quilts with well-sewn stitches; the availability of household help gave the women more time to be creative.

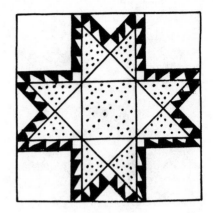

PINE CONE   See page 164.

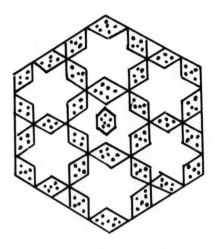

BOUTONNIERE   See page 275.

MOON FLOWER   See page 331.

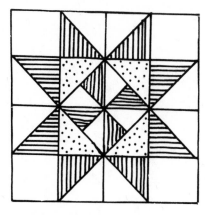

MARTHA WASHINGTON STAR
See page 65.

Square

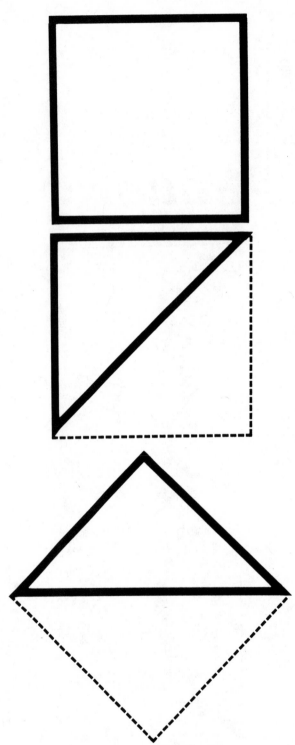

Square: Any pattern that obviously has a square or parts thereof will be considered a square. The original four-patch quilt is a square design.

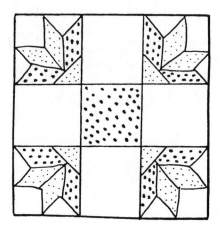

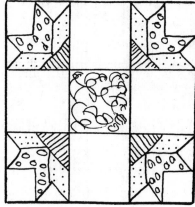

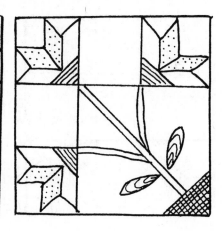

SAGE BUD

The Romance of the Patchwork Quilt in America, page 96, No. 13

TURKEY TRACKS

The Standard Book of Quilt Making and Collecting, page 232

NOON DAY LILY

Ladies Art Company, No. 51

One Hundred and One Patchwork Patterns, page 67

NOON DAY LILY

Ladies Art Company, No. 131 Also **DUCK PADDLE**

FANNY'S FAN

Grandmother Clark's Patchwork Quilt Designs, Book 20, 1931

FANCY FLOWERS

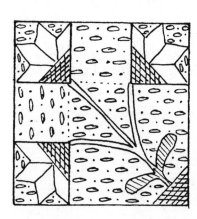

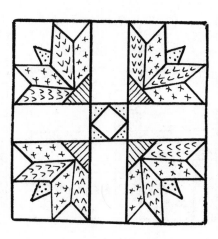

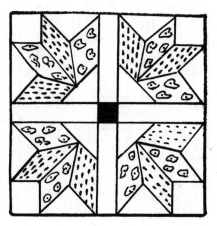

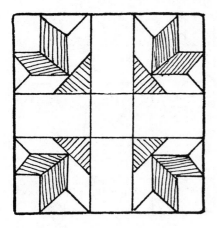 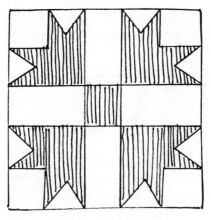 

GOOSE TRACKS

Ladies Art Company, No. 156

GOOSE TRACKS

One Hundred and One Patchwork Patterns, page 113
The Romance of the Patchwork Quilt in America, page 74, No. 3

BEAR'S FOOT

Ladies Art Company, No. 357

The Romance of the Patchwork Quilt in America, page 78, No. 20.
This name was used after 1850 in Western Pennsylvania and Ohio. Known as **DUCK'S FOOT-IN-THE-MUD** in Long Island and **HAND OF FRIENDSHIP** by the Quakers of Philadelphia.

The Standard Book of Quilt Making and Collecting, page 228

BEAR'S TRACK

BEAR'S PAW

The Perfect Patchwork Primer, page 32.
Also **BEAR'S PAW**

DUCK'S FOOT

 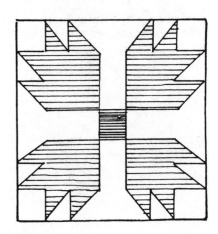

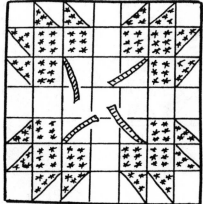

THE MAPLE LEAF

AUTUMN LEAF

*Ladies Art Company, No. 502
Old Patchwork Quilts and the
Women Who Made Them,* page
116

AUTUMN LEAF

*The Romance of the Patch-
work Quilt in America,* page
102, No. 16
Also **MAPLE LEAF**

*Ladies Art Company, No. 387
One Hundred and One Patchwork Patterns,* page 39
*The Romance of the Patch-
work Quilt in America,* page
126, No. 12*

GRAPE BASKET

*Ladies Art Company, No. 59
The Romance of the Patch-
work Quilt in America,* page
126, No. 1*

CAKE STAND

*The Standard Book of Quilt
Making and Collecting,* page
228

PEONY

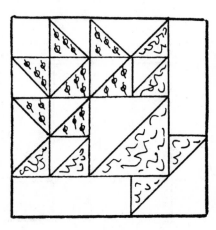

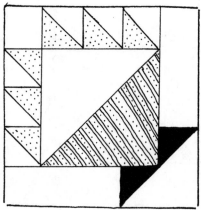

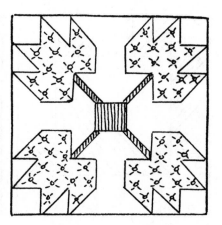

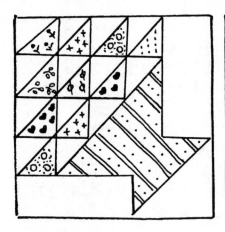

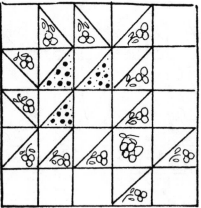

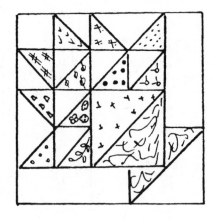

FLOWER POT

The Romance of the Patchwork Quilt in America, page 127, No. 17

FRUIT BASKET

The Perfect Patchwork Primer, page 62

MAY BASKET

Woman's World, February 1928, page 30
One Hundred and One Patchwork Patterns, page 108

The Household Magazine, November 1929, page 38

FRUIT BASKET

Needlecraft Magazine, April 1929, page 7

FLOWER BASKET

FRUIT BASKET

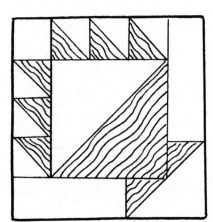

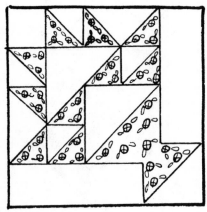

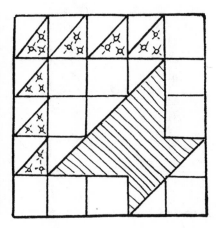

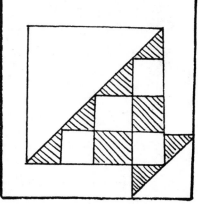

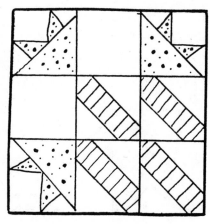

BASKET OF ORANGES

One Hundred and One Patchwork Patterns, page 85
The Romance of the Patchwork Quilt in America, page 126, No. 4

GRANDMOTHER'S BASKET

The Romance of the Patchwork Quilt in America, page 126, No. 3

TASSEL PLANT

Ladies Art Company, No. 389
The Romance of the Patchwork Quilt in America, page 106, No. 1

(Women's Christian Temperance Union)
Ladies Art Company, No. 161

W.C.T. UNION

Ladies Art Company, No. 517
The Romance of the Patchwork Quilt in America, page 106, No. 3
Nancy Cabot

ROSEBUD

Nancy Page, 1920-30

OZARK MAPLE LEAVES

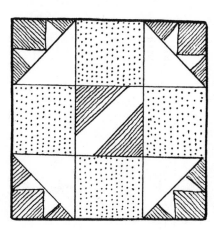

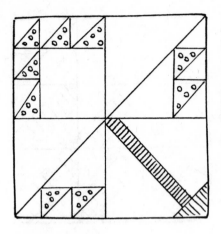

ENGLISH IVY

Kansas City Star, 1931
*The Romance of the Patch-
work Quilt in America*, page
102, No. 6

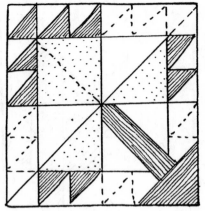

TREE OF LIFE

Nancy Cabot

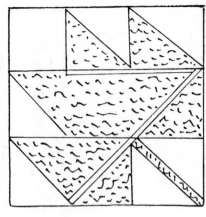

APPLE LEAF

Kansas City Star, 1935

Kansas City Star, 1931
*The Romance of the Patch-
work Quilt in America*, page
72, No. 15
*The Standard Book of Quilt
Making and Collecting*, page
234

CACTUS FLOWER

*One Hundred and One Patch-
work Patterns*, page 54
Also **AUTUMN LEAF**

MAPLE LEAF

The Perfect Patchwork Primer,
page 53

DAY LILY BLOCK

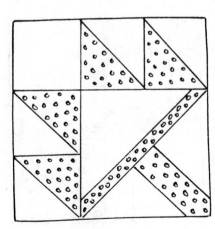

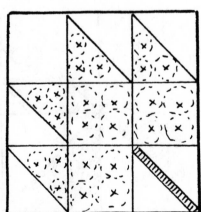

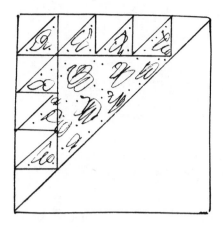

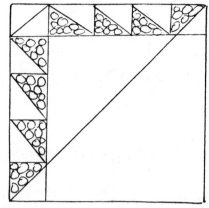

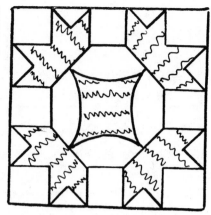

SAWTOOTH

The Perfect Patchwork Primer,
page 85

STAR OF HOPE

Ladies Art Company, No. 523
*The Romance of the Patch-
work Quilt in America,* page
58, No. 18

HANDS ALL ROUND

Ladies Art Company, No. 402
*The Romance of the Patch-
work Quilt in America,* page
94, No. 18
*The Standard Book of Quilt
Making and Collecting,* page
239
Stated to be a dance figure
popular in the pioneer days
in the Middle West.

*Grandmother Clark's Patch-
work Quilt Designs,* Book 20,
1931

Nancy Cabot

POT OF FLOWERS

BASKET OF TULIPS

THE BRIDE'S BOUQUET

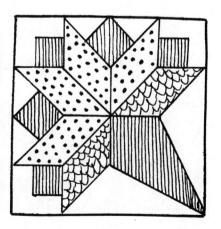

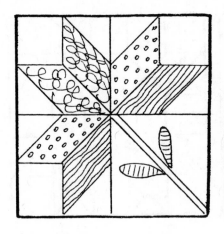

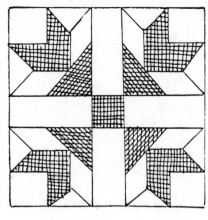

SINGLE LILY

Nancy Cabot

TRIPLE SUNFLOWER

The Perfect Patchwork Primer, page 103

BLUE BIRDS FLYING

The Household Magazine, July 1933, page 29

The Standard Book of Quilt Making and Collecting, page 242

DAVID AND GOLIATH

The Romance of the Patchwork Quilt in America, page 74, No. 21
Also **BULL'S EYE, DOE AND DARTS, FLYING DARTS, FOUR DARTS**

DAVID AND GOLIATH

Old Patchwork Quilts and the Women Who Made Them, page 95

DAVID AND GOLIATH

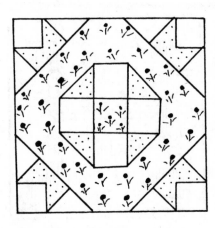

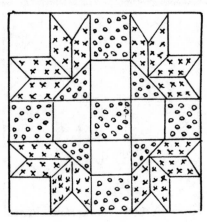

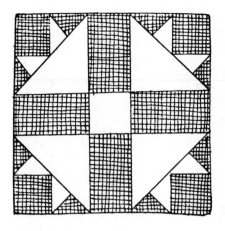

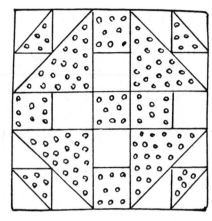

CROSS AND CROWN

Ladies Art Company, No. 151
The Romance of the Patchwork Quilt in America, page 68, No. 14
Also CROWNED CROSS
The Standard Book of Quilt Making and Collecting, page 227

DUCK PADDLE

The Romance of the Patchwork Quilt in America, page 70, No. 1
Also FANNY'S FAN

DUCK AND DUCKLINGS

Ladies Art Company, No. 245

Kansas City Star, 1929
The Romance of the Patchwork Quilt in America, page 72, No. 14
Also CORN AND BEANS, HANDY ANDY, HEN AND CHICKENS, SHOO-FLY

DUCK AND DUCKLINGS

The Romance of the Patchwork Quilt in America, page 70, No. 9
The Standard Book of Quilt Making and Collecting, page 230
Reminds us of the days when cream had to be hand-churned into butter.

CHURN DASH

Ladies Art Company, No. 362

KING'S CROWN

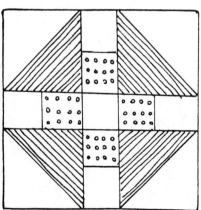

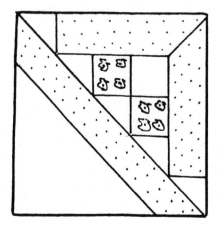

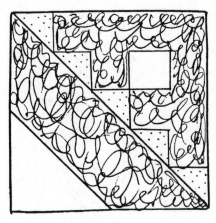

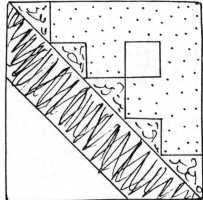

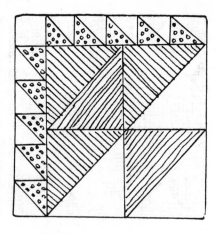

KING'S CROWN

The Romance of the Patchwork Quilt in America, page 68, No. 11

GREEK CROSS

The Standard Book of Quilt Making and Collecting, page 238

BIRTHDAY CAKE

Nancy Page

The Romance of the Patchwork Quilt in America, page 74, No. 7

CITY SQUARE

THE BASKET

DOVE OF PEACE

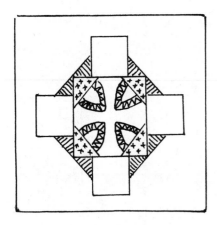

FOUR LITTLE BASKETS

The Romance of the Patchwork Quilt in America, page 126, No. 10
Ladies Art Company, No. 305

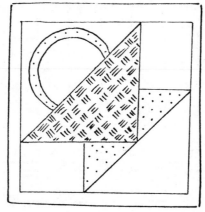

FLOWER BASKET

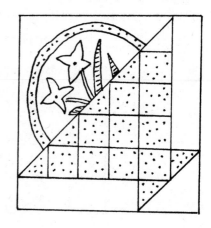

BASKET

The Perfect Patchwork Primer, page 100

Ladies Art Company, No. 58
One Hundred and One Patchwork Patterns, page 120
The Romance of the Patchwork Quilt in America, page 126, No. 14

CHERRY BASKET

Kansas City Star, 1930

THE CALICO PUZZLE

Nancy Page, 1920-30

TIC TAC TOC

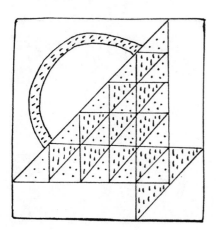

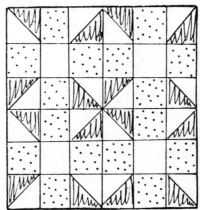

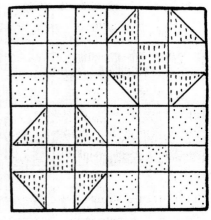

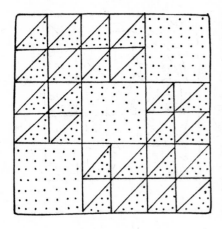 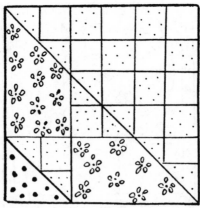 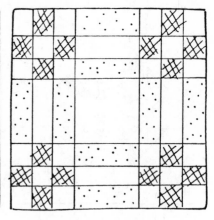

CUT GLASS DISH

Ladies Art Company, No. 7

STRAWBERRY BASKET

Grandmother Clark's Patchwork Quilt Designs, Book 20, 1931

BUILDING BLOCKS

The Household Magazine, November 1929, page 38

The Perfect Patchwork Primer, page 92

The Romance of the Patchwork Quilt in America, page 48, No. 14

The Romance of the Patchwork Quilt in America, page 70, No. 16
The Standard Book of Quilt Making and Collecting, page 232

PUSS IN THE CORNER

NINE PATCH

PUSS IN THE CORNER

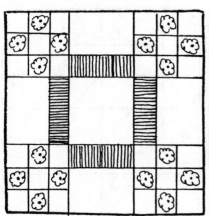 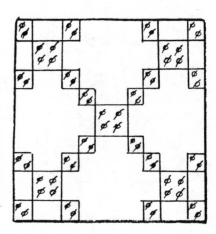

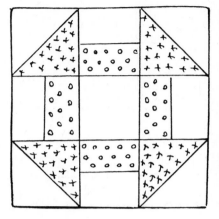

WRENCH

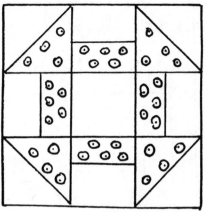

SHOO FLY

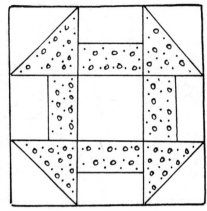

CHURN DASH

One Hundred and One Patchwork Patterns, page 121

Ladies Art Company, No. 276
Old Patchwork Quilts and the Women Who Made Them, page 80
The Romance of the Patchwork Quilt in America, page 100, No. 5
American Quilts and Coverlets, page 60
Also **CORN AND BEANS, DOUBLE MONKEY WRENCH, DUCK AND DUCKLINGS**

The Perfect Patchwork Primer, page 89
Also **HOLE IN THE BARN DOOR, DOUBLE MONKEY WRENCH**

SHERMAN'S MARCH

ALBUM

SHOO FLY

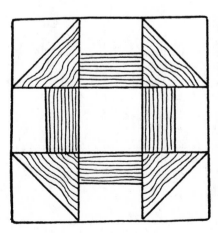

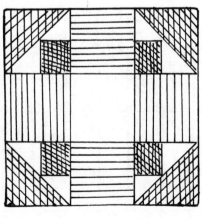

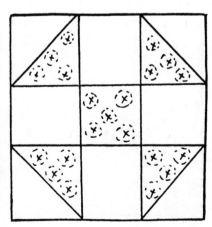

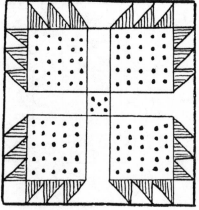

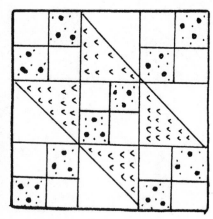

PRAIRIE QUEEN

The Romance of the Patchwork Quilt in America, page 72, No. 20
Nancy Cabot

PREMIUM STAR

The Romance of the Patchwork Quilt in America, page 58, No. 17
The Standard Book of Quilt Making and Collecting, page 229

TRAIL OF THE COVERED WAGON
Also **JACOB'S LADDER, TAIL OF BENJAMIN'S KITE**

Old Patchwork Quilts and the Women Who Made Them, page 71
The Romance of the Patchwork Quilt in America, page 64, No. 22
Also **JACOB'S LADDER**

Ladies Art Company, No. 206
One Hundred and One Patchwork Patterns, page 38
The Romance of the Patchwork Quilt in America, page 68, No. 12

Also **JACOB'S LADDER**

UNDERGROUND RAILROAD

STEPPING STONES

STEPS TO THE ALTAR

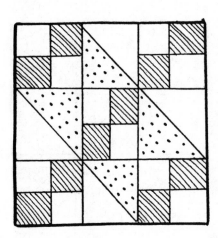

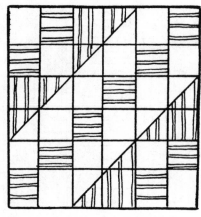

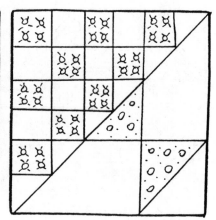

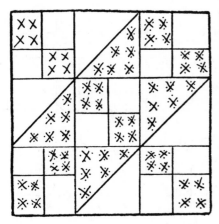

THE RAILROAD

Ladies Art Company, No. 207

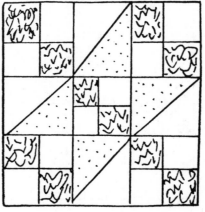

ROAD TO CALIFORNIA

The Household Magazine,
November 1929, page 38

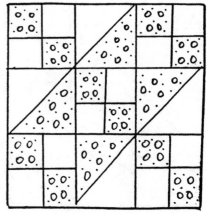

ROAD TO CALIFORNIA

*One Hundred and One Patch-
work Patterns,* page 28

The Perfect Patchwork Primer,
page 89

ROAD TO CALIFORNIA

Farm Journal, January 1938

**ROAD TO THE WHITE
HOUSE**

Also **JACOB'S LADDER,
TRAIL OF THE COVERED
WAGON**

TAIL OF BENJAMIN'S KITE

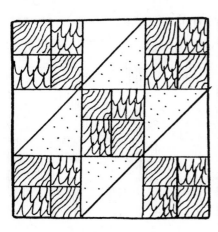

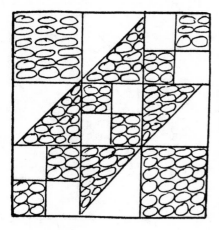

ROCKY ROAD TO CALIFORNIA

Ladies Art Company, No. 237
Also **DRUNKARD'S PATH**

CONTRARY WIFE

WORLD'S FAIR

Early American Quilts, page 14

The Romance of the Patch-work Quilt in America, page 92, No. 1
Also **FOUR FROGS**

Nancy Cabot

RAILROAD

Nancy Page, 1920-30

GOING TO CHICAGO

FLYING CLOUDS

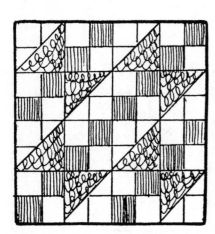

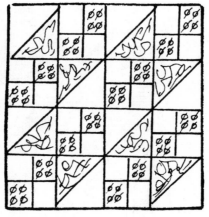

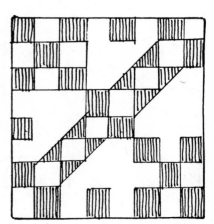

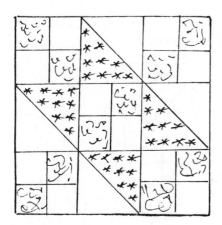

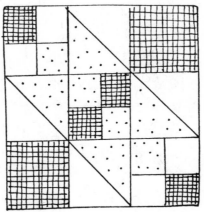

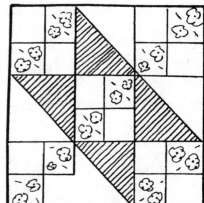

THE BROKEN SUGAR BOWL

Kansas City Star, 1932

DOUBLE HOUR GLASS

Grandmother Clark's Patchwork Quilt Designs, Book 20

JACOB'S LADDER

The Standard Book of Quilt Making and Collecting, page 231-232

Old Patchwork Quilts and the Women Who Made Them, page 71
The Romance of the Patchwork Quilt in America, page 64, No. 20
Pattern dates from the pre-Revolutionary days. The design is made in two tones only—very dark and very light patches since the fundamental idea is of a series of dark "ladders" running up and down or diagonally across the quilt.

JACOB'S LADDER

Quilts and Coverlets, page 63
In New England and Virginia called **STEPPING STONES**; in Pennsylvania **THE TAIL OF BENJAMIN'S KITE**; in Mississippi and the prairie states **TRAIL OF THE COVERED WAGON** or **WAGON TRACKS**; and in Kentucky the **UNDERGROUND RAILROAD.**

JACOB'S LADDER

Bureau Farmer, February 1930

CONVENTIONAL BLOCK

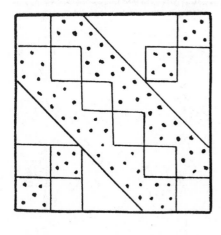

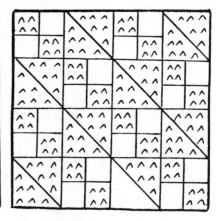

MILL AND STAR

Progressive Farmer

OHIO STAR

Capper's Weekly Quilt Block Service, 1930s

WORLD'S FAIR BLOCK

Ladies Art Company, No. 66

Nancy Page, 1920-30

Kansas City Star

SUNNY LANES

COG WHEELS

CHRISTMAS STAR

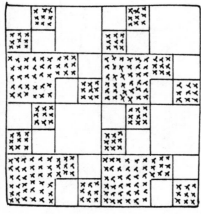

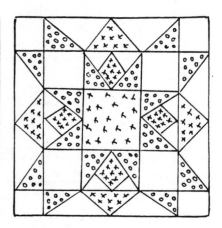

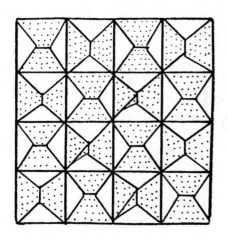

HONEYCOMB

Ladies Art Company, No. 197

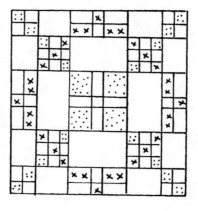

TRIPLE IRISH CHAIN

One Hundred and One Patch-work Patterns, page 27

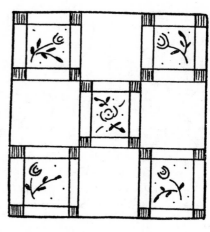

PUSS IN THE CORNER

Quilts: Their Story and How to Make Them, page 64, plate

Ladies Art Company, No. 227

TICK-TACK-TOE

FRAME-A-PRINT QUILT

Kansas City Star, 1938

FAIR AND SQUARE

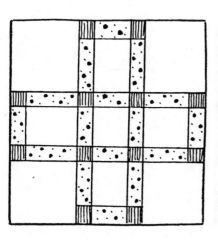

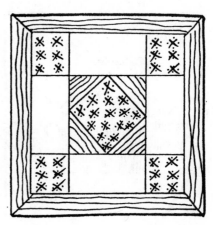

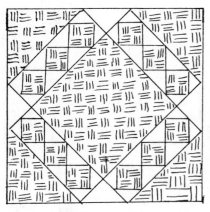

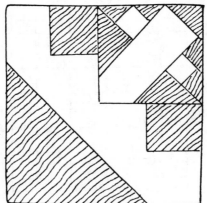

BLUE FIELDS

Nancy Cabot

CROSS AND CROWN

Old Patchwork Quilts and the Women Who Made Them, page 107
One Hundred and One Patchwork Patterns, page 69

SARAH'S FAVORITE

Ladies Art Company, No. 280

Kansas City Star, 1936

Needlecraft Magazine, June 1931, page 18

Nancy Cabot

THE MAYFLOWER

LITTLE SHIP O'DREAMS

SHIPS AT SEA

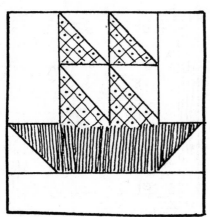

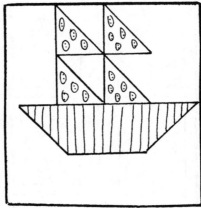

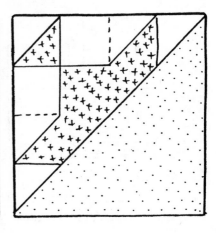

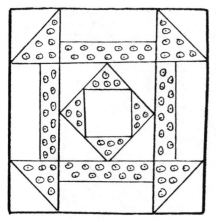

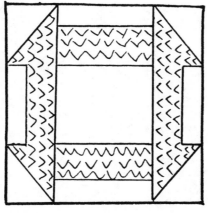

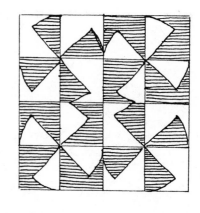

TRIANGLES AND STRIPES

Ladies Art Company, No. 229

HOLE IN THE BARN DOOR

Also **SHERMAN'S MARCH**

ELECTRIC FANS

The Perfect Patchwork Primer,
page 107

*The Romance of the Patch-
work Quilt in America,* page
100, No. 2

BRIDAL STAIRWAY

Nancy Page, 1920-30

JULY 4th

*The Romance of the Patch-
work Quilt in America,* page
86, No. 12

PIN WHEELS

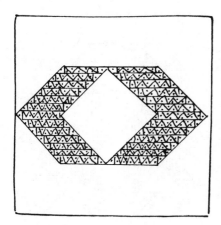

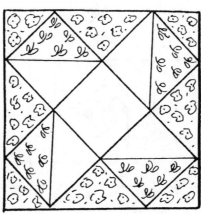

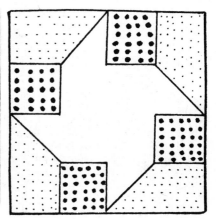

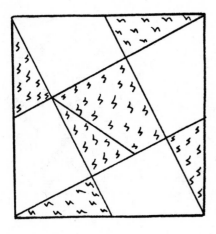

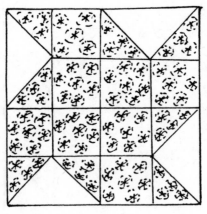

WASHINGTON'S PUZZLE

Ladies Art Company, No. 32

CHURN DASH

Old Patchwork Quilts and the Women Who Made Them, page 75

THE PRIMROSE PATH

Old Patchwork Quilts and the Women Who Made Them, page 73
The Romance of the Patchwork Quilt in America, page 96, No. 9

Old Patchwork Quilts and the Women Who Made Them, page 77

FLYING CLOUDS

SQUARE DEAL

BROWN GOOSE

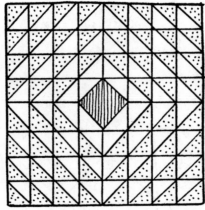

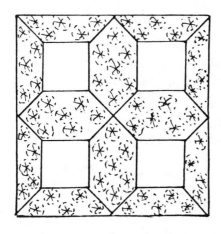

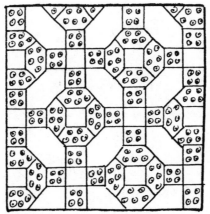

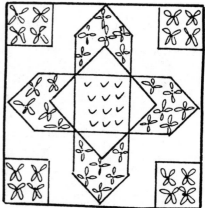

GRANDMOTHER'S OWN

Ladies Art Company, No. 166

PUZZLE TILE

Ladies Art Company, No. 289

AUNT SUKEY'S CHOICE

The Romance of the Patch-work Quilt in America, page 70, No. 20
The Standard Book of Quilt Making and Collecting, page 244

Old Patchwork Quilts and the Women Who Made Them, page 115
Kansas City Star, 1939

Laura Wheeler

ROLLING STONE

WATER WHEEL

PINWHEEL QUILT

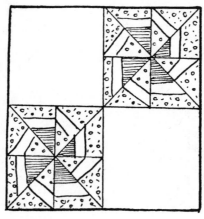

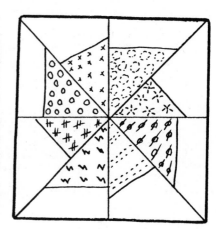

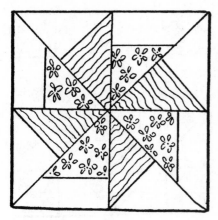

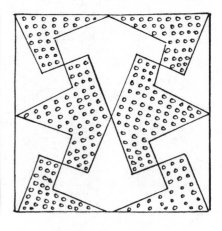

PIN WHEEL

Grandmother Clark's Patchwork Quilt Designs, Book 20, 1931

CUPID'S ARROWPOINT

The Romance of the Patchwork Quilt in America, page 94, No. 10

ARABIC LATTICE

Ladies Art Company, No. 413
One Hundred and One Patchwork Patterns, page 87
The Romance of the Patchwork Quilt in America, page 84, No. 18

One Hundred and One Patchwork Patterns, page 62
The Romance of the Patchwork Quilt in America, page 86, No. 4
Nancy Cabot

Ladies Art Company, No. 86
Old Fashioned Quilts, page 21

Ladies Art Company, No. 369

T QUARTETTE

T QUILT

DOUBLE T

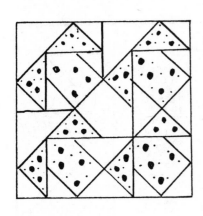

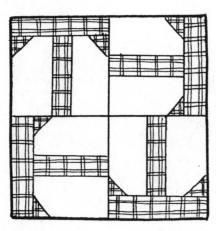

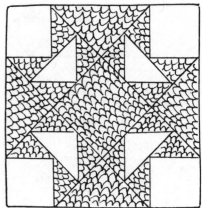

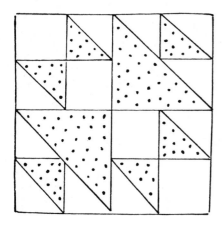 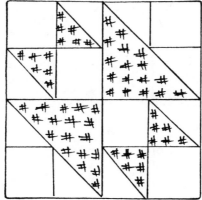 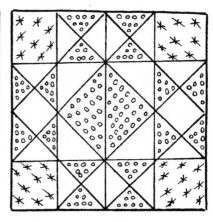

DOUBLE X

Ladies Art Company, No. 77
The Standard Book of Quilt
Making and Collecting, page
243

DOUBLE X

Ladies Art Company, No. 78

GEORGETOWN CIRCLE

The Romance of the Patch-
work Quilt in America, page
76, No. 18
Also **CROWN OF THORNS**

Modern Patchwork, page 30

TWELVE CROWNS

The Perfect Patchwork Primer,
page 77

PIECED STAR

Nancy Cabot

ROCKY MOUNTAIN
PUZZLE

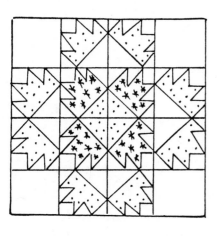  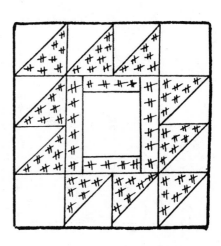

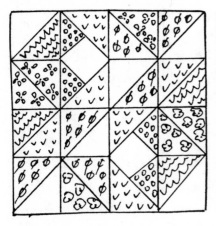

CHINESE PUZZLE

Grandmother Clark's Patchwork Quilt Designs, Book 21, 1931

SLANTED DIAMOND

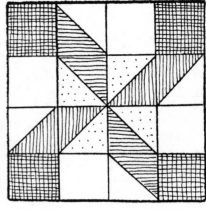

STAR OF THE WEST

Also **CLAY'S CHOICE**

Ladies Art Company, No. 16
Nancy Cabot

SHOOTING STAR

Nancy Page, 1920-30

STARDUST

Kansas City Star, 1941

THE ARKANSAS CROSS ROADS

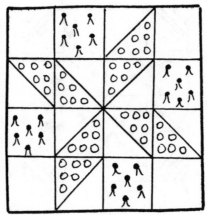

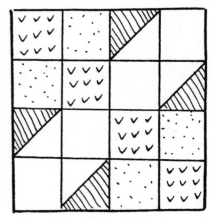

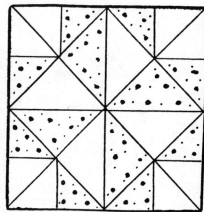

MOSAIC

Ladies Art Company, No. 22

OCEAN WAVES

Ladies Art Company, No. 182

WINDMILL

Ladies Art Company, No. 127

Also **CRIMSON RAMBLER**

SPRING BEAUTY

Kansas City Star, 1941

THE PERIWINKLE

BROKEN SASH

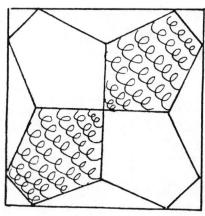

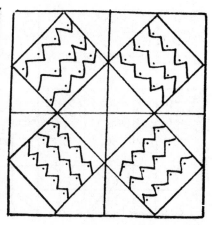

MARION'S CHOICE

Nancy Page, 1920-30

TURKEY GIBLETS

Nancy Cabot

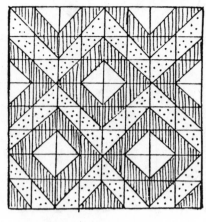

DEPRESSION

Kansas City Star

Farmer's Wife, 1920

THE ARROWHEAD

Kansas City Star, 1934

DOGWOOD BLOSSOM

Grandmother Clark's Patchwork Quilt Designs, Book 20, 1931

REVERSE X

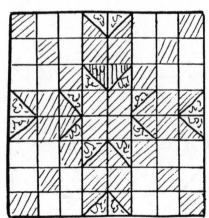

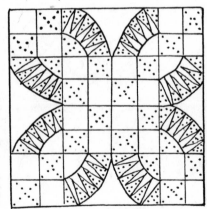

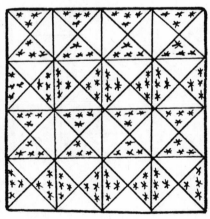

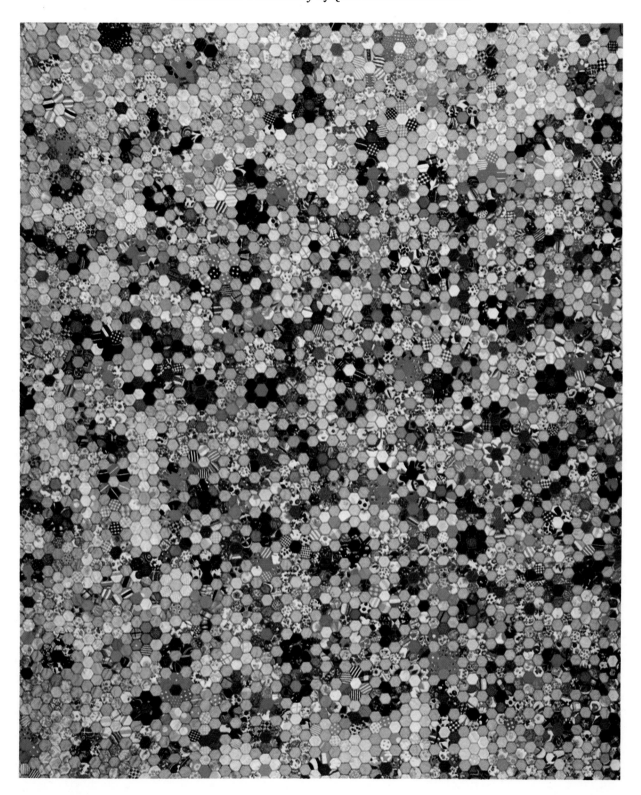

PLATE 9   **MOSAIC**

Pieced by Yvonne M. Khin. The tiny hexagons were outlined in the buttonhole stitch in red cotton thread. The 6-petal hexagons are sewn together to form a flower with a plain colored center. This was backed together with another hexagon flower. It is not quilted.

PLATE 10   **DRUNKARD'S TRAIL**

Pieced in a variety of cotton prints in shades of blue with a dark sky-blue "trail", and quilted by Yvonne M. Khin.

PLATE 11 **MRS. HOOVER'S COLONIAL QUILT**   Courtesy of Mrs. Minerva I. Axe

Pieced and quilted by Yvonne M. Khin. Blue calico printed with white daisies and unbleached muslin. Design similar to the Double Irish Chain. At an exhibition of handicrafts of the neighborhood women held in 1925 at the Neighborhood House, a social settlement in Washington, D.C., Mrs. Herbert Hoover so admired the original quilt that she ordered an exact copy to be presented to her son as a wedding gift. Hence the pattern came to be known as MRS. HOOVER'S COLONIAL QUILT.

PLATE 12 **PEKING QUILT**

Appliqued by Yvonne M. Khin and quilted by U Khin. The original quilt was brought across from Peking, China, by Mrs. Chuan O. Chao in the 1940's.

PLATE 13   **MORNING GLORIES**

Courtesy of Daw Khin Nyunt

Appliqued and quilted by Yvonne M. Khin.

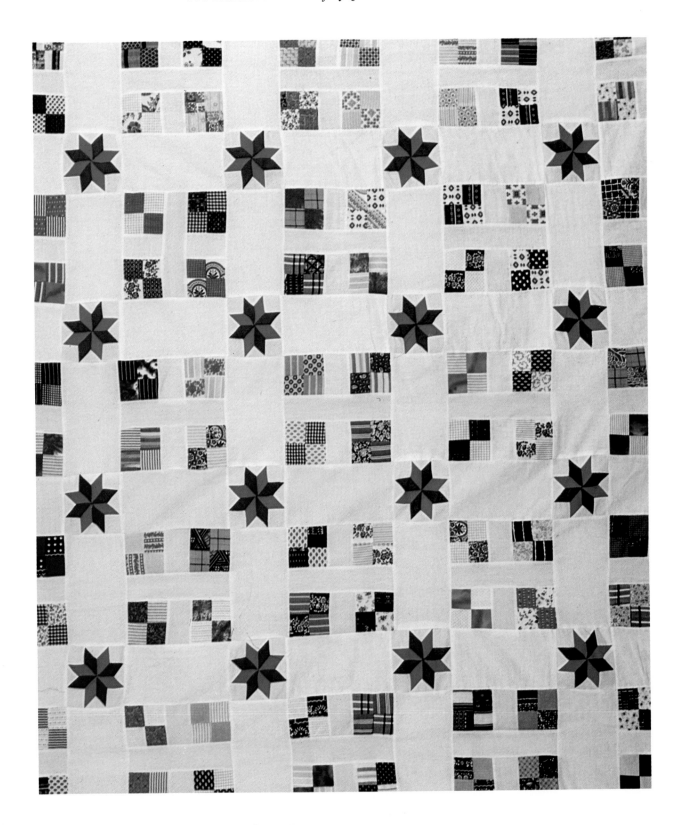

PLATE 14 **STAR AND FOUR-PATCH**

Pieced by Yvonne M. Khin and quilted by U Khin. Original design came from the State of Ohio.

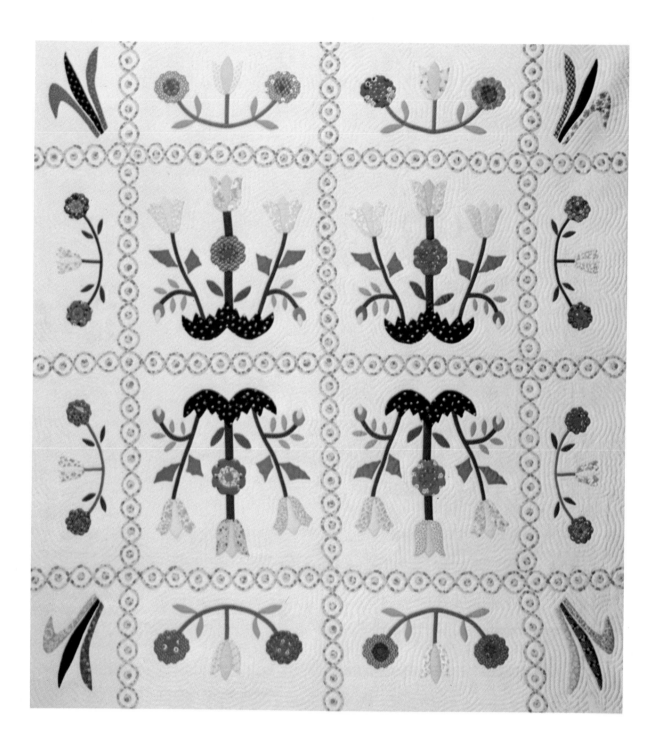

PLATE 15   **CONVENTIONAL TULIPS**

Collection of the Khins

Designed and quilted by Yvonne M. Khin.

PLATE 16   **BICENTENNIAL QUILT**

Designed, embroidered and quilted by U Khin. This quilt was made in 1976 to commemorate the Bicentennial Year of American Independence. The theme was the stars, the stripes and the American Eagle.

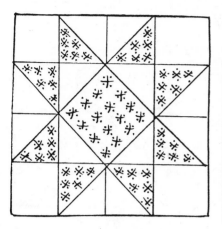

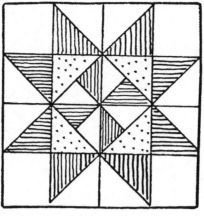

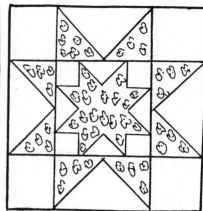

CRYSTAL STAR

Kansas City Star, 1934

MARTHA WASHINGTON STAR

American Quilts and Coverlets, page 27
Nancy Cabot

RISING STAR

Old Patchwork Quilts and the Women Who Made Them, page 77
Also **STARS AND SQUARES**
The Standard Book of Quilt Making and Collecting, page 236

The Romance of the Patchwork Quilt in America, page 94, No. 5
The Standard Book of Quilt Making and Collecting, page 237

The Romance of the Patchwork Quilt in America, page 98, No. 3

NELSON'S VICTORY

STAR FLOWER

SAW TOOTH

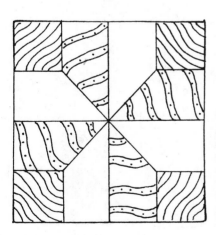

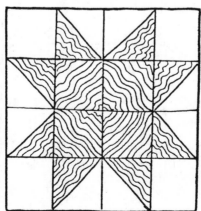

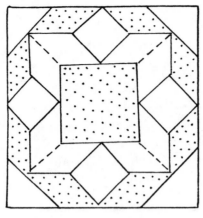

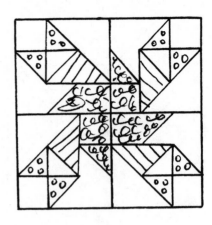

EVENING STAR

Ladies Art Company, No. 5
*The Romance of the Patch-
work Quilt in America*, page
54, No. 4

BATON ROUGE BLOCK

Ladies Art Company, No. 474

ROLLING PINWHEEL

The Perfect Patchwork Primer,
page 92

Ladies Art Company, No. 271
*The Romance of the Patch-
work Quilt in America*, page
94, No. 4
*The Standard Book of Quilt
Making and Collecting*, page
232
Nancy Page
Also **FEATHER STAR**

Ladies Art Company, No. 85
*The Romance of the Patch-
work Quilt in America*, page
86, No. 7

SAW TOOTH

SHOO FLY

MIXED T

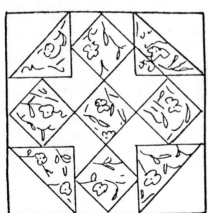

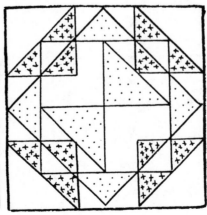

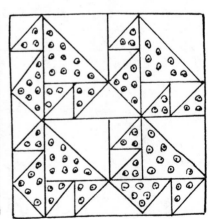

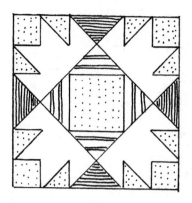

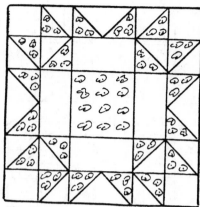

UNION SQUARES

The Perfect Patchwork Primer,
page 96

UNION SQUARE

Ladies Art Company, No. 160
Nancy Cabot
The Romance of the Patchwork Quilt in America, page 90, No. 19

ROBBING PETER TO PAY PAUL

Ladies Art Company, No. 154
The Romance of the Patchwork Quilt in America, page 64, No. 3

Nancy Page, 1920-30

ARIZONA

Nancy Page

CHAINED DOMINOS

Ladies Art Company, No. 457
Nancy Cabot

STONE MASON'S PUZZLE

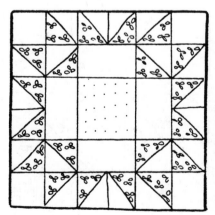

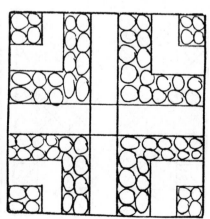

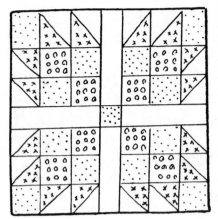

ROSEBUD

Nancy Page, 1920-30

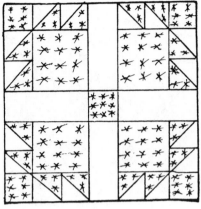

DOVE IN THE WINDOW

Ladies Art Company, No. 215

**QUEEN VICTORIA'S
CROWN**

Progressive Farmer

FOUR QUEENS

The Perfect Patchwork Primer,
page 76

ROAD TO CALIFORNIA

*The Romance of the Patch-
work Quilt in America,* page
96, No. 12
Also **INDIAN TRAIL,
STORM AT SEA**

PRICKLY PEAR

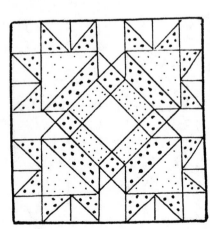

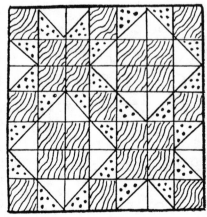

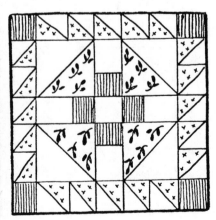

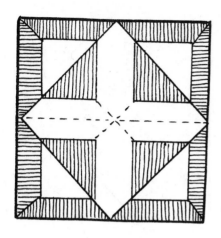

NIGHT AND DAY

Nancy Cabot

ARKANSAS TRAVELER

Ladies Art Company, No. 205
Also known as **COWBOY'S
STAR, TRAVEL STAR**
Nancy Page

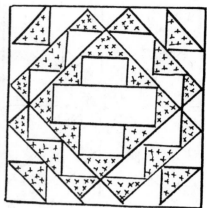

MEMORY BLOCKS

Ladies Art Company, No. 87
*The Romance of the Patch-
work Quilt in America,* page
82, No. 1

Nancy Cabot

GRAPE VINES

Mrs. Danner's Quilts, Book 5,
page 14

**GRANDMOTHER'S PIN
WHEEL**

Ladies Art Company, No. 359

LINTON

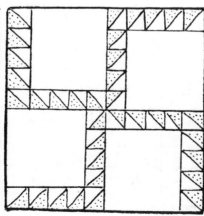

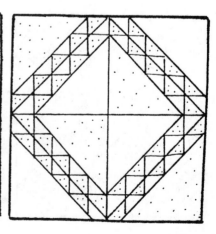

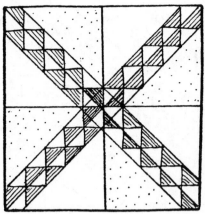

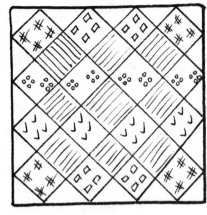

PATH THRU THE WOODS

OLD MAID'S RAMBLE

THE GARDEN PATCH

Early American Quilts, page 14

Kansas City Star, 1940

1946

Nancy Cabot

RED CROSS

CROSS PATCH QUILT

INDIAN SQUARES

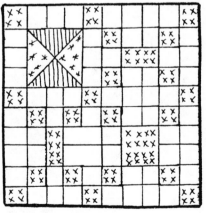

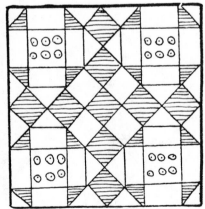

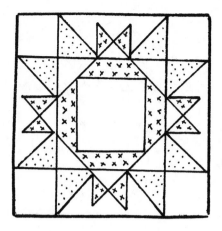

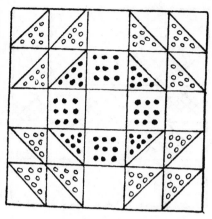

KING DAVID'S CROWN

Old Patchwork Quilts and the Women Who Made Them, page 106

The Romance of the Patchwork Quilt in America, page 64, No. 15

The Standard Book of Quilt Making and Collecting, page 238

CROWN AND THORNS

The Standard Book of Quilt Making and Collecting, page 239

GEORGETOWN CIRCLE

The Perfect Patchwork Primer, page 83

The Romance of the Patchwork Quilt in America, page 64, No. 8
Also **GEORGETOWN CIRCLE, SINGLE WEDDING RING, MEMORY WREATH**

CROWN OF THORNS

Ladies Art Company, No. 163
The Romance of the Patchwork Quilt in America, page 60, No. 10

FOUR X STAR

The Perfect Patchwork Primer, page 85

5-PATCH STAR

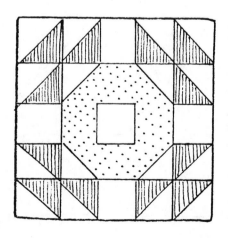

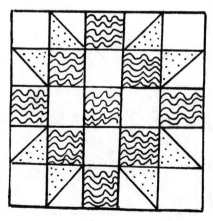

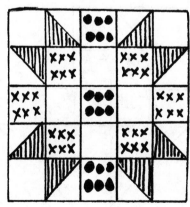

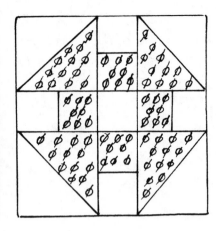

NINE-PATCH STAR

ODD SCRAPS PATCHWORK

Ladies Art Company, No. 159
Nancy Cabot

DOUBLE WRENCH

Ladies Art Company, No. 148

Nancy Page, 1920-30

FRENCH 4'S

Nancy Cabot
Also **INDIAN PUZZLE,
MONKEY WRENCH**

CHINESE COIN

Nancy Cabot

CHINESE COIN

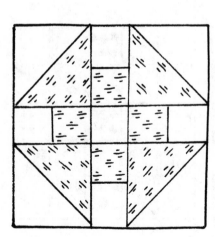

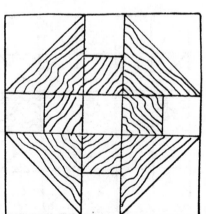

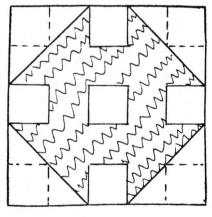

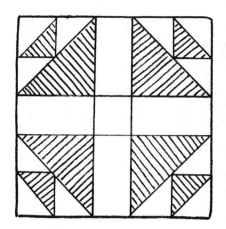

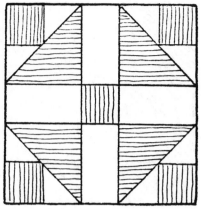

DUCKS AND DUCKLINGS

Old Patchwork Quilts and the Women Who Made Them, page 80

GRANDMOTHER'S CHOICE

Ladies Art Company, No. 129
The Romance of the Patchwork Quilt in America, page 70, No. 17
The Standard Book of Quilt Making and Collecting, page 230

BUTTERFLY AT THE CROSSROADS

Hearth and Home Magazine, 1928

The Perfect Patchwork Primer, page 84

PIGEON TOES

Also **CROWN OF THORNS, WHEEL**

SINGLE WEDDING RING

Farmer's Wife Magazine
Also **BLOCK CIRCLE**

ROLLING STONE

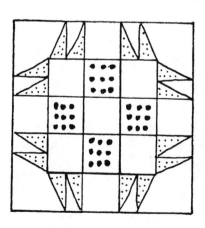

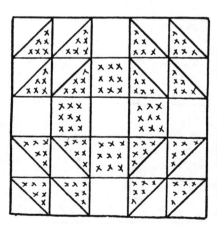

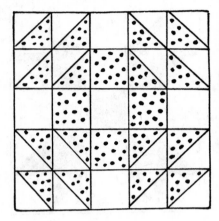

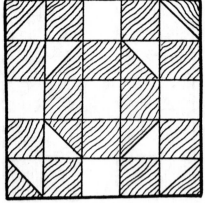

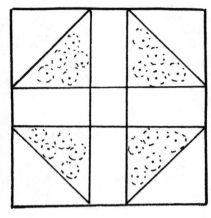

WEDDING RING

Early American Quilts, page 14
Ladies Art Company, No. 48
Nancy Cabot

WISHING RING

Mrs. Danner's Quilts, Book 2,
page 12

SHOO FLY

Ladies Art Company Catalog,
No. 392
The Romance of the Patch-work Quilt in America, page
68, No. 16
The Standard Book of Quilt Making and Collecting, page
230

Ladies Art Company, No. 506
The Romance of the Patch-work Quilt in America, page
82, No. 16

Ladies Art Company Catalog,
No. 248

PROPELLER

WIDOWER'S CHOICE

RED CROSS

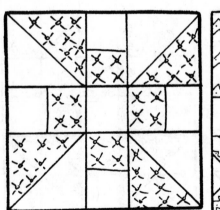

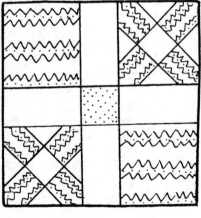

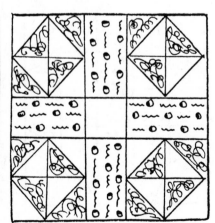

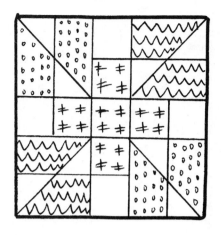

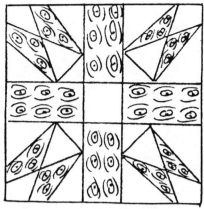

Z-CROSS

The Perfect Patchwork Primer,
page 85

NEW STAR

Ladies Art Company Catalog,
No. 17
The Romance of the Patch-
work Quilt in America, page
62, No. 4

PINWHEEL SQUARE

Ladies Art Company Catalog,
No. 231

Ladies Art Company, No. 507
One Hundred and One Patch-
work Patterns, page 76
The Romance of the Patch-
work Quilt in America, page
72, No. 2

The Romance of the Patch-
work Quilt in America, page
82, No. 14
The Standard Book of Quilt
Making and Collecting, page
239

JAPANESE POPPY

MILKY WAY

HANDY ANDY

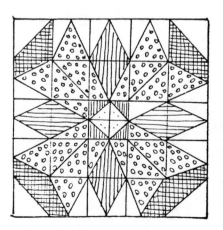

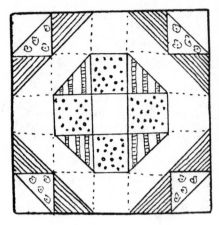

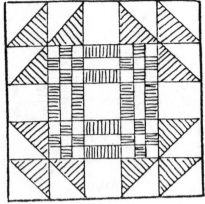

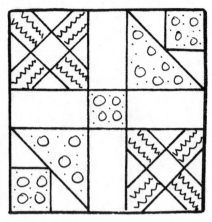

WEDDING RINGS

The Perfect Patchwork Primer, page 83

YOUNG MAN'S FANCY

Old Patchwork Quilts and the Women Who Made Them, page 81
The Romance of the Patchwork Quilt in America, page 222, Plate LXXXV
Also **GOOSE IN THE POND**

LEAP FROG

Ladies Art Company, No. 250

One Hundred and One Patchwork Patterns, page 46
The Romance of the Patchwork Quilt in America, page 70, No. 18. Also **WHIRLIGIG.**
The Standard Book of Quilt Making and Collecting, page 230

The Romance of the Patchwork Quilt in America, page 72, No. 9

Nancy Cabot

BACHELOR'S PUZZLE

HEAVENLY PROBLEM

JACK IN THE BOX

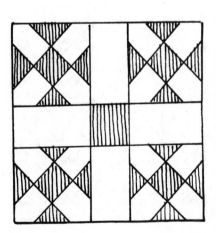

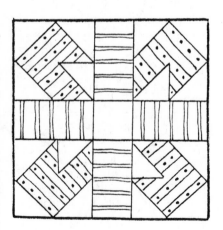

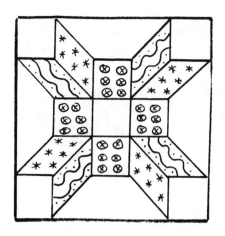

FARMER'S DAUGHTER

Ladies Art Company, No. 21

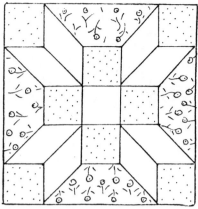

ROLLING STAR

Joseph Doyle & Co., N.J.

JACK'S BLOCKS

Grandmother Clark's Patchwork Quilt Designs, Book 20, 1931

Ladies Art Company, No. 258
The Romance of the Patchwork Quilt in America, page 58, No. 4

WILD ROSE AND SQUARE

ODD STAR

PINE BURR

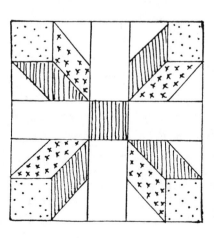

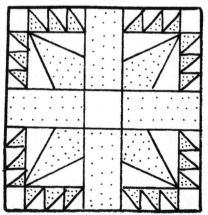

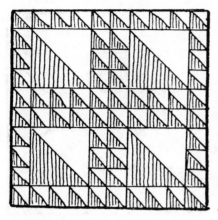

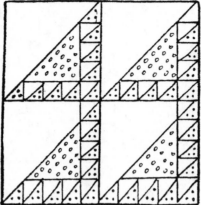

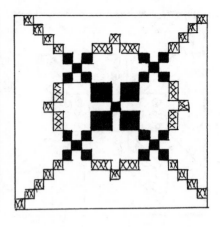

BASKET OF TRIANGLES

LITTLE SAW TOOTH

BURGOYNE SURROUNDED

The Romance of the Patchwork Quilt in America, page 84, No. 2
Also **INDIAN MEADOW, LEND AND BORROW, LOST SHIP, ROCKY GLEN**

One Hundred and One Patchwork Patterns, page 98
The Romance of the Patchwork Quilt in America, page 98, No. 4
British General John Burgoyne tried to take the city of Albany, New York, but on being surrounded by the Americans he surrendered at Saratoga on October 17, 1777. This pattern is also known as **BURGOYNE'S SURRENDER** and dates from the early 19th century. About 1850 the name was changed to **WHEEL OF FORTUNE.** The early settlers took the pattern to the West where it came to be known as **THE ROAD TO CALIFORNIA.**

Spinning Wheel Magazine, July-August, 1968, page 16
The Western migration during the 1860's suggested wagons rolling; so quilt patterns made up of stylized versions of wagon wheels and chains were created.

Ladies Art Company, No. 285

AN ODD PATCHWORK

ROAD TO CALIFORNIA

SAVE-ALL

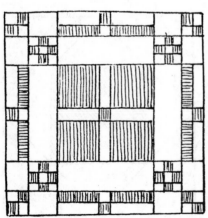

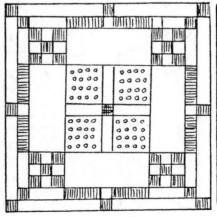

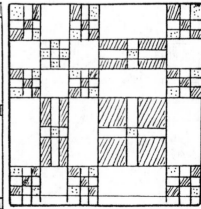

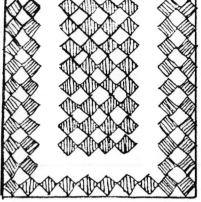

STRIPES AND SQUARES

PHILADELPHIA PAVEMENT

Old Fashioned Quilts, page 17

RAILROAD CROSSING

Old Patchwork Quilts and the Women Who Made Them, page 71
Nancy Cabot

Good Housekeeping Magazine, January 1930, page 77

STREETS OF NEW YORK

The Romance of the Patchwork Quilt in America, page 52, No. 1

HIT AND MISS

Also **HAIRPIN CATCHER**

HIT OR MISS

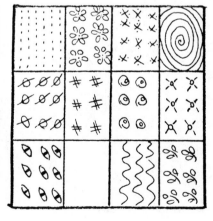

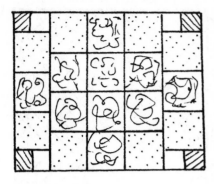

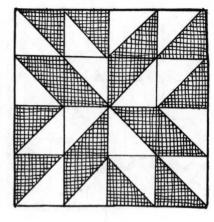

JERICHO WALLS

Kansas City Star, 1942

POSTAGE STAMP

*The Romance of the Patch-
work Quilt in America,* page
52, No. 18

SQUARE AND COMPASS

Kansas City Star, 1924

ANNA'S CHOICE QUILT

JULY 4TH

WINDMILL

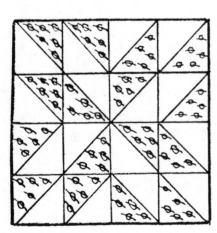

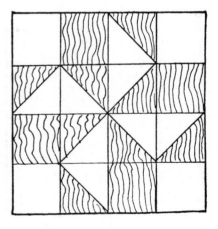

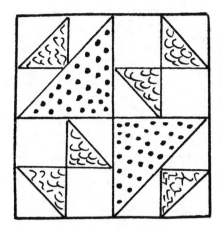

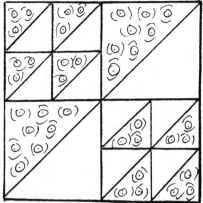

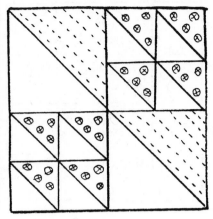

OLD MAID'S PUZZLE

Ladies Art Company Catalog, No. 25
The Romance of the Patch-work Quilt in America, page 70, No. 8
One Hundred and One Patch-work Patterns, page 6
The Standard Book of Quilt Making and Collecting, page 237
Nancy Cabot

FLOCK OF GEESE

Old Patchwork Quilts and the Women Who Made Them, page 72
The Romance of the Patch-work Quilt in America, page 74, No. 9

FLOCK

The Perfect Patchwork Primer, page 80

The Romance of the Patch-work Quilt in America, page 84, No. 12

DOUBLE X

Quilts: Their Story and How to Make Them, plate facing page 33

DOUBLE X

Pattern named after the old fox who raided barnyards.

FOX AND GEESE

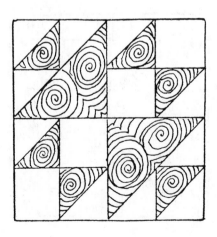

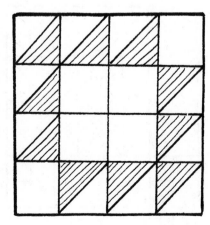

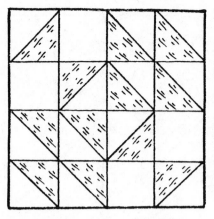

LADIES' WREATH

Ladies Art Company, No. 322

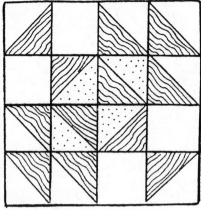

FLYING DUTCHMAN

Nancy Cabot

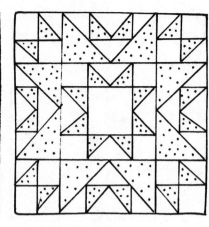

ODD FELLOW'S CHAIN

Ladies Art Company, No. 61

Old Patchwork Quilts and the Women Who Made Them, page 111
The Romance of the Patchwork Quilt in America, page 98, No. 1

FREE TRADE BLOCK

The Standard Book of Quilt Making and Collecting, page 238

JAGGED EDGE

Nancy Page, 1920-30

KALEIDOSCOPE

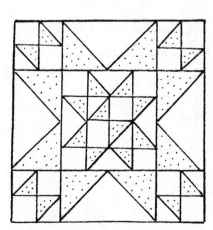

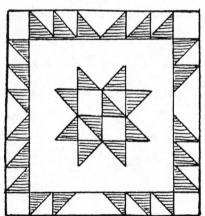

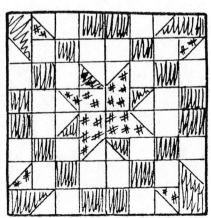

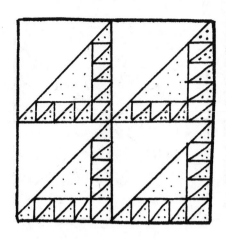

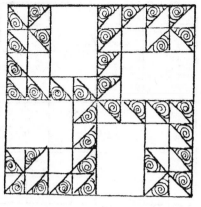

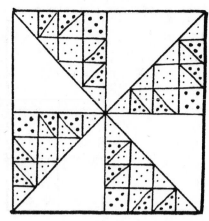

LEND AND BORROW

Women's World Magazine, January 1930, page 21
Also **LITTLE SAW TOOTH**

MERRY-GO-ROUND

One Hundred and One Patchwork Patterns, page 123
Also **ETERNAL TRIANGLE**

GRAND RIGHT AND LEFT

Named after the old square dance.

Ladies Art Company, No. 27
The Romance of the Patchwork Quilt in America, page 80, No. 4. Also **KANSAS TROUBLES.**
The Standard Book of Quilt Making and Collecting, page 244

IRISH PUZZLE

Nancy Cabot

FLASHING WINDMILLS

The Romance of the Patchwork Quilt in America, page 86, No. 6

PIN WHEELS

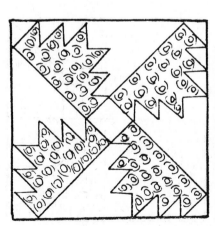

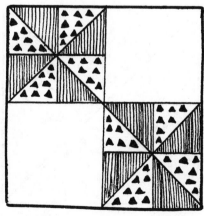

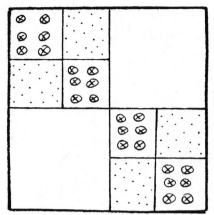

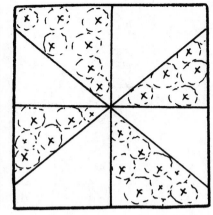

FOUR-PATCH

The Romance of the Patchwork Quilt in America, page 48, No. 4
The earliest basic design is the square, which is used in a variety of shapes and arrangements. To enhance the pattern, light and dark patches are employed. This design is called the original **Four-Patch** for obvious reasons.

FOUR-PATCH

SUGAR BOWL

The Romance of the Patchwork Quilt in America, page 82, No. 13
Called **FLY** in Ohio; **KATHY'S RAMBLE** in New York; **CROW'S FOOT** in Maryland; and **FAN MILL** in Pennsylvania.

Progressive Farmer Magazine,

OLD WINDMILL

Ladies Art Company, No. 519

TURNSTILE

Nancy Page, 1920-30

THE SPINNER

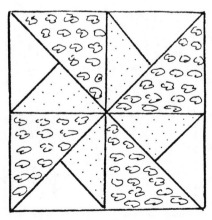

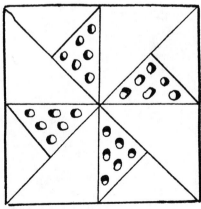

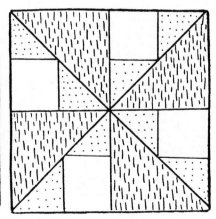

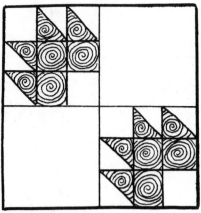

THE TEA LEAF

Modern Priscilla, August 1928, page 18

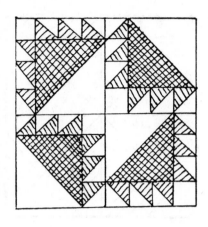

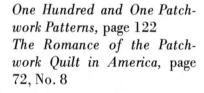

STORM AT SEA

Old Patchwork Quilts and the Women Who Made Them, page 103
Also called **INDIAN TRAIL, PRICKLY PEAR, RAMBLING ROAD, WINDING WALK, WEATHER VANE**

THE SAW

One Hundred and One Patchwork Patterns, page 122
The Romance of the Patchwork Quilt in America, page 72, No. 8

Ladies Art Company, No. 30

WORLD'S FAIR PUZZLE

WHIRLWIND

WINDMILL

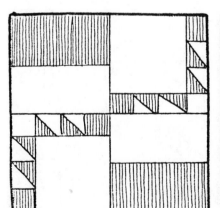

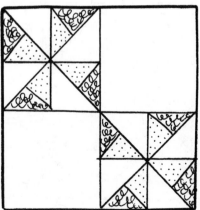

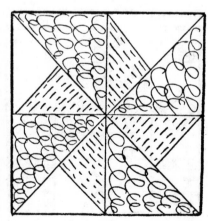

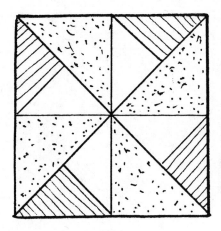

THE WHIRLIGIG

Kansas City Star, 1930's

WHIRLWIND

Woman's World, February 1928, page 30

NEW ALBUM

Ladies Art Company, No. 36

Old Patchwork Quilts and the Women Who Made Them, page 78

Kansas City Star, 1937

TEMPLE COURT

GEORGETOWN WREATH

INDIAN STAR

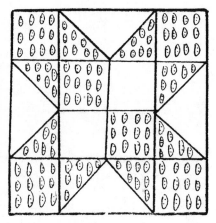

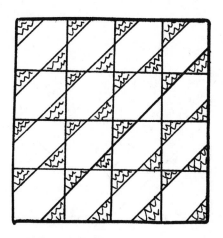

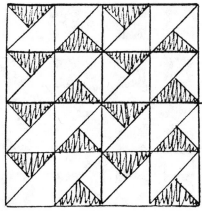

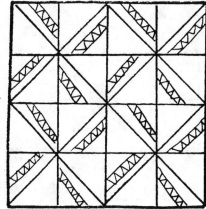

THE X-QUISITE

WILD WAVES

MOSAIC

Ladies Art Company, No. 281
The Romance of the Patch-
work Quilt in America, page
84, No. 15

Ladies Art Company, No. 9

Ladies Art Company, No. 17

Ladies Art Company, No. 140
The Romance of the Patch-
work Quilt in America, page
62, No. 9

Woman's World Magazine

MOSAIC

MOTHER'S FANCY STAR

TRUE LOVER'S KNOT

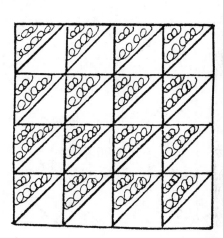

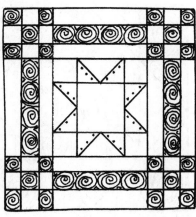

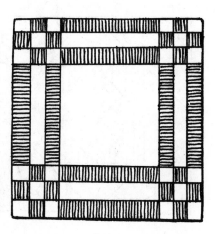

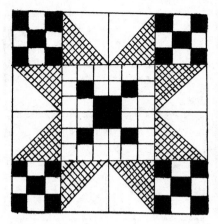

BRIDAL PATH

Kansas City Star, 1935

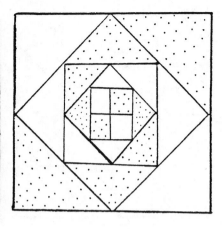

ECONOMY

SNAIL TRAIL

Ladies Art Company, No. 504

Nancy Page, 1920-30

Nancy Cabot

SHADOW BOXES

SUMMER'S DREAM

THE PYRAMIDS

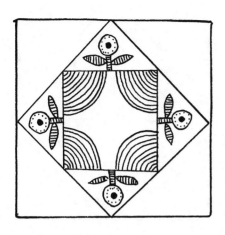

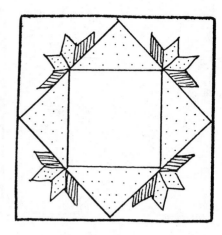

THE POSY QUILT

Kansas City Star

POSIES ROUND THE SQUARE

Needlecraft Magazine, July 1934, page 8
Also called **SPICE PINKS**

SWALLOWS IN A WINDOW

The Romance of the Patchwork Quilt in America, page 74, No. 6

Also **POSIES ROUND THE SQUARE**

SPICE PINKS

AIRPLANES

Ladies Art Company, No. 196

HOUR GLASS

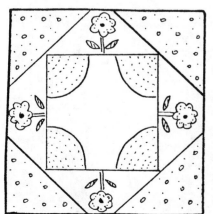

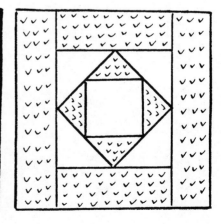

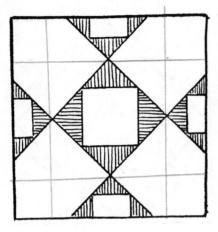

HANDY ANDY

The Perfect Patchwork Primer,
page 79

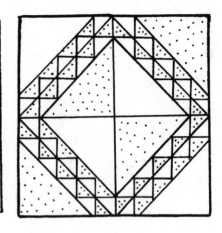

THE GOOSE TRACK

SUN AND SHADE

Nancy Page, 1920-30

Old Fashioned Quilts, page 23

SCOTCH PLAID

*Farm Journal and Farmer's
Wife,* Pa.

THREE CHEERS

Nancy Cabot

NIGHT AND DAY

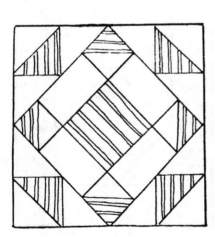

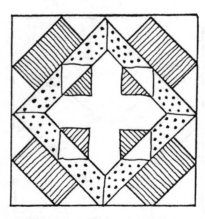

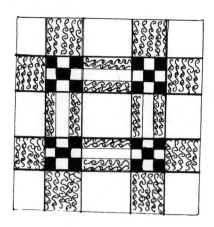

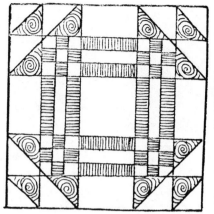

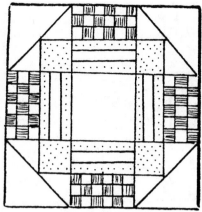

ALBUM PATCH

The Romance of the Patch-work Quilt in America, page 92, No. 7
Also **AUTOGRAPH PATCH**

PATCHWORK FANTASY

The Household Magazine, November 1929, page 38

GOLDEN GATES

Ladies Art Company, No. 117
The Romance of the Patch-work Quilt in America, page 100, No. 10
Also **WINGED SQUARE**

Nancy Cabot

ODD PATCHWORK

The Standard Book of Quilt Making and Collecting, page 233

OHIO STAR

The Perfect Patchwork Primer, page 96

FRIENDSHIP STAR

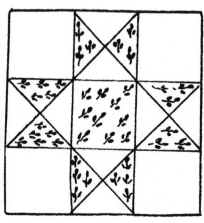

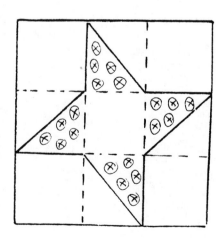

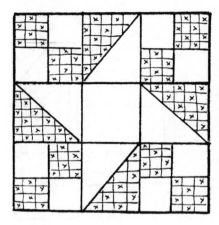

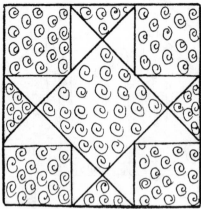

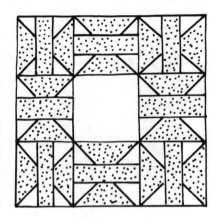

INDIAN PUZZLE

Also **CHINESE COIN,
MONKEY WRENCH**

AUNT ELIZA'S STAR

Ladies Art Company, No. 13
The Romance of the Patch-work Quilt in America, page 58, No. 10

BEGGAR BLOCK

Ladies Art Company, No. 68

Old Patchwork Quilts and the Women Who Made Them, page 84
The Romance of the Patch-work Quilt in America, page 82, No. 3

BEGGAR'S BLOCKS

Ladies Art Company, No. 238

LONDON ROADS

Ladies Art Company, No. 315
The Romance of the Patch-work Quilt in America, page 78, No. 1
Nancy Page

MOLLIE'S CHOICE

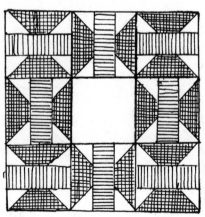

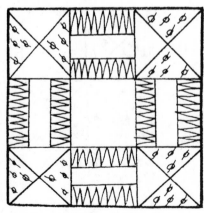

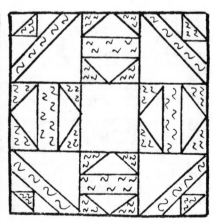

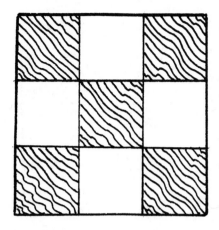

**FUNDAMENTAL NINE-
PATCH**

*Old Patchwork Quilts and the
Women Who Made Them,* page
80

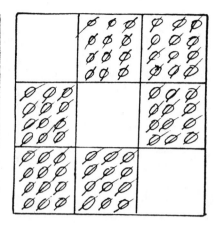

HOMEWARD BOUND

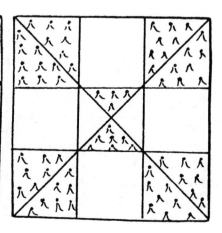

PATIENCE 9-PATCH

The Perfect Patchwork Primer,
page 94

Ladies Art Company, No. 82

FIVE PATCH

Also **THE YO-YO QUILT**

PINWHEEL

Ladies Art Company, No. 141
Nancy Cabot

THE PRACTICAL ORCHARD

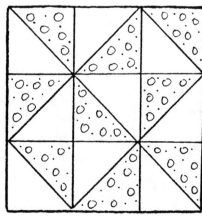

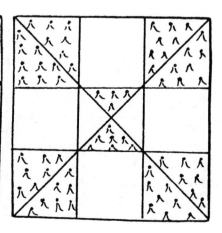

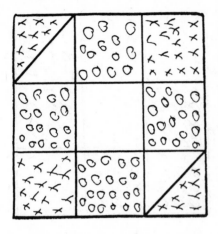

HOUR GLASS

Old Patchwork Quilts and the Women Who Made Them, page 80

NINE-PATCH VARIATION

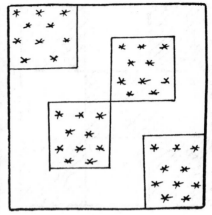

PATIENCE CORNER

The Standard Book of Quilt Making and Collecting, page 236

The Romance of the Patchwork Quilt in America, page 84, No. 10

PATIENCE CORNERS

The Standard Book of Quilt Making and Collecting, page 232

NINE PATCH

Kansas City Star

FLAG IN, FLAG OUT

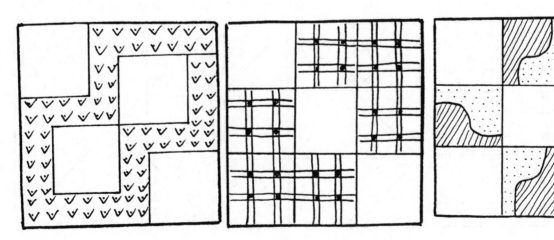

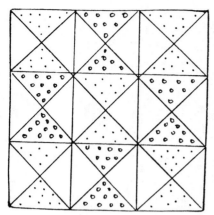

COTTON REEL

Used as borders or sewn together in strips to make an all-over quilt.

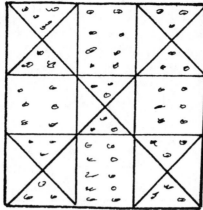

THE LETTER X

Ladies Art Company, No. 279

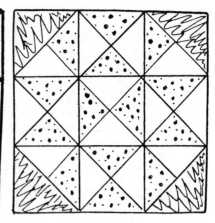

OLD TIPPECANOE

The Romance of the Patchwork Quilt in America, page 98, No. 13

Kansas City Star, 1934

NEW ALBUM

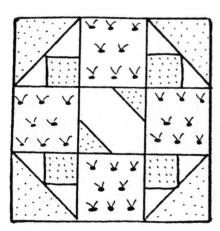

The Progressive Farmer

WYOMING VALLEY

Nancy Cabot

FOUR WINDS

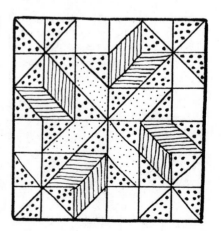

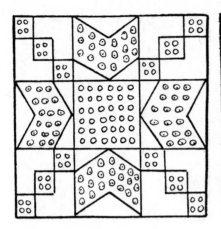

ARROWHEADS

The Romance of the Patchwork Quilt in America, page 77, No. 5

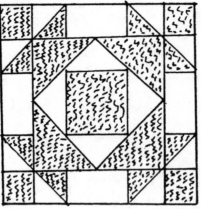

BROKEN DISHES

Needlecraft Magazine, February 1930, page 8

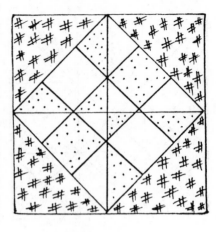

STORM SIGNAL

Progressive Farmer

Grandmother Clark's Patchwork Quilt Designs, Book 20, 1931

ARBOR WINDOW

The Perfect Patchwork Primer, page 91

BOXES

The Romance of the Patchwork Quilt in America, page 90, No. 16

LONDON SQUARE

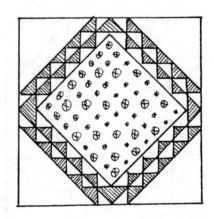

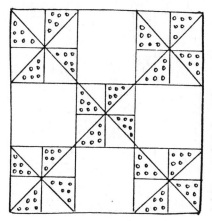

FLUTTER WHEEL

Ladies Art Company, No. 39
Early American Quilts, page 14

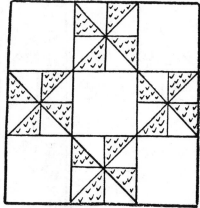

FOUR-LEAF CLOVER

Farm Journal and *Farmer's Wife,* 1942

Old Patchwork Quilts and the Women Who Made Them, page 80

The Romance of the Patchwork Quilt in America, page 94, No. 11. Also **LOVE KNOT, HOLE-IN-THE-BARN-DOOR, LINCOLN'S PLATFORM, PUSS-IN-THE-CORNER, SHERMAN'S MARCH, SHOO-FLY**

DOUBLE MONKEY WRENCH

PIN WHEELS

One Hundred and One Patchwork Patterns, page 74

The Standard Book of Quilt Making and Collecting, page 33

MONKEY WRENCH

Joseph Doyle & Co., N.J.

THE WINDMILL

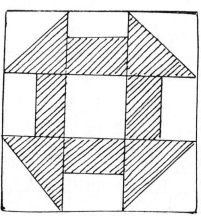

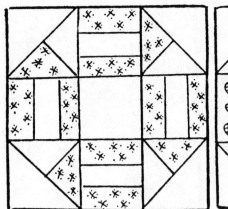

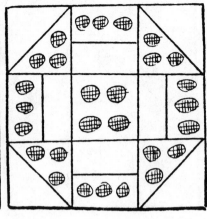

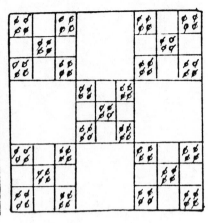

MOSAIC

Ladies Art Company, No. 8

GRECIAN DESIGNS

Ladies Art Company, No. 152
Nancy Cabot

DOUBLE NINE-PATCH

The Romance of the Patchwork Quilt in America, page 48, No. 10

Also **DOUBLE NINE PATCH**

IRISH CHAIN

NEW NINE PATCH

Nancy Cabot

INDEPENDENCE SQUARE

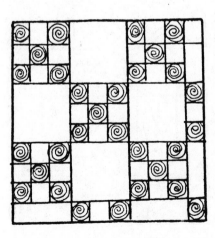

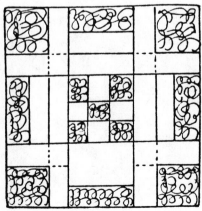

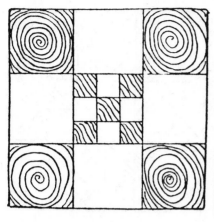

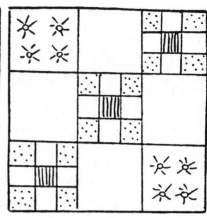

DOUBLE NINE-PATCH

The Romance of the Patchwork Quilt in America, page 48, No. 11

NINE PATCH

9-PATCH CHAIN

The Perfect Patchwork Primer, page 90

The Romance of the Patchwork Quilt in America, page 48, No. 6

American Needlewoman, April 1926, page 19

NINE PATCH

STAR PATTERN

RAILROAD CROSSING

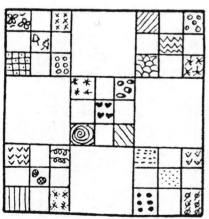

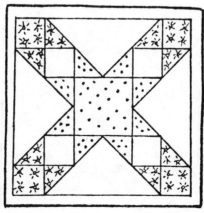

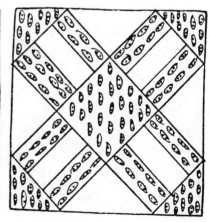

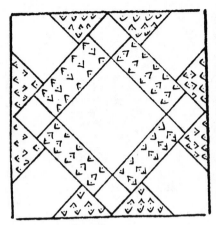

FOUR POINTS

ARKANSAS

ST. GREGORY'S CROSS

Ladies Art Company, No. 106
Also **CRAZY STAR QUILT**

Kansas City Star, 1933

Mrs. Danner's Quilts, Book 4,
page 18

The Perfect Patchwork Primer,
page 91

THE FOUR X QUILT

BLOCKS AND STARS

CROSSROADS

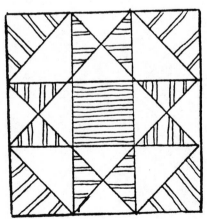

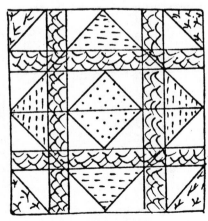

ROYAL STAR

Ladies Art Company, No. 462
The Romance of the Patch-
work Quilt in America, page
58, No. 12
The Standard Book of Quilt
Making and Collecting, page
240

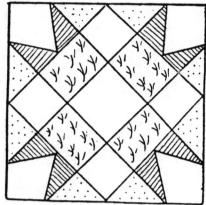

ROYAL STAR

The Perfect Patchwork Primer,
page 93

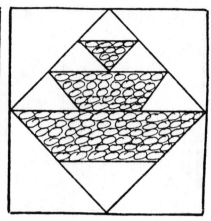

SAILBOAT

The Romance of the Patch-
work Quilt in America, page
76, No. 22

Ladies Art Company, No. 195
The Romance of the Patch-
work Quilt in America, page
52, No. 16

RIGHT AND LEFT

Nancy Cabot

FOUR POINTS

Kansas City Star, 1939

THE PRIDE OF OHIO

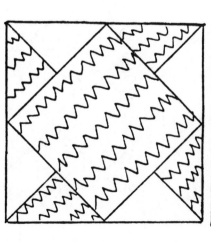

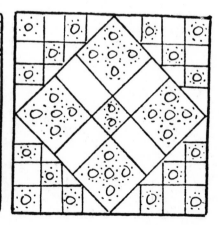

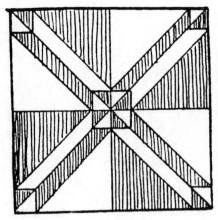

GRETCHEN

LADY OF THE LAKE

The Romance of the Patchwork Quilt in America, page 100, No. 14

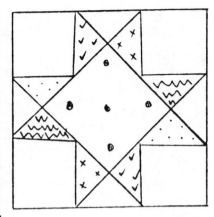

TIPPECANOE AND TYLER TOO

Old Patchwork Quilts and the Women Who Made Them, plate 28
When William Henry Harrison was running for the Presidency, he was portrayed as a battle-scarred hero. The conquest of the great Indian Chief Tecumseh at Tippecanoe in 1881 was one of the most important battles. John Tyler was Harrison's running mate and the catch slogan under which they campaigned provided the quilters with this name for a pattern.

One Hundred and One Patchwork Patterns, page 41

SUSANNAH

Ladies Art Company, No. 485

SUSANNAH PATCH

Ladies Art Company, No. 277

A SNOWFLAKE

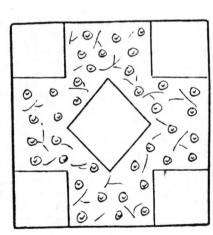

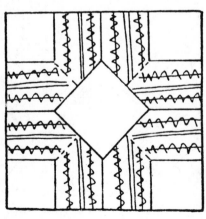

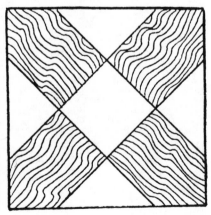

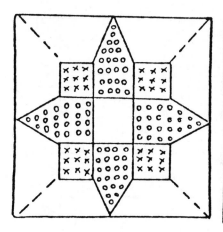

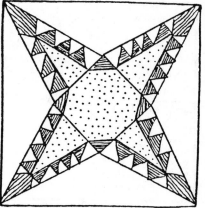

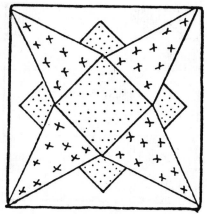

GRANDMOTHER'S CROSS

One Hundred and One Patch-work Patterns, page 21

THE PINE BURR

Kansas City Star

GEOMETIC STAR

The Romance of the Patch-work Quilt in America, page 54, No. 10
The Standard Book of Quilt Making and Collecting, page 244

Old Patchwork Quilts and the Women Who Made Them, page 81

ODD FELLOW'S CROSS

Grandmother Clark's Patch-work Quilt Designs, Book 20, 1931

DAD'S BOW TIE

Nancy Cabot

NECKTIE

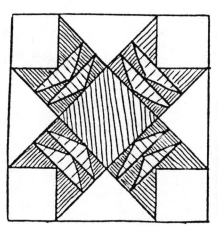

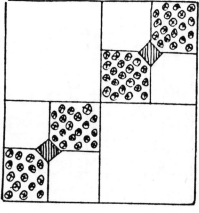

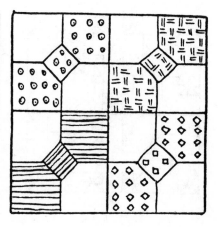

BOW-TIE

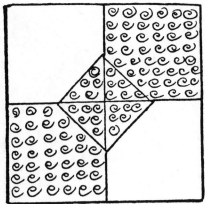

NECKTIE

Ladies Art Company, No. 119
Old Patchwork Quilts and the
Women Who Made Them, page
76
The Romance of the Patch-
work Quilt in America, page
82, No. 5

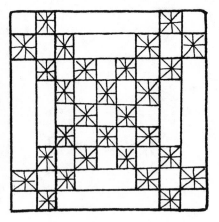

GARDEN PATH

Nancy Page, 1920-30

Nancy Cabot

DUBLIN CHAIN

The Romance of the Patch-
work Quilt in America, page
78, No. 8

GOLDEN GLOW

MORNING STAR

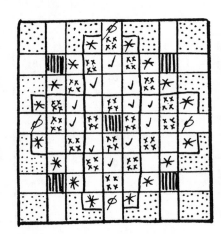

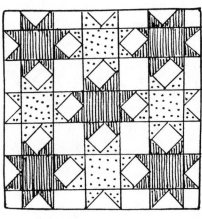

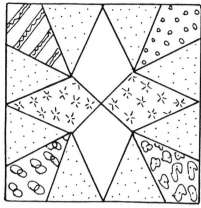

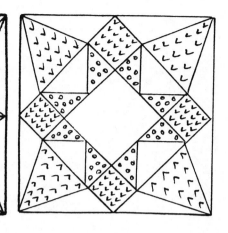

TIME AND TIDE

ST. LOUIS

Yesterday's Quilts in Homes of Today, page 6
Also **MOTHER'S DELIGHT**

DOG TOOTH VIOLET

Nancy Cabot

The Romance of the Patch-work Quilt in America, page 84, No. 1
Also **SPOOLS, SECRET DRAWER**

Practical Needlework Quilt Patterns, Vol. 3

EXEA'S STAR

Kansas City Star, 1930

THE SECRET DRAWER

ARKANSAS TRAVELER

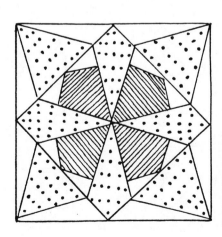

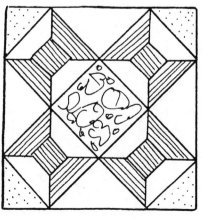

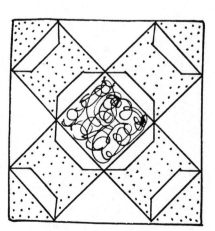

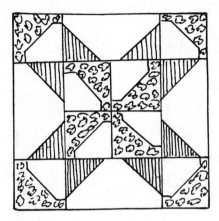

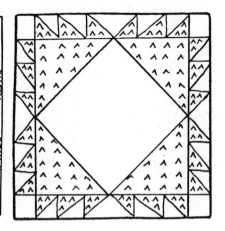

COLUMBIA PUZZLE

Ladies Art Company, No. 31
The Romance of the Patch-
work Quilt in America, page
80, No. 9

HOME TREASURE

Ladies Art Company, No. 114
Nancy Page

SUNSHINE

Ladies Art Company, No. 121

Laura Wheeler

FRIENDSHIP STAR

Ladies Art Company, No. 158

CENTENNIAL

Ladies Art Company, No. 40
Old Fashioned Quilts, page 21

WHEEL OF FORTUNE

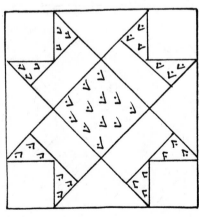

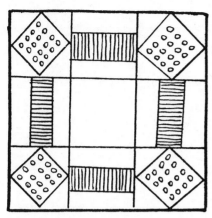

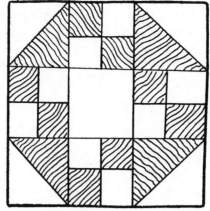

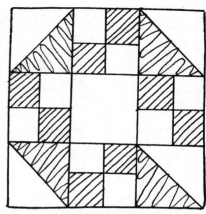

KITTY CORNER

Old Patchwork Quilts and the Women Who Made Them, page 81

PRAIRIE QUEEN

Old Patchwork Quilts and the Women Who Made Them, page 80

DOUBLE   THREE   PATCH

Ladies Art Company, No. 202
One Hundred and One Patchwork Patterns, page 35
The Romance of the Patchwork Quilt in America, page 74, No. 4
Also **YOUNG MAN'S FANCY**

Ladies Art Company, No. 254

JACK KNIFE

GOOSE IN THE POND

HANDY ANDY

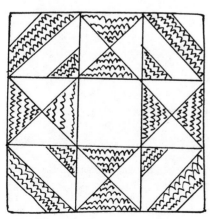

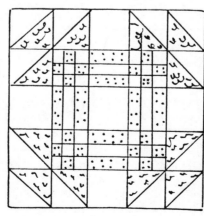

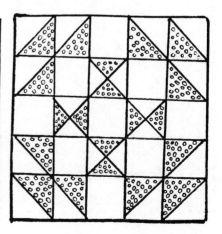

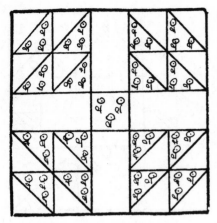

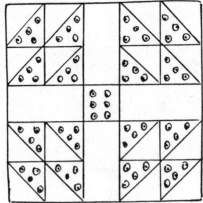

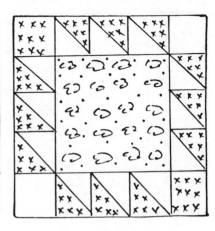

HANDY ANDY

FLYING GEESE

DOUBLE SAWTOOTH

Old Patchwork Quilts and the Women Who Made Them, page 81
The Romance of the Patchwork Quilt in Ameria, page 82, No. 19
Also **CORN AND BEANS, DUCK AND DUCKLINGS**

The Standard Book of Quilt Making and Collecting, page 239

The Perfect Patchwork Primer, page 87

Ladies Art Company, No. 174

Nancy Page, 1920-30

The Perfect Patchwork Primer, page 87

LADY OF THE LAKE

HILLS OF VERMONT

HANDY ANDY

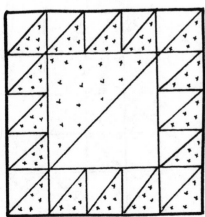

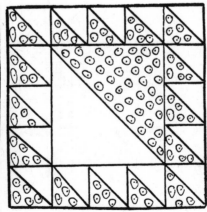

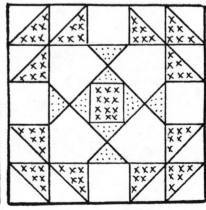

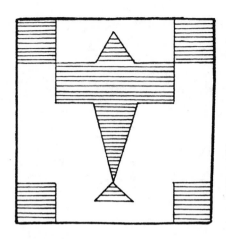

AIRPLANE

The Romance of the Patch-work Quilt in America, page 82, No. 17

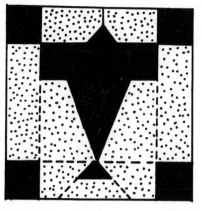

AIRCRAFT QUILT

Kansas City Star

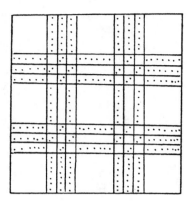

ALBUM QUILT

Ladies Art Company, No. 267

The Romance of the Patch-work Quilt in America, page 92, No. 7
Also **AUTOGRAPH PATCH**

ALBUM PATCH

Nancy Cabot

BRICK PAVEMENT

The Romance of the Patch-work Quilt in America, page 68, No. 13

GREEK CROSS

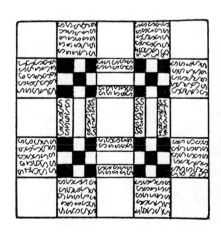

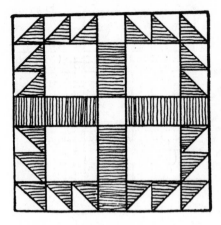

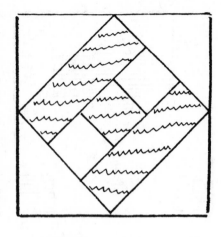

HEN AND CHICKENS

Ladies Art Company, No. 385
The Romance of the Patch-work Quilt in America, page 72, No. 23
The Standard Book of Quilt Making and Collecting, page 228

NEBRASKA

Nancy Cabot

LETTER H

Ladies Art Company, No. 164

Kansas City Star, 1935
Laura Wheeler

SHADED TRAIL

Ladies Art Company, No. 101

AIR CASTLE

Ladies Art Company, No. 452

LOCK AND CHAIN

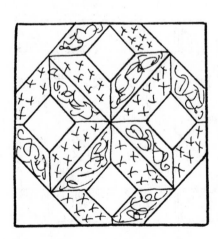

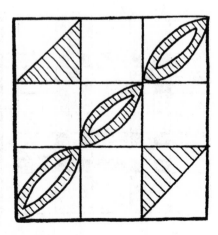

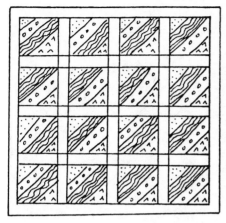

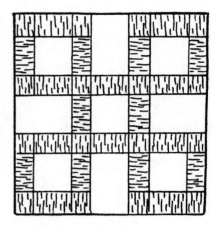

SQUARES WITH STRIPES

ROMAN SQUARE

Old Patchwork Quilts and the Women Who Made Them, page 50

STRIP SQUARES

Ladies Art Company, No. 226 *The Romance of the Patchwork Quilt in America,* page 90, No. 2

Ladies Art Company, No. 390 *The Romance of the Patchwork Quilt in America,* page 82, No. 18

Nancy Cabot

Ladies Art Company, No. 234

TILE PATCHWORK

WOODLAND PATH

ROAD TO CALIFORNIA

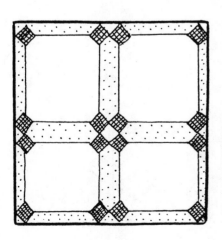

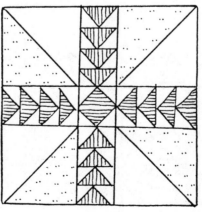

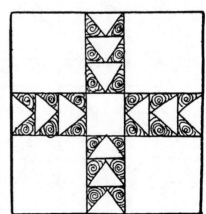

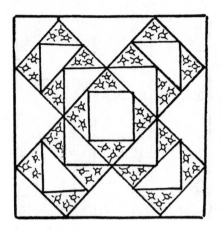

IXL or I EXCEL

Circa 1936

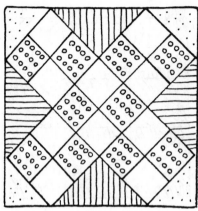

GRANDMOTHER'S CROSS

Kansas City Star, 1945

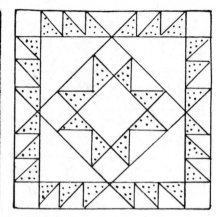

BLINDMAN'S FANCY

Ladies Art Company, No. 201
The Romance of the Patchwork Quilt in America, page 84, No. 24

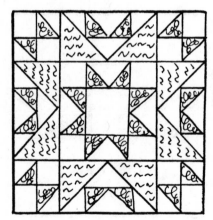

Nancy Page, 1920-30

SAN DIEGO

Old Patchwork Quilts and the Women Who Made Them, page 113 Also **LITTLE SAW TOOTH**

ROCKY GLEN

Ladies Art Company, No. 162
One Hundred and One Patchwork Patterns, page 15
The Perfect Patchwork Primer, page 32
Also **DUCK'S FOOT**

BEAR'S PAW

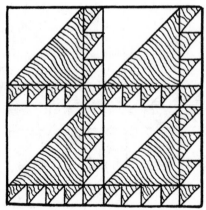

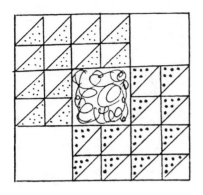

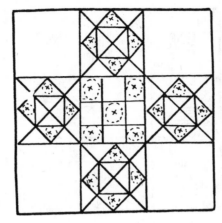

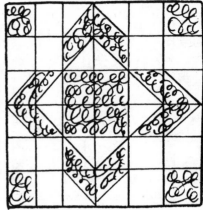

WINGED SQUARE

Old Patchwork Quilts and the Women Who Made Them, page 77
One Hundred and One Patchwork Patterns, page 28
The Romance of the Patchwork Quilt in America, page 90, No. 1

SANTE FE BLOCK

Ladies Art Company, No. 467

PUSS IN THE CORNER

The Romance of the Patchwork Quilt in America, page 80, No. 7
Also **PUSS-IN-BOOTS**

Anne Cabot

The Perfect Patchwork Primer, page 99

Ladies Art Company, No. 399

DOUBLE STAR

CHAIN

STAR A

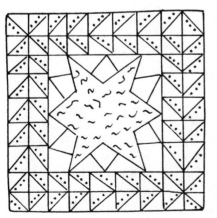

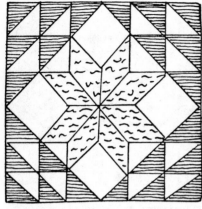

DIAMOND STAR

STEPPING STONES

The Romance of the Patch-work Quilt in America, page 84, No. 3
The Standard Book of Quilt Making and Collecting, page 229

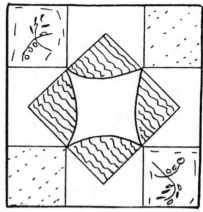

WINDOW SQUARES

Grandmother Clark's Patch-work Quilt Designs, Book 21, 1931

Grandmother Clark's Patch-work Quilt Designs, Book 21, 1931

PUSSY IN THE CORNER

Also **JACOB'S LADDER**

WAGON TRACKS

Ladies Art Company, No. 172

DOMINO

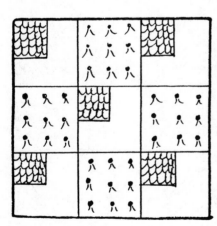

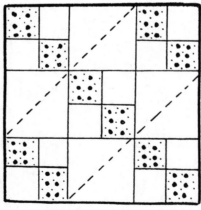

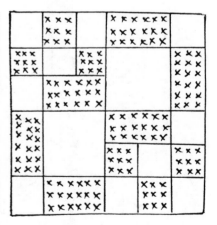

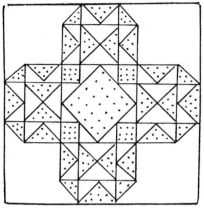

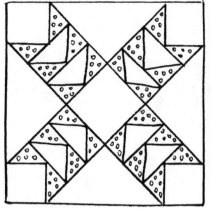

COUNTRY FARM

Ladies Art Company, No. 209

ODD FELLOWS PATCH

Ladies Art Company, No. 269
The Romance of the Patch-work Quilt in America, page 100, No. 19

JOSEPH'S COAT

Ladies Art Company, No. 146
The Standard Book of Quilt Making and Collecting, page 230
Nancy Cabot

Ladies Art Company, No. 256
One Hundred and One Patch-work Patterns, page 75
The Romance of the Patch-work Quilt in America, page 74, No. 5

Ladies Art Company, No. 257
The Romance of the Patch-work Quilt in America, page 70, No. 12
The Standard Book of Quilt Making and Collecting, page 238

The Standard Book of Quilt Making and Collecting, page 229

BIRD'S NEST

SISTER'S CHOICE

MEXICAN STAR

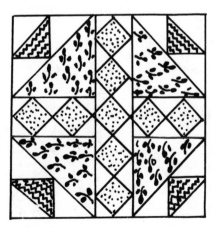

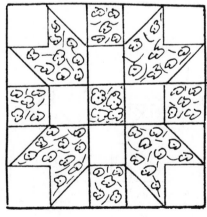

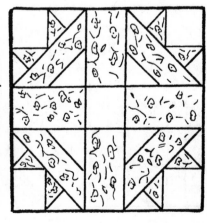

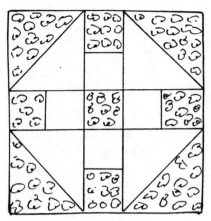

WRENCH

One Hundred and One Patchwork Patterns, page 90

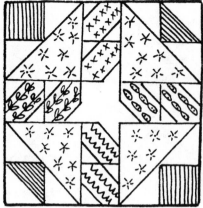

MARE'S NEST

The Perfect Patchwork Primer, page 83

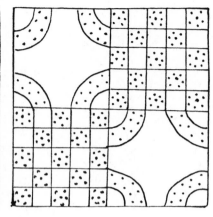

DOGWOOD BLOSSOMS

The Romance of the Patchwork Quilt in America, page 74, No. 16

Nancy Cabot

FEDERAL CHAIN

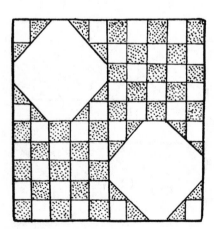

Ladies Art Company, No. 60

DOUBLE IRISH CHAIN

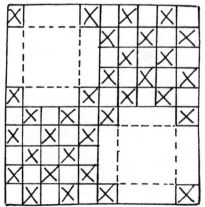

One Hundred and One Patchwork Patterns, page 42

DOUBLE IRISH CROSS

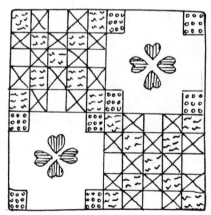

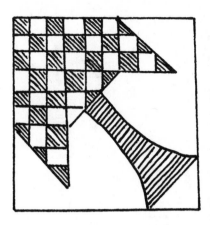

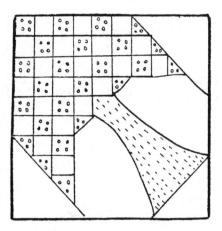

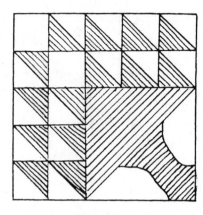

LITTLE BEECH TREE

One Hundred and One Patchwork Patterns, page 102

LITTLE BEECH TREE

Ladies Art Company, No. 223
The Romance of the Patchwork Quilt in America, page 102, No. 11

PINE TREE

The Perfect Patchwork Primer, page 103

The Romance of the Patchwork Quilt in America, page 102, No. 8
Also **TEMPERANCE TREE**
The Standard Book of Quilt Making and Collecting, page 43

PINE TREE

Modern Priscilla, August 1928, page 18

THE TREE OF PARADISE

The Romance of the Patchwork Quilt in America, page 102, No. 18

TREE OF PARADISE

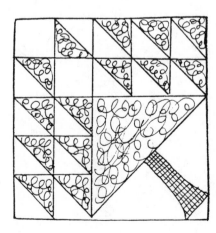

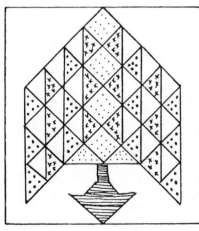

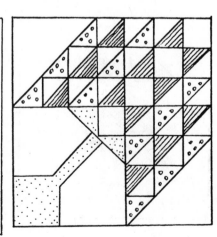

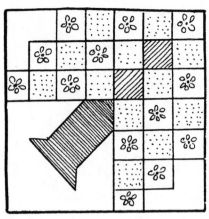

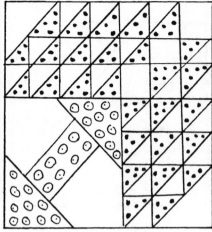

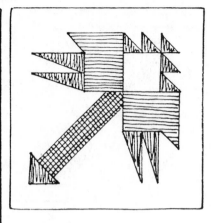

TREE OF TEMPTATION

The Romance of the Patchwork Quilt in America, page 102, No. 13

TREE OF PARADISE

Old Fashioned Quilts, page 12

TREE OF LIFE

The Perfect Patchwork Primer, page 85

Kansas City Star, 1934

PINE TREE

PINE TREE

CHRISTMAS TREE

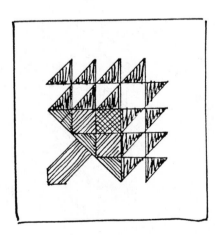

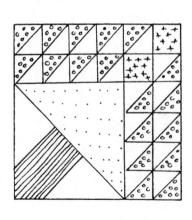

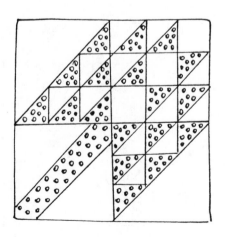

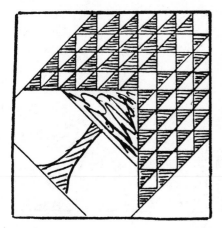

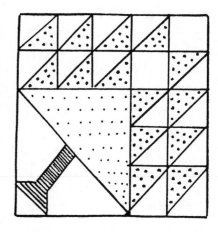

PINE TREE

The **Pine Tree,** one of the oldest quilt patterns used in the United States, was developed during the Revolutionary War period. It honored the colonists' Pine Tree flag, which centered a pine tree above the legend, "An Appeal to Heaven."

CHRISTMAS TREE

The Romance of the Patchwork Quilt in America, page 102, No. 19
Also **TREE OF LIFE**

TEMPERANCE TREE

Also **PINE TREE**

The Romance of the Patchwork Quilt in America, page 118, No. 8

LILY OF THE FIELD

The Romance of the Patchwork Quilt in America, page 80, No. 2

CROSSWORD PUZZLE

TRIPLE IRISH CHAIN

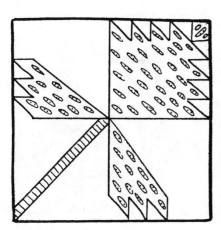

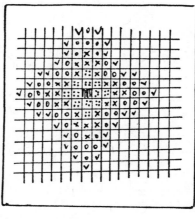

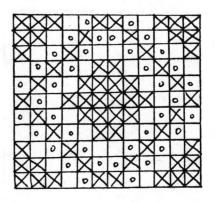

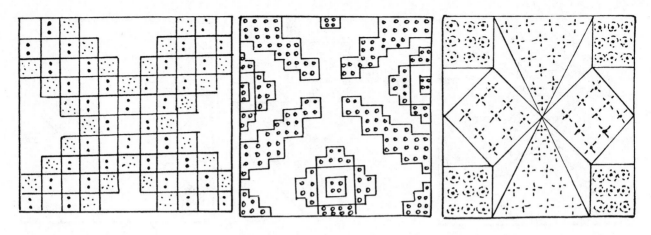

TRIPLE IRISH CHAIN

The Romance of the Patchwork Quilt in America, page 94, No. 7

CROSS PATCH

A BUTTERFLY IN ANGLES

Kansas City Star, 1944

Ladies Art Company, No. 244
The Romance of the Patchwork Quilt in America, page 60, No. 8

Nancy Cabot

BROKEN CRYSTALS

DIAMOND STAR

FLYING BARN SWALLOWS

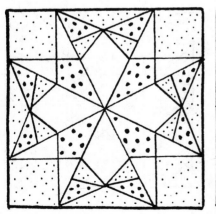
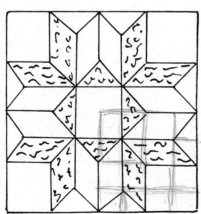

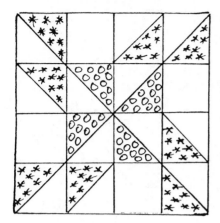 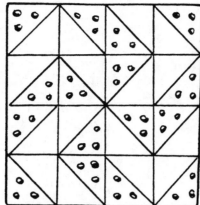 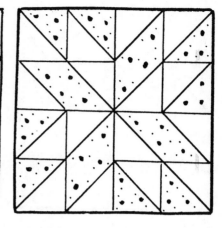

YEAR'S FAVORITE **SPIDER** **STAR OF THE MILKY WAY**

Modern Patchwork, page 19

Nancy Page, 1920-30 *Modern Patchwork*, page 46 Nancy Cabot

WILD DUCK **PEACE AND PLENTY** **FLYING FISH**

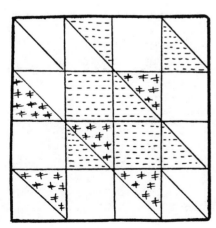 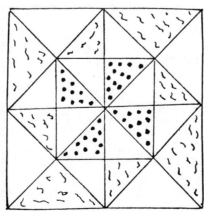 

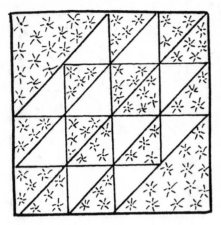

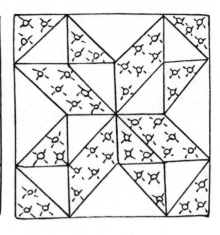

HOVERING HAWKS

Old Patchwork Quilts and the Women Who Made Them, page 72
Also **TRIPLE X**
The Romance of the Patchwork Quilt in America, page 74, No. 12

END OF THE DAY

Modern Patchwork, page 21

STAR PUZZLE

Ladies Art Company, No. 10
The Romance of the Patchwork Quilt in America, page 62, No. 1

Nancy Cabot

CUBIST ROSE

Laura Wheeler

THE WINDFLOWER

Modern Patchwork, page 44

WINDMILL—VARIATION

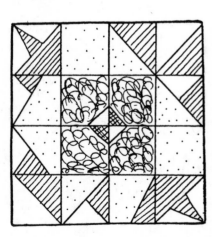

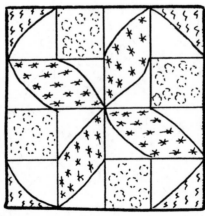

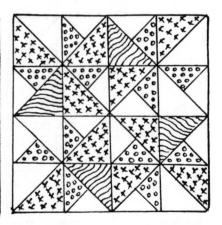

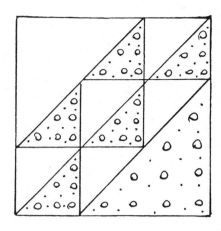

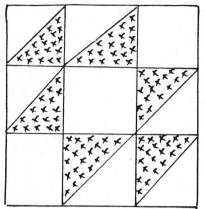

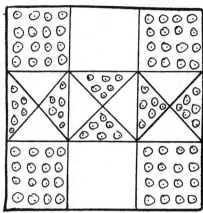

NORTH WIND

Nancy Page, 1920-30

DOUBLE X

Ladies Art Company, No. 76

TRIPLET

Kansas City Star, 1933

Ladies Art Company, No. 394
The Romance of the Patchwork Quilt in America, page 96, No. 15
The Standard Book of Quilt Making and Collecting, page 236

Nancy Cabot

SHOO FLY

TULIP LADY FINGERS

YANKEE CHARM

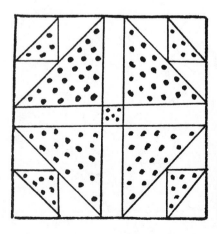

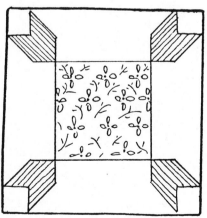

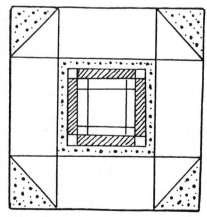

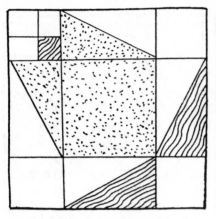 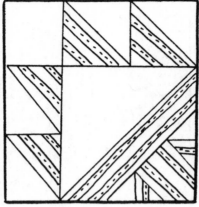 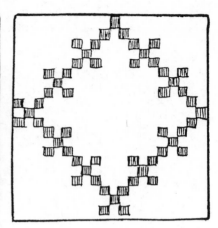

MAGNOLIA BUDS

Kansas City Star

TEXAS FLOWER

Ladies Art Company, No. 304
The Romance of the Patch-work Quilt in America, page 120, No. 6
Also **TEXAS TREASURE**

SINGLE IRISH CHAIN

The Romance of the Patch-work Quilt in America, page 94, No. 2
Also **CHAINED FIVE PATCH**

DOUBLE IRISH CHAIN

TRIPLE IRISH CHAIN

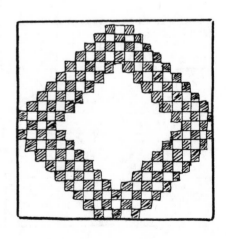

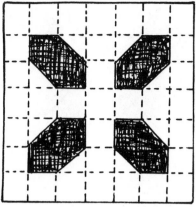

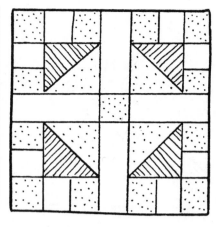

**MRS. HOOVER'S
COLONIAL QUILT**

Needlecraft Magazine, May
1926, page 9
Similar in design to the
DOUBLE IRISH CHAIN

LONE-X

ABE LINCOLN'S PLATFORM

A housewife from the state of
Illinois, impressed with the
honesty of Abe Lincoln, designed a quilt pattern and
dedicated it to "Honest Abe"
around 1860.

Ladies Art Company, No. 147
*The Romance of the Patch-
work Quilt in America,* page
98, No. 2
*The Standard Book of Quilt
Making and Collecting,* page
228

LINCOLN'S PLATFORM

Nancy Page

TABLE FOR FOUR

Modern Patchwork, page 47

FORMAL GARDEN

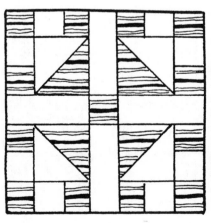

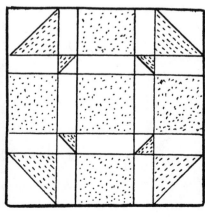

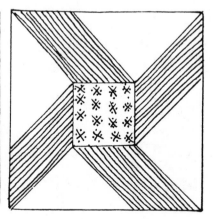

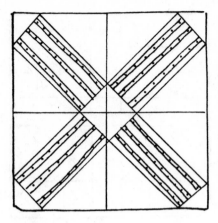

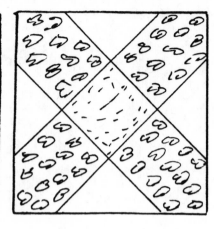

DEVIL'S PUZZLE

MOTHER'S DREAM

THE MOUNTAIN PEAK

Ladies Art Company, No. 24
The Romance of the Patchwork Quilt in America, page 80, No. 11
Also **FLY FOOT**

The Romance of the Patchwork Quilt in America, page 100, No. 7

Old Patchwork Quilts and the Women Who Made Them, page 74

Nancy Page, 1920-30

Kansas City Star, 1936

INDIAN HATCHET

PIN WHEEL

THE FLYING X QUILT

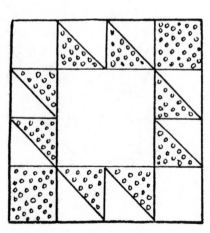

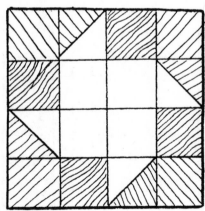

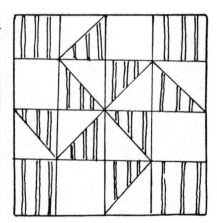

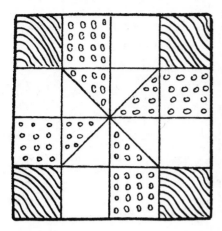

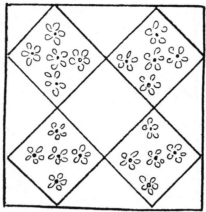

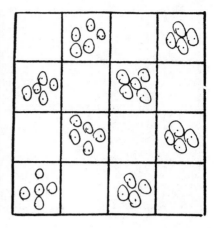

NELSON'S VICTORY

Old Patchwork Quilts and the Women Who Made Them, page 75

MOSAIC

Ladies Art Company, No. 3

MOSAIC

Ladies Art Company, No. 20

The Perfect Patchwork Primer, page 79

Kansas City Star, 1936

HOVERING BIRDS

BIRDS IN AIR

THE SICKLE

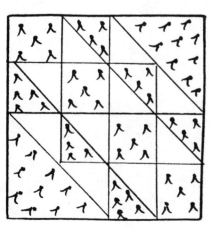

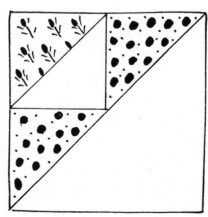

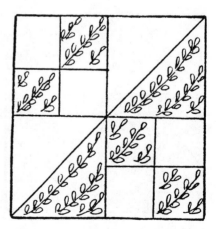

 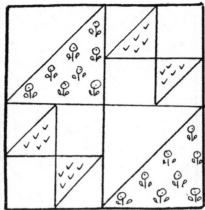 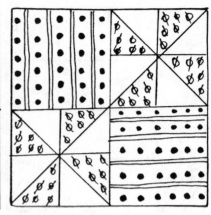

AUTUMN TINTS

The Romance of the Patchwork Quilt in America, page 96, No. 16

FOX AND GEESE

Nancy Page, 1920-30
Also **CROSSES AND LOSSES**

DOUBLE T

The Standard Book of Quilt Making and Collecting, page 238

Ladies Art Company, No. 63
Old Patchwork Quilts and the Women Who Made Them, page 81
The Romance of the Patchwork Quilt in America, page 82, No. 15
Also **LAWYER'S PUZZLE**

BARRISTER'S BLOCK

The Romance of the Patchwork Quilt in America, page 82, No. 4

HOUR GLASS

Ladies Art Company, No. 320

BIG DIPPER

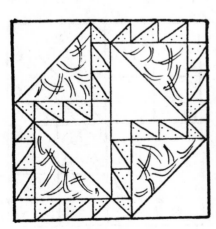  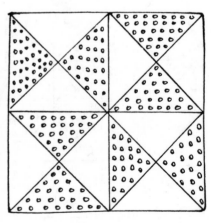

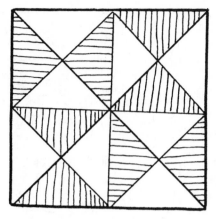

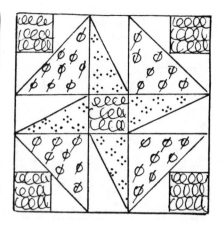

YANKEE PUZZLE

Old Patchwork Quilts and the Women Who Made Them, page 74

FOLLOW-THE-LEADER

Old Patchwork Quilts and the Women Who Made Them, page 109
The Romance of the Patchwork Quilt in America, page 94, No. 9
Named after a children's game.

CRAZY ANN

One Hundred and One Patchwork Patterns, page 4
The Romance of the Patchwork Quilt in America, page 84, No. 6
The Standard Book of Quilt Making and Collecting, page 236

Ladies Art Company, No. 126
The Romance of the Patchwork Quilt in America, page 78, No. 3
Nancy Cabot

LADIES' DELIGHT

Ladies Art Company, No. 516

CRAZY HOUSE

Ladies Art Company, No. 388

BLACKFORD'S BEAUTY

BLACK BEAUTY

Nancy Cabot

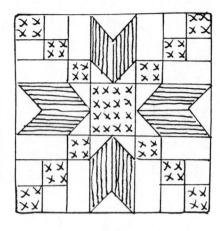

GOOD CHEER

Needlecraft Magazine, circa 1910

ARROW POINTS

The Romance of the Patchwork Quilt in America, page 82, No. 21

AIRCRAFT

Ladies Art Company, No. 251
Kansas City Star, 1929
One Hundred and One Patchwork Patterns, *The Romance of the Patchwork Quilt in America*, page 68, No. 17
Also **FOX AND GEESE**

CROSSES AND LOSSES

BOUNCING BETTY

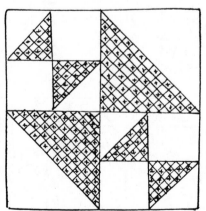

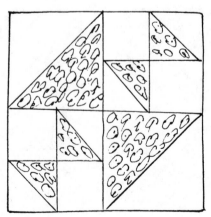

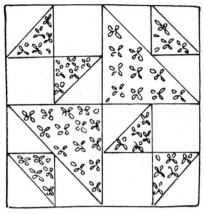

CROSSES AND LOSSES

The Perfect Patchwork Primer,
page 60

LADIES' WREATH

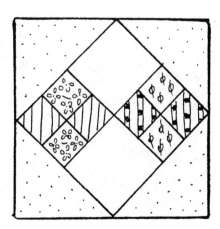

BROKEN DISHES

One Hundred and One Patch-
work Patterns, page 90

FLOCK OF GEESE

RETURN OF THE
SWALLOWS

FOUR PATCH BLOCK

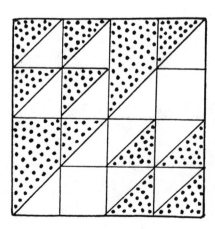

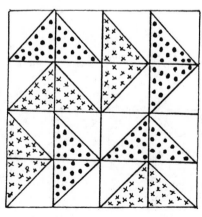

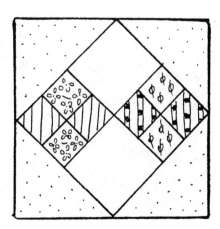

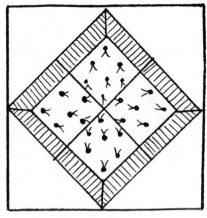

FOUR-PATCH

COFFIN STAR

FRIDAY 13TH

Kansas City Star, 1935

Kansas City Star, 1941

COLORADO QUILT

COLORADO BLOCK

YANKEE PUZZLE

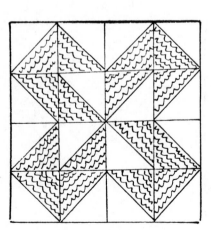

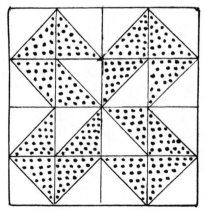

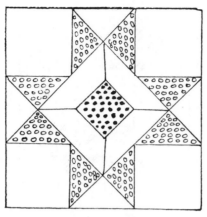

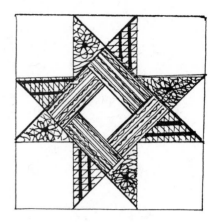

SHOOTING STAR

BRACED STAR

Ladies Art Company, No. 486
The Romance of the Patch-
work Quilt in America, page
60, No. 18

ANOTHER STAR

The Perfect Patchwork Primer,
No. 175

The Romance of the Patch-
work Quilt in America, page
58, No. 20
Also **STAR-OF-MANY-**
POINTS

ARROWHEAD STAR

Ladies Art Company, No. 323

EIGHT POINT DESIGN

Ladies Art Company, No. 88

IMPERIAL T

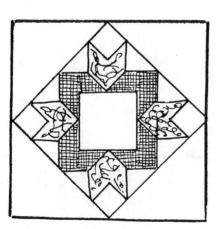

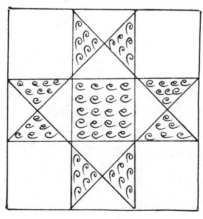

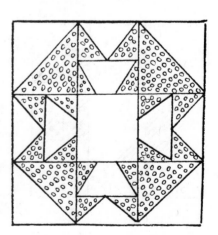

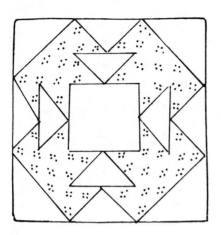

CAPITAL T

The Romance of the Patchwork Quilt in America, page 86, No. 15

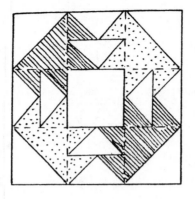

DOUBLE T

The Perfect Patchwork Primer, page 97
Also **WILD GEESE**

FOUR T'S

The Perfect Patchwork Primer, page 97

The Perfect Patchwork Primer, page 93

FLYING BIRD

The Romance of the Patchwork Quilt in America, page 100, No. 17

DOUBLE PYRAMIDS

Nancy Page, 1920-30

DOUBLE PYRAMID

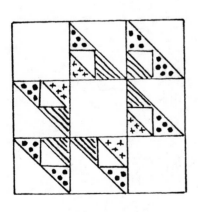

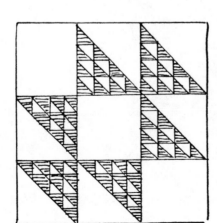

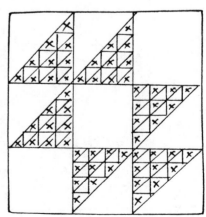

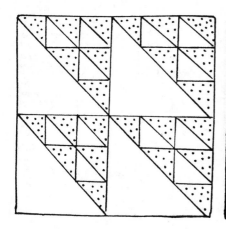

BIRDS IN THE AIR

The Romance of the Patchwork Quilt in America, page 96, No. 14

THE 1941 NINE PATCH

Kansas City Star, 1941

HAPPY HOME

Practical Needlework Quilt Patterns, Vol. 3

Modern Patchwork, page 39

OPTICAL ILLUSION

The Perfect Patchwork Primer, page 90

JEFFREY'S 9-PATCH

Ladies Art Company, No. 79

DOUBLE X

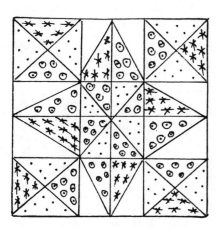

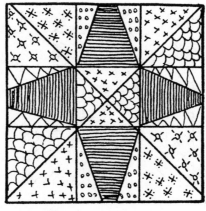

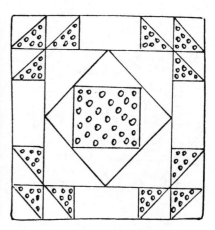

  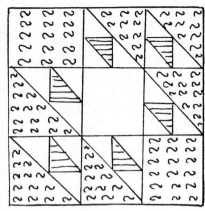

MRS. CLEVELAND'S CHOICE

Ladies Art Company, No. 144
Old Patchwork Quilts and the Women Who Made Them, page 87
The Romance of the Patchwork Quilt in America, page 78, No. 11. Also **COUNTY FAIR.** President Cleveland was married while in the White House and a quilt block was designed for Mrs. Cleveland.

KING'S CROWN

Nancy Page, 1920-30

CAT'S CRADLE

Kansas City Star, 1934

The Perfect Patchwork Primer, page 91

Ladies Art Company, No. 208

HANDY ANDY

GENTLEMAN'S FANCY

JACK KNIFE BLOCK

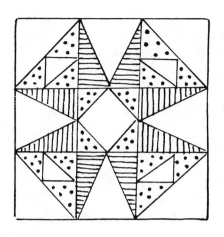

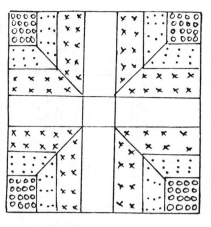

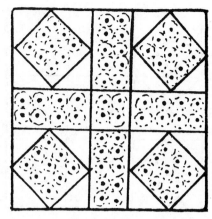

MALTESE STAR

Hearth and Home, 1922

CITY STREETS

Nancy Page, 1920-30

GARDEN OF EDEN

Ladies Art Company, No. 203
The Romance of the Patch-work Quilt in America, page 64, No. 4

Old Patchwork Quilts and the Women Who Made Them, page 74
The Romance of the Patch-work Quilt in America, page 80, No. 13
Also **FARMER'S PUZZLE.** Very similar to **SWASTIKA.**

BOW KNOT

Ladies Art Company, No. 12

CROSSES AND STAR

Ladies Art Company, No. 19
The Standard Book of Quilt Making and Collecting, page 233
Also **ORNATE STAR**

COMBINATION STAR

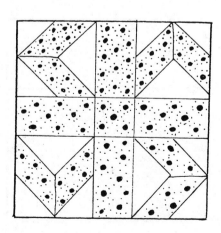

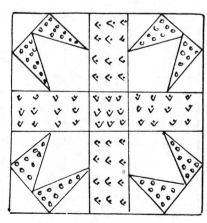

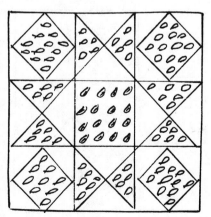

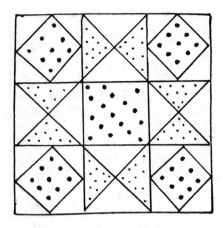

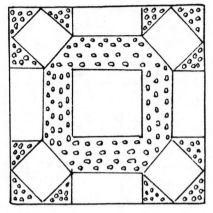

ORNATE STAR

The Romance of the Patch-work Quilt in America, page 76, No. 1
Also **COMBINATION STAR**

BROKEN WHEEL

Hearth and Home, 1926

PEEK-A-BOO

Joseph Doyle & Co., N.J.

The popular slogan in the 1830s-1840s, during the boundary dispute between the United States and Great Britain over the Oregon Territory, was "Fifty-Four Forty Or Fight." Quilt patterns were often named after the political issues of the day.

The Perfect Patchwork Primer, page 96

8-POINTED STAR

The Romance of the Patch-work Quilt in America, page 56, No. 9
Also **TEXAS STAR**

LONE STAR

54-40 OR FIGHT

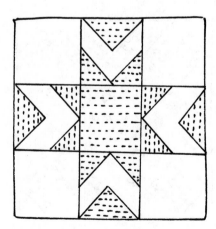

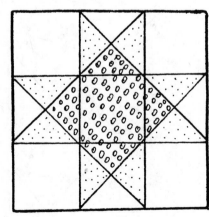

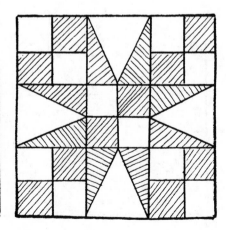

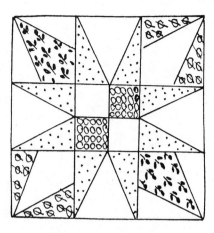

CLAWS

The Perfect Patchwork Primer,
page 99

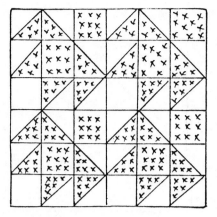

DARTING BIRDS

Nancy Page, 1920-30

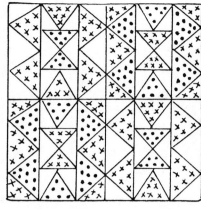

LOST SHIP PATTERN

Ladies Art Company, No. 318

Kansas City Star, 1933

FOUR CROWNS

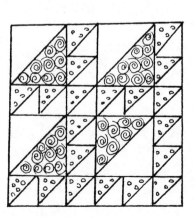

Modern   Patchwork,   page   9

FRAMED X

SIGNAL LIGHTS

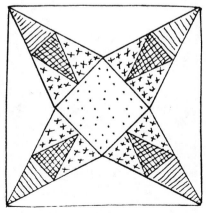

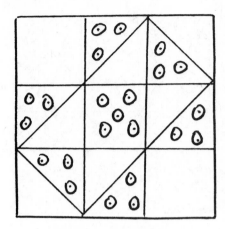 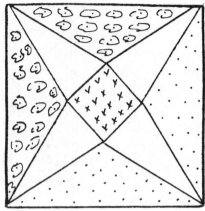 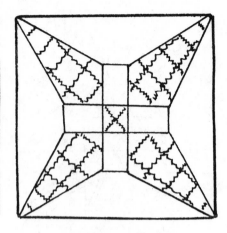

SPLIT NINE-PATCH

The Romance of the Patchwork Quilt in America, page 48, No. 12

KALEIDOSCOPE

One Hundred and One Patchwork Patterns, page 44

KING DAVID'S CROWN

The Romance of the Patchwork Quilt in America, page 60, No. 19
The Standard Book of Quilt Making and Collecting, page 229

Nancy Cabot

INDIAN CANOES

FLOWERING NINE-PATCH

DUMBELL BLOCK

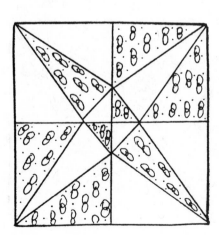 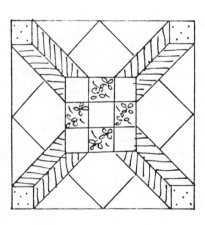 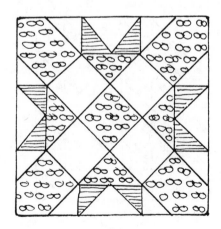

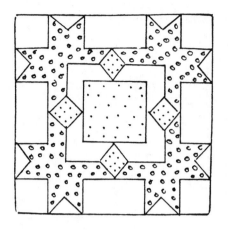

GOLGOTHA

Old Patchwork Quilts and the Women Who Made Them, page 107
The Romance of the Patchwork Quilt in America, page 64, No. 18
Also **THE THREE CROSSES, CROSS UPON CROSS**
Nancy Cabot

EASY WAYS

Farm Journal and *Farmer's Wife,* 1942

ALBUM PATCH

The Romance of the Patchwork Quilt in America, page 94, No. 12

One Hundred and One Patchwork Patterns, page 5
In olden times when a girl was about to be married, a group of her friends would get together and each contribute a quilt block to be pieced together and made into an album quilt. It was customary to embroider the name of the donor on the block.

The Perfect Patchwork Primer, page 91
Also **TRIP AROUND THE WORLD**

The Romance of the Patchwork Quilt in America, page 90, No. 17
The Standard Book of Quilt Making and Collecting, page 243

CHECKERBOARD

COURTHOUSE SQUARE

ALBUM

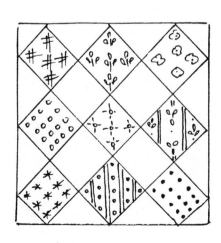

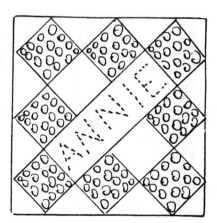

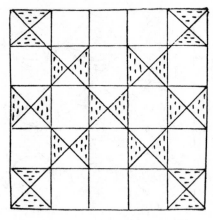

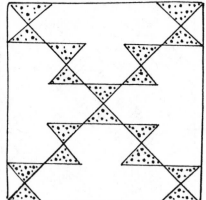

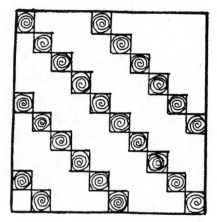

CLOWN

Ladies Art Company, No. 524

CLOWN'S CHOICE

The Romance of the Patch-work Quilt in America, page 78, No. 12

KITE'S TAIL

The Romance of the Patch-work Quilt in America, page 180, Plate XLVI

American Quilts and Cover-lets, page 27

MOTHER GOOSE

STAR TULIP

WINDING WALK

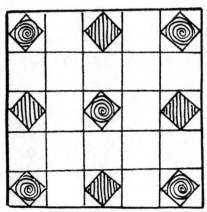

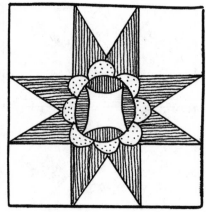

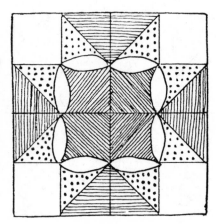

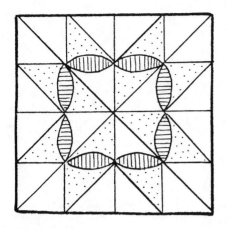

WINDING WALK

CATHEDRAL WINDOW

STAR FLOWER

Ladies Art Company, No. 409
Also **INDIAN TRAILS,
STORM AT SEA**

Laura Wheeler   1937

PINWHEEL

COLONIAL ROSE

QUILT WITHOUT A NAME

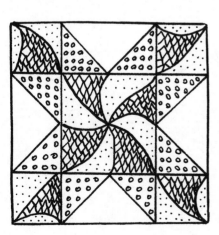

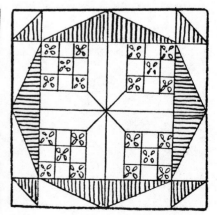

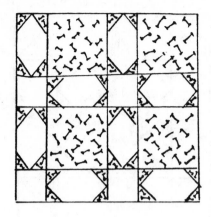

VESTIBULE

Ladies Art Company, No. 383

OLD MISSOURI

INTERWOVEN PUZZLE

Ladies Art Company, No. 83
The Romance of the Patch-work Quilt in America, page 48, No. 16
There are a number of variations of the original **NINE PATCH.** The design is created by the use of different sizes of patches and the arrangement of colors.

Ladies Art Company, No. 284
The Romance of the Patch-work Quilt in America, page 60, No. 11

Nancy Cabot

STAR AND CROSS

GRANDMOTHER'S DREAM

NINE PATCH

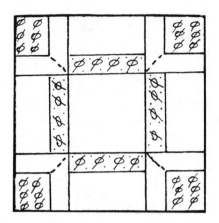

HAND WEAVE

Ladies Art Company, No. 526

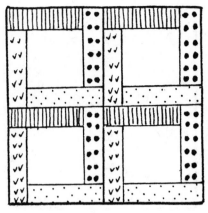

BRIGHT HOPES

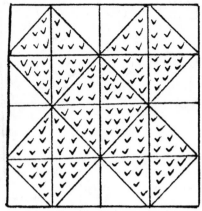

OLD TIPPECANOE

Ladies Art Company, No. 194
The Romance of the Patch-
work Quilt in America, page
98, No. 11

The Standard Book of Quilt
Making and Collecting, page
235

OLD TIPPECANOE

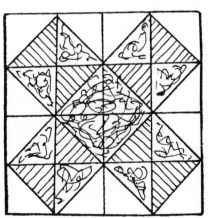

The Perfect Patchwork Primer,
page 81

TAM'S PATCH

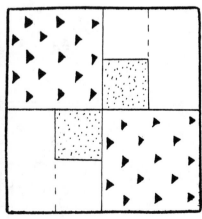

Modern Patchwork, page 15

BRAVE WORLD

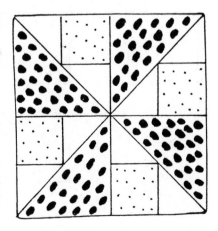

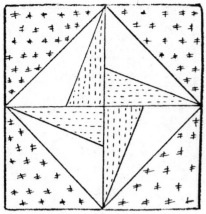

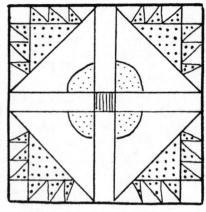

WASTE NOT

Nancy Page, 1920-30

MALTESE CROSS

Ladies Art Company, No. 272
The Romance of the Patch-work Quilt in America, page 68, No. 1
The Standard Book of Quilt Making and Collecting, page 241

WORLD'S FAIR QUILT

The Romance of the Patch-work Quilt in America, page 84, No. 9
This pattern commemorates the 1893 Chicago World Fair.

Ladies Art Company, No. 4

MOSAIC

HILL AND VALLEY

DOUBLE CROSS

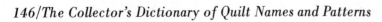

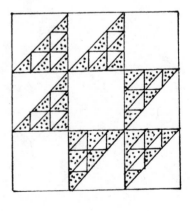

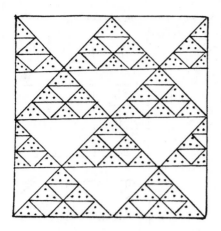

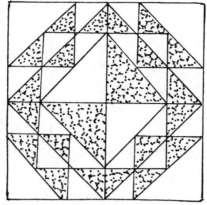

FLYING GEESE

The Standard Book of Quilt Making and Collecting, page 228

CORN AND BEANS

Ladies Art Company, No. 100 One Hundred and One Patchwork Patterns, page 105
The Romance of the Patchwork Quilt in America, page 78, No. 9
Also **SHOO-FLY, HANDY ANDY, HEN AND CHICKENS, DUCK AND DUCKLINGS**

GEORGETOWN CIRCLES

The Perfect Patchwork Primer, page 80

HITHER AND YON

Ladies Art Company, No. 268

RIBBON STAR

Ladies Art Company, No. 19

MOSAIC

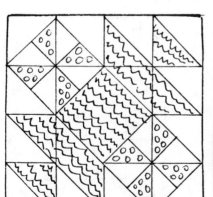

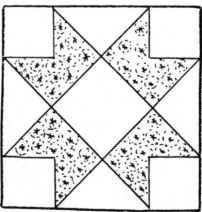

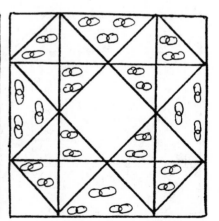

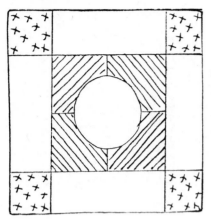

CIRCLE IN A FRAME

Kansas City Star, 1945

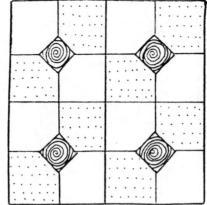

TRUE LOVER'S KNOT

Ladies Art Company, No. 262
The Romance of the Patchwork Quilt in America, page 70, No. 14
In Kentucky called **SASSAFRAS LEAF**; in New England, the **HAND**; and in the Middle West, the **CALIFORNIA OAK LEAF.**

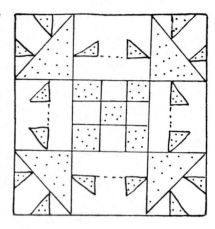

FOUR CLOWNS

Nancy Cabot

The Romance of the Patchwork Quilt in America, page 74, No. 8

MRS. KELLER'S NINE-PATCH

Ladies Art Company, No. 112

CHURN DASH

Ladies Art Company, No. 407

THE CROSS

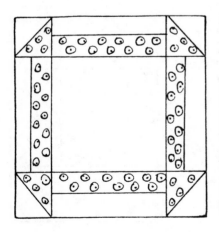

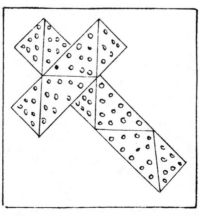

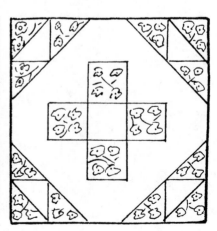

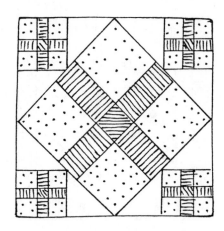

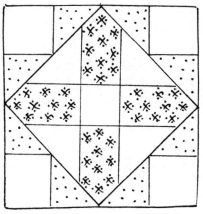

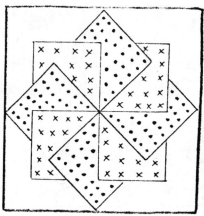

CABIN WINDOWS

Kansas City Star, 1940

CROSS WITHIN A CROSS

Ladies Art Company, No. 313
The Romance of the Patch-work Quilt in America, page 68, No. 3

TWISTING STAR

Variations of this pattern include **DOUBLE MONKEY WRENCH, DUCK AND DUCK-LINGS, HANDY ANDY, SHOO FLY**
Also **CAPITAL T, IMPERIAL T, T QUARTETTE**

The Perfect Patchwork Primer, page 98

The Perfect Patchwork Primer, page 92

CARD TRICK

T BLOCK

CASTLE IN AIR

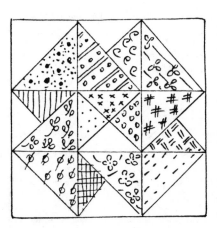

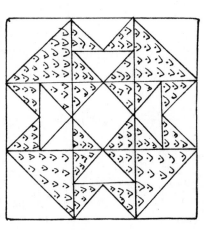

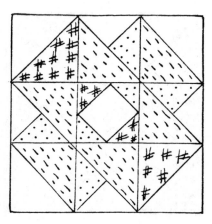

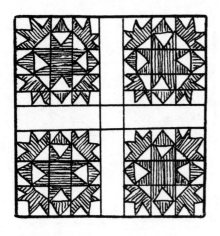

SUNBURST

American Quilts, page 111

INDIAN PLUME

SQUARES

The Romance of the Patch-work Quilt in America, page 82, No. 8
The Standard Book of Quilt Making and Collecting, page 238

DEVIL'S CLAWS

WHIRLING PINWHEEL

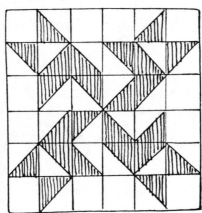

Nancy Cabot

LADIES WREATH

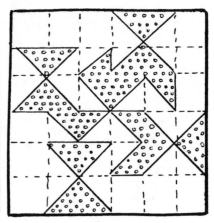

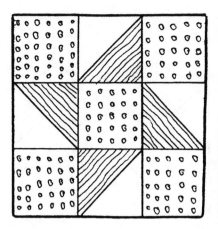

WINGS IN A WHIRL

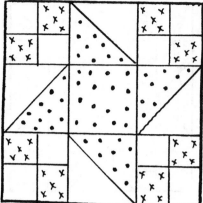

WATER WHEEL

Nancy Cabot

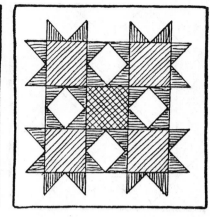

DEVIL'S CLAWS

Ladies Art Comapny, No. 142

Old Patchwork Quilts and the Women Who Made Them, page 70
The Romance of the Patchwork Quilt in America, page 56, No. 8

Nancy Page, 1920-30

STAR OF HOPE

VARIABLE STAR

A WISHING STAR

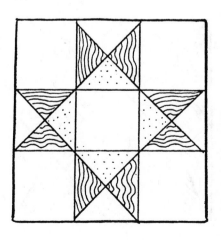

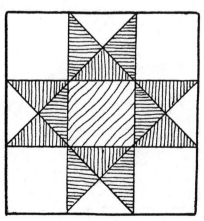

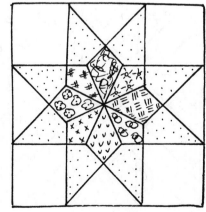

FOUR T'S

Nancy Cabot

STARRY LANE

The Romance of the Patchwork Quilt in America, page 60, No. 16

MORNING STAR

Kansas City Star

Woman's World, February 1928, page 30
One Hundred and One Patchwork Patterns, page 51
The Romance of the Patchwork Quilt in America, page 92, No. 6

The Standard Book of Quilt Making and Collecting, page 231

MEXICAN ROSE

LOCKED STAR

SKYROCKET

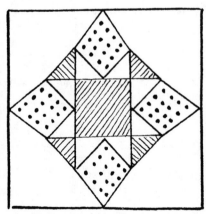

SKY ROCKET

The Perfect Patchwork Primer,
page 97

SMALL BUSINESS

The Perfect Patchwork Primer,
page 80

SQUARE AND STAR

Ladies Art Compay, No. 263

Modern Patchwork, page 32

PEACEFUL HOURS

Early American Quilts, page
14

TRIANGLE

Nancy Cabot

BALKAN PUZZLE

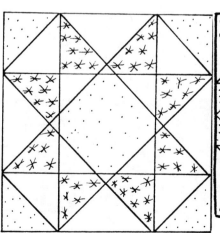

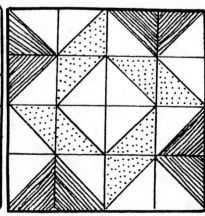

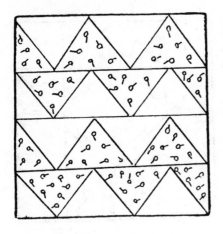

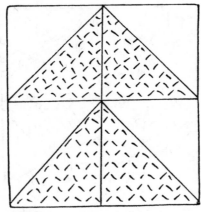

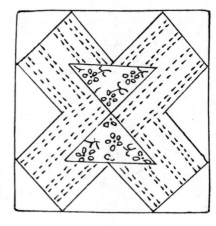

LIGHTNING

Nancy Cabot

CHEVRON

DOUBLE Z

The Standard Book of Quilt Making and Collecting, page 244

Grandmother Clark's Patchwork Quilt Designs, Book 21, 1931

Ladies Art Company, No. 393 *The Romance of the Patchwork Quilt in America,* page 56, No. 16

Ladies Art Company, No. 22 *The Romance of the Patchwork Quilt in America,* page 58, No. 16

CRISS-CROSS

CLUSTER OF STARS

CHICAGO STAR

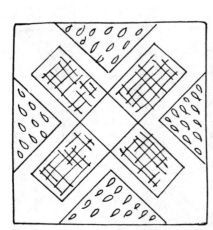

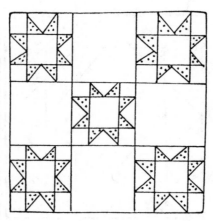

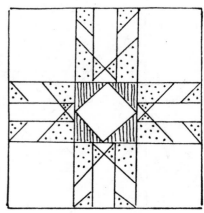

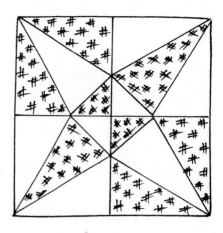

STAR

The Perfect Patchwork Primer,
page 80

EXPLODING STARS

CROSSED CANOES

Ladies Art Company, No. 89
One Hundred and One Patch-
work Patterns, page 114
The Romance of the Patch-
work Quilt in America, page
94, No. 1

Ladies Art Company, No. 317
The Romance of the Patch-
work Quilt in America, page
72, No. 21
The Standard Book of Quilt
Making and Collecting, page
241

CATS AND MICE

Ladies Art Company, No. 236
Also **JOB'S TEARS**
The Romance of the Patch-
work Quilt in America, page
76, No. 15

ROCKY ROAD TO KANSAS

Weekly Star Farmer, 1954

THE DRAGON FLY

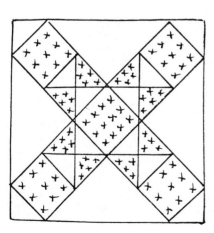

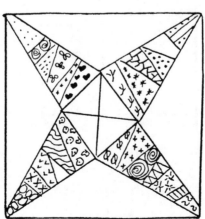

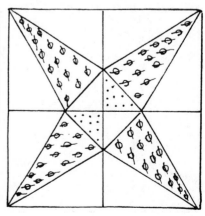

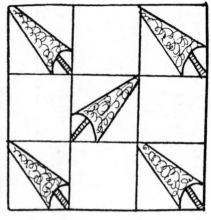

ROCKY ROAD TO KANSAS **FORGOTTEN STAR** **OLD INDIAN TRAIL**

The Standard Book of Quilt Making and Collecting, page 240

Ladies Art Company, No. 145   Nancy Page

JOSEPH'S NECKTIE **WINDMILL** **GOOD LUCK BLOCK**

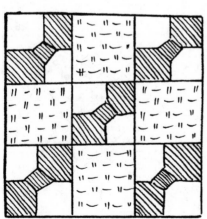

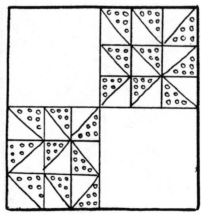

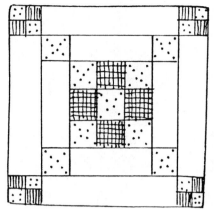

NINE PATCH PLAID

COUNTERPANE

Nancy Cabot

MADAM X

The Romance of the Patchwork Quilt in America, page 92, No. 13

Also **CHECKERBOARD, GRANDMA'S DREAM**

TRIP AROUND THE WORLD

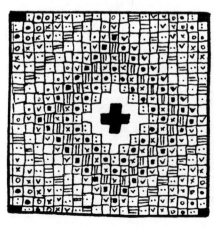

NINE PATCH BLOCK

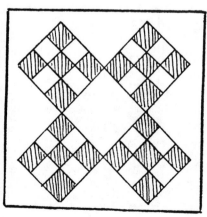

Ladies Art Company, No. 233

FLYING SQUARES

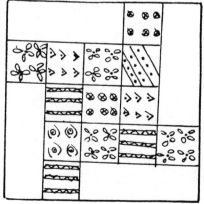

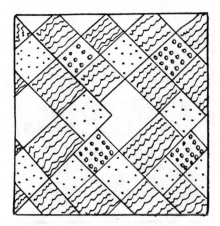

AUNT MARY'S SQUARES

Grandmother Clark's Patchwork Quilt Designs, Book 21, 1931

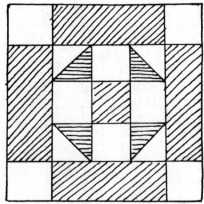

PHILADELPHIA PAVEMENT

Old Patchwork Quilts and the Women Who Made Them, page 80
The Romance of the Patchwork Quilt in America, page 100, No. 1

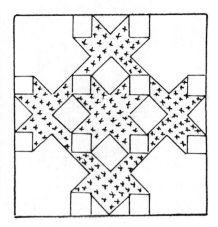

DOUBLE STAR

Hearth and Home, 1924

Ladies Art Company, No. 84

CAPITAL T

Kansas City Star

ARMY STAR

Needlecraft Magazine, February 1934, page 8

LILY POOL

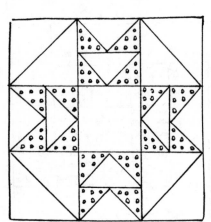

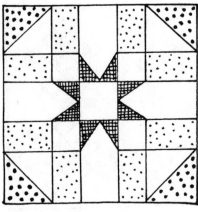

JOSEPH'S COAT

The Romance of the Patch-work Quilt in America, page 64, No. 13
Also **SCRAP-BAG** in Pennsylvania

WINGED SQUARE

Laura Wheeler

LEMON STAR

Ladies Art Company, No. 247
The Romance of the Patch-work Quilt in America, page 92, No. 5
The Standard Book of Quilt Making and Collecting, page 232

Kansas City Star, 1933

THE OLD SPANISH TILE PATTERN

This pattern is similar to **SNAIL TRAIL**

VIRGINIA REEL

FLYING DUTCHMAN

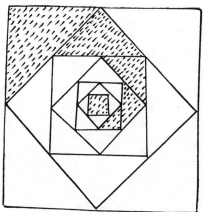

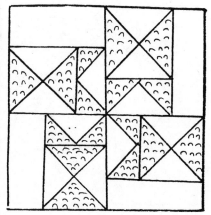

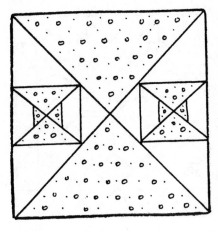

SPOOLS

Ladies Art Company, No. 398

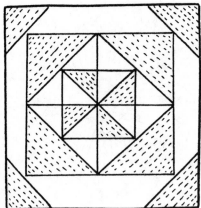

SQUARE WITHIN SQUARES

ZIG-ZAG

Ladies Art Company, No. 513

NAVAJO

Kansas City Star, 1936

SOLOMON'S TEMPLE

KENTUCKY CROSSROADS

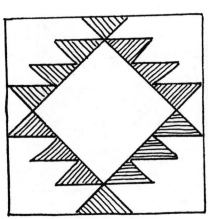

PROSPERITY

Nancy Cabot

SNOW BALL

The Romance of the Patchwork Quilt in America, page 78, No. 18
Also **JOB'S TROUBLES, PULLMAN PUZZLE**

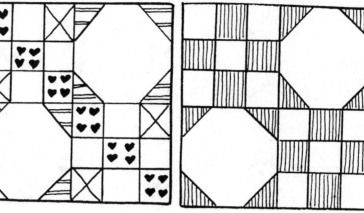

FLAGSTONES

Ladies Art Company, No. 514

Old Patchwork Quilts and the Women Who Made Them, page 81

JOSEPH'S COAT

American Needlewoman, April 1926, page 19

ATTIC WINDOW

Joseph Doyle & Co., N.J.

GRANDMOTHER'S PUZZLE

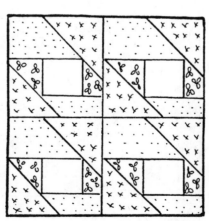

PROVIDENCE QUILT BLOCK

Ladies Art Company, No. 478
Nancy Cabot

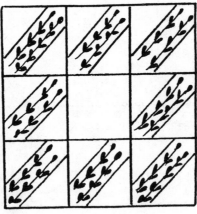

NONSUCH

Ladies Art Company, No. 363

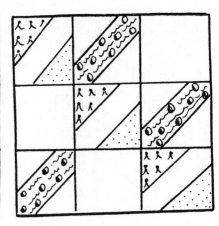

INDIAN TOMAHAWK

Old Patchwork Quilts and the Women Who Made Them, page 79
The Romance of the Patchwork Quilt in America, page 68, No. 18
As a compliment to Queen Charlotte, wife of King George III of England, a group of Virginian ladies named this quilt design **QUEEN CHARLOTTE'S CROWN.** Later, after 1770, it came to be known as **INDIAN MEADOW.**

QUEEN CHARLOTTE'S CROWN

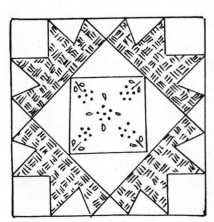

CONTRARY WIFE

Nancy Cabot

OLD FASHIONED DAISY

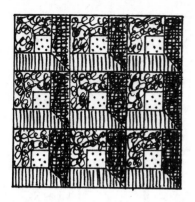

SHADOW BOX

QUADRILLE

Nancy Cabot

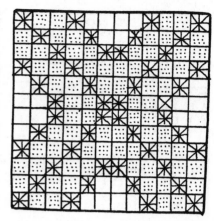

STEPS TO THE GARDEN

Nancy Cabot

Old Patchwork Quilts and the Women Who Made Them, page 72

THE SWALLOW

The Romance of the Patchwork Quilt in America, page 86, No. 13
Also **SINGLE WEDDING RING**

WHEEL

Grandmother Clark's Patchwork Quilt Designs, Book 21, 1931

WATERMILL

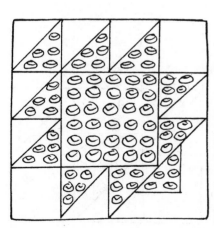

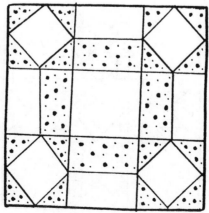

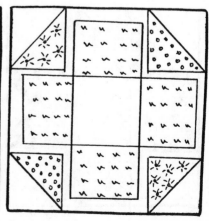

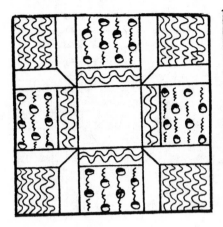 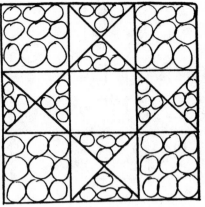 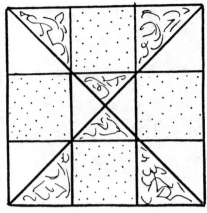

INTERWOVEN

Nancy Page, 1920-30

SHOO FLY

HOUR GLASS

Practical Needlework Quilt Patterns, Vol. 3

Old Patchwork Quilts and the Women Who Made Them, page 85
The Romance of the Patchwork Quilt in America, page 56, No. 1
Dolly Madison acted as hostess at the White House during her husband's term of office, and again for President Thomas Jefferson, who was a widower. She was the "First Lady" to be honored with a quilt pattern.

Kansas City Star, 1935

Ladies Art Company, No. 20

DOLLY MADISON STAR

PINE CONE

JOINING STAR

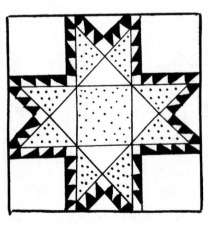 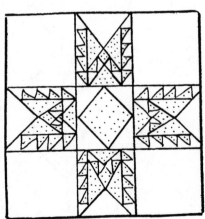 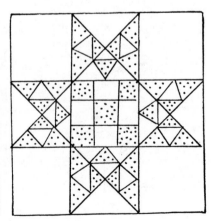

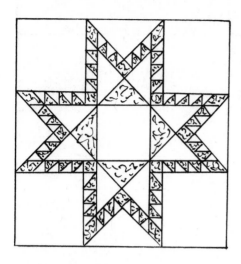

FEATHER EDGE STAR

Kansas City Star, 1934

CALIFORNIA STAR

The Romance of the Patchwork Quilt in America, page 92, No. 8

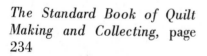
The Standard Book of Quilt Making and Collecting, page 234

CALIFORNIA STAR

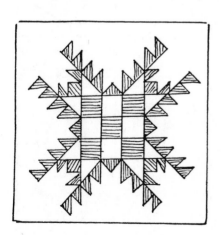

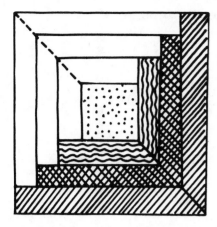

STRAIGHT FURROW   See page 172.

Rectangle

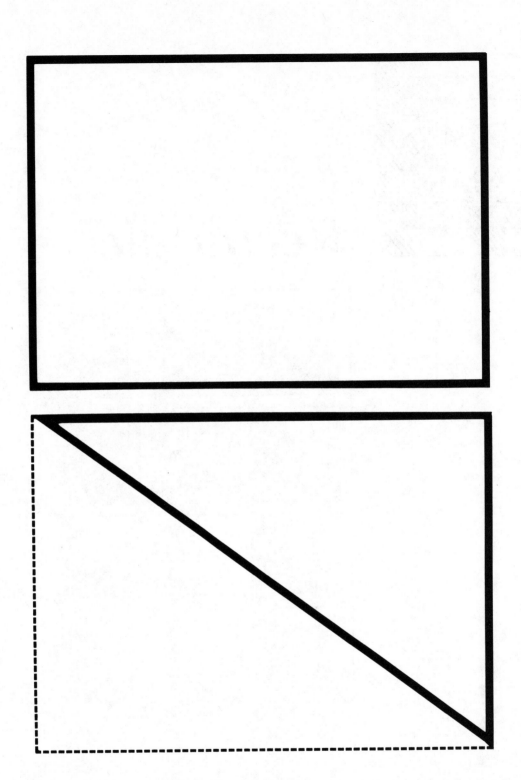

Rectangle: Any pattern that contains a rectangle (a four-sided regular figure) or parts thereof, such as a log cabin quilt, will be shown under "rectangle."

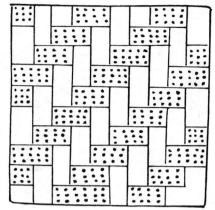

BRICK WORK

Ladies Art Company, No. 293
The Romance of the Patch-work Quilt in America, page 52, No. 2 and 3

COARSE WOVEN PATCHWORK

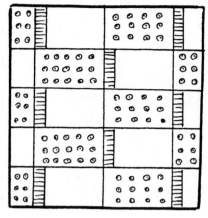

BASKET WEAVE

The Romance of the Patch-work Quilt in America, page 52, No. 7
Also **COARSE WOVEN**

Nancy Cabot

ENDLESS STAIR

FINE WOVEN

Nancy Cabot

SPIRIT OF ST LOUIS

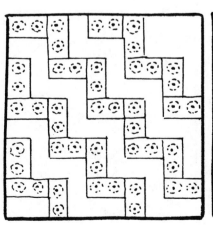

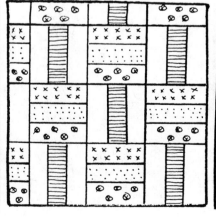

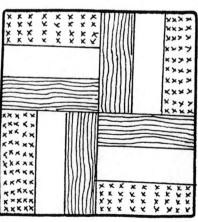

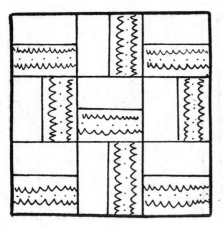

LONDON STAIRS

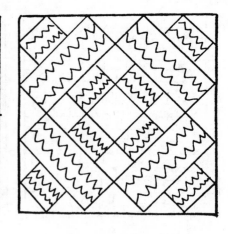

FOUR H

Nancy Page
Kansas City Star, 1940

WASHINGTON SIDEWALK

Ladies Art Company, No.
175

Ladies Art Company, No.
171
Also **LITTLE SAW TOOTH**

ROCKY GLEN

Nancy Cabot

FRIENDSHIP CHAIN

Ladies Art Company, No.
364
*The Romance of the Patch-
work Quilt in America,* page
68, No. 7

ROMAN CROSS

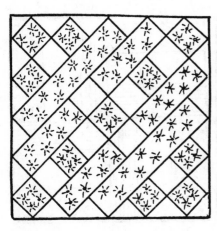

SWASTIKA PATCH

Ladies Art Company, No. 455
The Romance of the Patchwork Quilt in America, page 94, No. 21
Also **WIND POWER OF THE OSAGES**

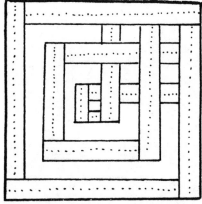

INTERLOCKED BLOCKS

Ladies Art Company, No. 326
Nancy Cabot

The pattern dates from the 18th century—most probably created by the earliest settlers who made early patterns from worn-out usable woolen material and clothing. From the middle of the 19th to the early 20th century (the Victorian Era), scraps of brocades, silks, and velvets were then used with elaborate embroidery. The use of light and dark material in piecing the square block together created various designs.

LOG CABIN — BASIC PATCH

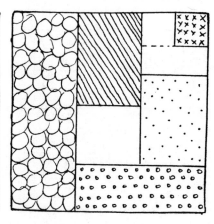

BECKY'S 9-PATCH

The Perfect Patchwork Primer, page 89

Old Patchwork Quilts and the Women Who Made Them, page 48

BRICK WALL

Ladies Art Company, No. 168

THE LOG PATCH

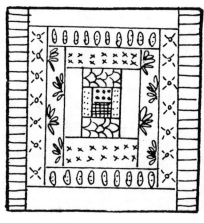

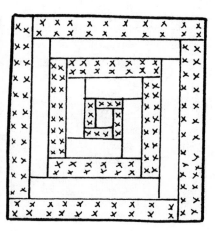

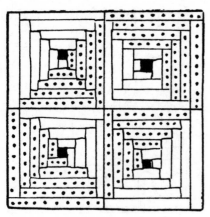

**AMERICAN LOG.
PATCHWORK**

Ladies Art Company, No.
374

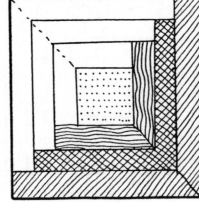

STRAIGHT FURROW

Nancy Cabot
Also **LOG CABIN**

STREAK OF LIGHTNING

Also **ZIG-ZAG**

Ladies Art Company, No. 240

FINE WOVEN PATCHWORK

A Log Cabin variation

CAPITAL STEPS

Ladies Art Company, No.
242

**COARSE WOVEN
PATCHWORK**

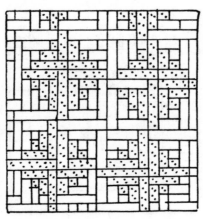

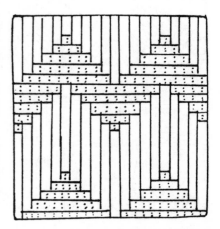

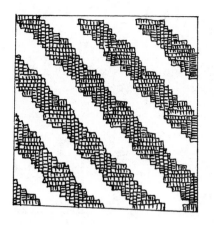

FALLING TIMBERS

Also **LOG CABIN**

BARN-RAISING

Old Patchwork Quilts and the Women Who Made Them, Plate 2

FINE WOVEN PATCH

Old Patchwork Quilts and the Women Who Made Them, Plate 3
The Romance of the Patchwork Quilt in America, page 52, No. 5

The Romance of the Patchwork Quilt in America, page 52, No. 4

LOG CABIN—BARN RAISING

LOG CABIN—STRAIGHT FURROW—FALLING TIMBERS

LOG CABIN —CAPITAL STEPS —COURTHOUSE STEPS

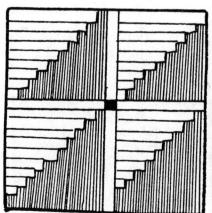

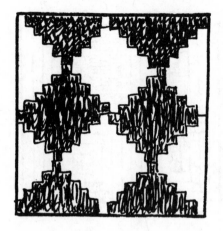

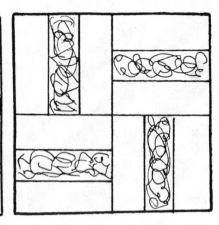

LOG CABIN—LIGHT AND
DARK

LOG CABIN—ZIG ZAG

INTERLOCKED SQUARES

The Perfect Patchwork Primer,
page 28

*The Romance of the Patch-
work Quilt in America,* page
106, No. 10
Also **SPRING BEAUTY**

Ladies Art Company, No.
139

ROMAN STRIPE ZIG-ZAG

CRIMSON RAMBLER

FIVE STRIPES

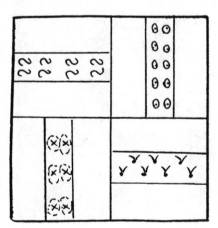

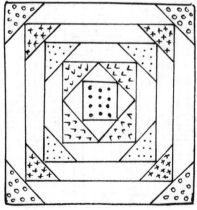

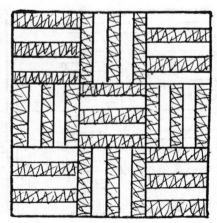

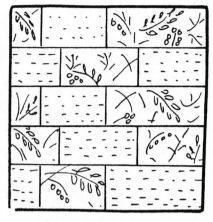

ROMAN STRIPE

RAINBOW

ZIGZAG BLOCKS

The Romance of the Patch-work Quilt in America, page 52, No. 9

Grandmother Clark's Patch-work Quilt Designs, Book 20, 1931

Ladies Art Company, No. 327

Ladies Art Company, No. 378

Progressive Farmer

AUNT SUKEY'S PATCH

ALBUM

TENNALLYTOWN

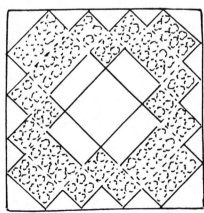

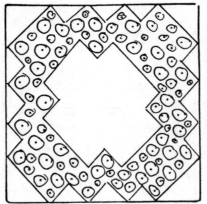

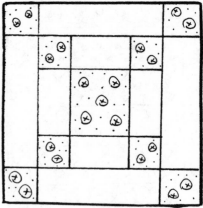

DOMINO AND SQUARE

Ladies Art Company, No. 278
Nancy Cabot

CHIMNEY SWEEP

*The Romance of the Patch-
work Quilt in America,* page
100, No. 6

PENNSYLVANIA

Nancy Page, 1920-30

Laura Wheeler

WHITE HOUSE STEPS

Woman's World, November
1926, page 38

YELLOW LILY

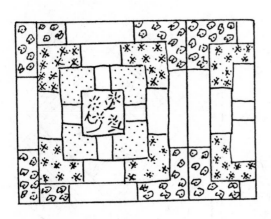

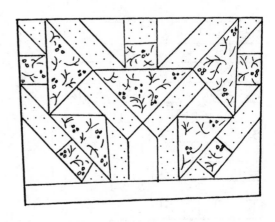

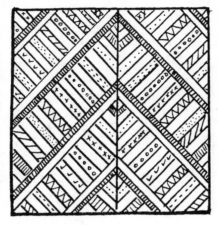

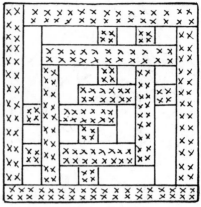

CHILDREN'S DELIGHT

Ladies Art Company, No. 319
The Romance of the Patch-work Quilt in America, page 70, No. 13

HIT AND MISS

CARPENTER'S SQUARE

Ladies Art Company, No. 395
The Romance of the Patch-work Quilt in America, page 90, No. 3

Progressive Farmer

CRAZY LOONS

Ladies Art Company, No. 35

E BLOCK

WEDDING RING TILE

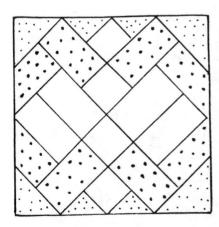

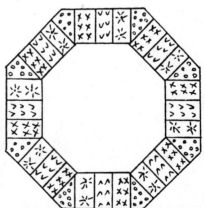

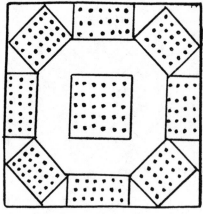

NONSENSE

Ladies Art Company, No. 153

ROLLING STONE

Ladies Art Company, No. 216
Early American Quilts, page 14
The Romance of the Patchwork Quilt in America, page 76, No. 2
Also **BLOCK CIRCLE, JOHNNIE-ROUND-THE-CORNER, JOSEPH'S COAT**
The Standard Book of Quilt Making and Collecting, page 245

FOUR-LEAF CLOVER

Needlecraft Magazine, February 1935, page 9

Kansas City Star, 1930

THE GOBLET QUILT

The Romance of the Patchwork Quilt in America, page 52, No. 10

ROMAN SQUARE

Needlecraft Magazine, February 1934, page 8

TREES IN THE PARK

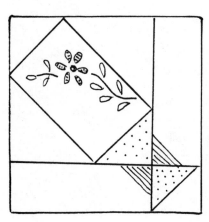

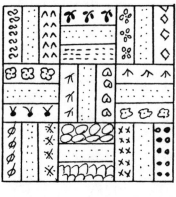

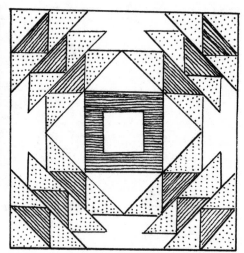

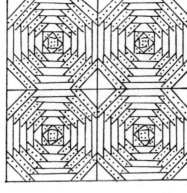

PINEAPPLE

The Romance of the Patch-work Quilt in America, page 68, No. 15
Also **MALTESE CROSS**

CHESTNUT BURR

Mrs. Danner's Quilts, Book 2

PINEAPPLE

The Household Magazine, November 1929, page 38

The Romance of the Patch-work Quilt in America, page 96, No. 18
Also **MALTESE CROSS**

Nancy Cabot

COLONIAL PINEAPPLE

PINEAPPLE

ALTAR STEPS

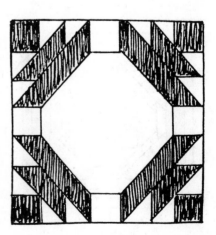

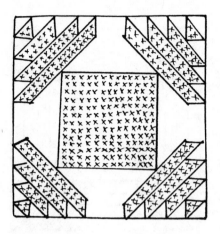

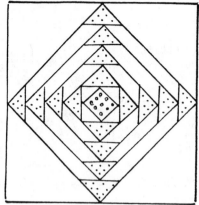

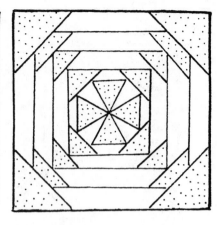

PINE BURR

The Romance of the Patchwork Quilt in America, page 120, No. 18

CHURCH STEPS

The Romance of the Patchwork Quilt in America, page 92, No. 14
A variation of the **LOG CABIN** pattern

A MALTESE CROSS

Ladies Art Company, No. 354
Also **PINEAPPLE**

Ladies Art Company, No. 1

PINEAPPLE

Kansas City Star, 1931

PINEAPPLE QUILT

Grandmother Clark's Patchwork Quilt Designs, Book 20, 1931

PINEAPPLES

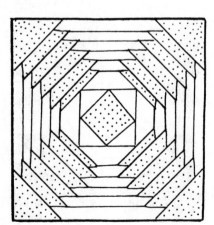

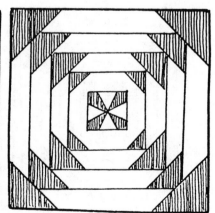

BLAZING STAR See page 217.

Diamond

Diamond/181

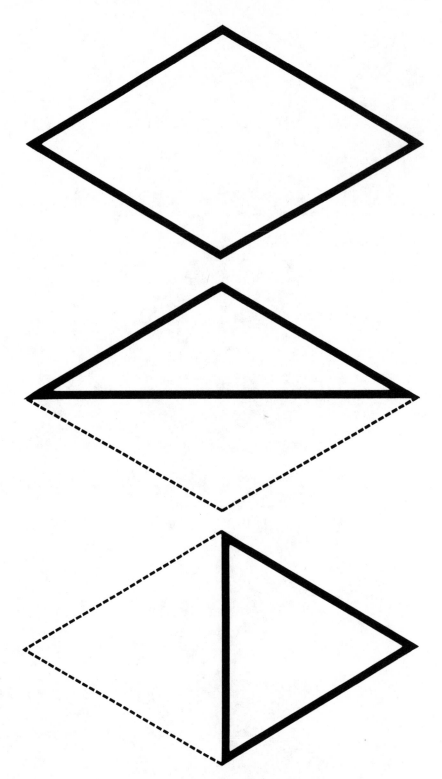

Diamond: The diamond pattern looks like two isosceles triangles with a common base. Most star patterns are diamond patterns.

STARS UPON STARS

Ladies Art Company, No. 211

American Quilts and Coverlets, page 26

SUMMER SUN

PRAIRIE STAR

The Romance of the Patchwork Quilt in America, page 62, No. 6
Also **HARVEST SUN** in the Middle West and **SHIP'S WHEEL** in Massachusetts

Ladies Art Company, No. 530

LONE STAR

Diamond/183

**WORLD'S FAIR PATTERN
(CHICAGO)**

Laura Wheeler

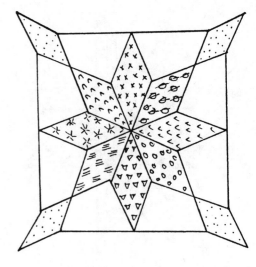

WANDERING DIAMOND

*The Romance of the Patch-
work Quilt in America,* page
58, No. 8
Also **THE LONE STAR**
*Grandmother Clark's Patch-
work Quilt Designs,* Book 21,
1931

STAR OF THE EAST

*The Romance of the Patch-
work Quilt in America,* page
58, No. 5
*The Standard Book of Quilting
and Collecting,* page 234

ST LOUIS STAR

Ladies Art Company, No. 181

THE KING'S CROWN

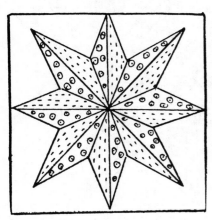

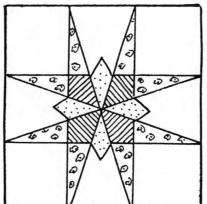

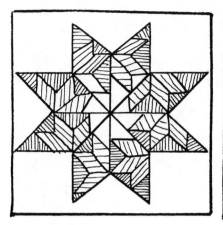

ROLLING STAR

FLYING SWALLOW

WOOD LILY

Old Patchwork Quilts and the Women Who Made Them, page 94

Ladies Art Company, No. 503
Also **FALLING STAR**

Kansas City Star, 1936
Also **INDIAN HEAD**

The Romance of the Patchwork Quilt in America, page 60, No. 3
Also **CIRCLING SWALLOWS, FLYING STAR, FLYING SWALLOW.** Dates from 1800, a favorite design in New England and Pennsylvania.

Grandmother Clark's Patchwork Quilt Designs, Book 20, 1931

The Romance of the Patchwork Quilt in America, page 60, No. 17
Also **DUTCH ROSE**

The Romance of the Patchwork Quilt in America, page 60, No. 14
Also **ROLLING STAR, STAR AND CHAINS**

STAR WITH DIAMOND

OCTAGONAL STAR

RING AROUND THE STAR

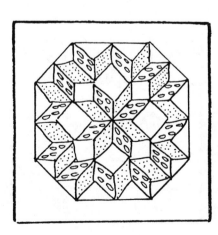

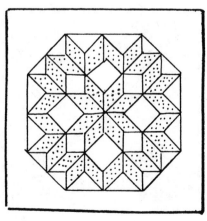

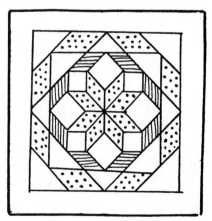

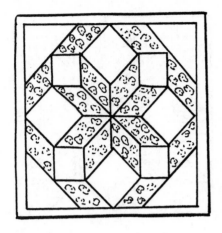

ROLLING STAR

DOUBLE PAEONY

PINEYS

Ladies Art Company, No. 4
The Romance of the Patch-work Quilt in America, page 58, No. 9
Also **BRUNSWICK STAR, CHAINED STAR, 8-POINTED STAR, RING AROUND THE STAR**

Ladies Art Company, No. 178
The Romance of the Patch-work Quilt in America, page 110, No. 5

Ladies Art Company, No. 53

Modern Priscilla, August 1928, page 18

Ladies Art Company, No. 55

CLEVELAND LILIES

THE DOUBLE TULIP

BASKET OF LILIES

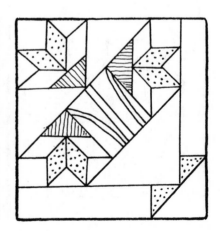

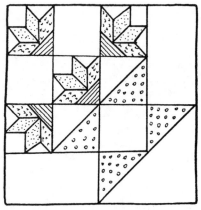

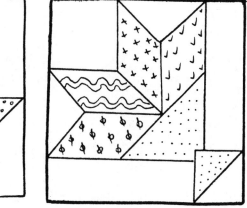

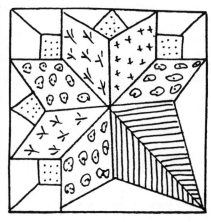

BASKET OF LILIES

The Romance of the Patch-work Quilt in America, page 126, No. 13

BASKET OF SCRAPS

The Perfect Patchwork Primer, page 99

THE NOSEGAYS

Kansas City Star, 1937

The Romance of the Patch-work Quilt in America, page 62 No. 3

Nancy Cabot

OLD COLONY STAR

SIX-POINTED STAR

OLD POINSETTIA BLOCK

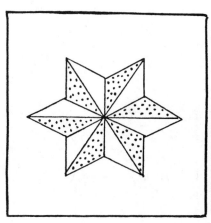

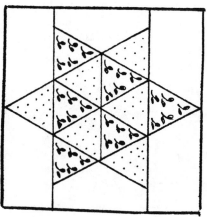

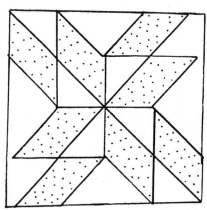

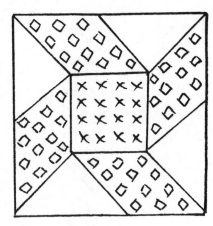

ECCENTRIC STAR

BOX QUILT PATTERN

THE OPEN BOX

The Romance of the Patchwork Quilt in America, page 62, No. 15

Ladies Art Company, No. 351

Also **ECCENTRIC STAR**

The Romance of the Patchwork Quilt in America, page 70, No. 11

The Romance of the Patchwork Quilt in America, page 78, No. 5

SPINNING TRIANGLES

SUNBURST

SASHED STAR

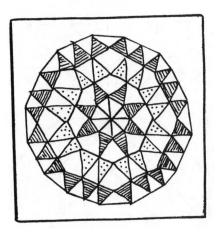

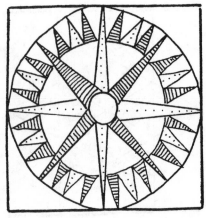

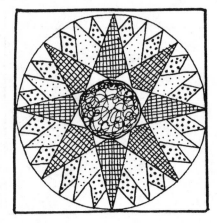

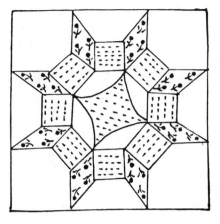

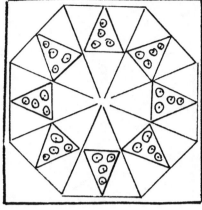

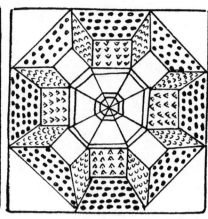

DOGWOOD

Lockport Cotton Batting Company, 1941

EVENING STAR

Kansas City Star, 1931

CASTLE WALL

The Romance of the Patchwork Quilt in America, page 94, No. 19
The Standard Book of Quilt Making and Collecting, page 250

The Romance of the Patchwork Quilt in America, page 72, No. 10

The Romance of the Patchwork Quilt in America, page 78, No. 4

One Hundred and One Patchwork Patterns, page 99

KALEIDOSCOPE

SUNBEAM

SUNBEAM BLOCK

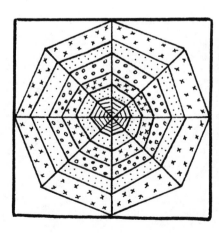

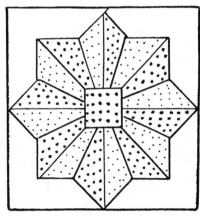

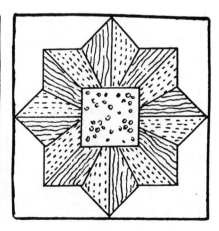

TENNESSEE STAR

The Romance of the Patchwork Quilt in America, page 58, No. 21
The Standard Book of Quilt Making and Collecting, page 248

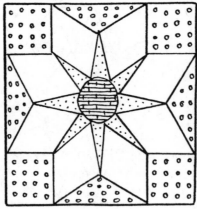

SUNFLOWER

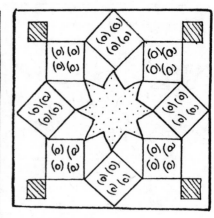

STARLIGHT

The Romance of the Patchwork Quilt in America, page 54, No. 8

Practical Needlework Quilt Patterns, Vol. 3

WESTERN SPY

Ladies Art Company, No. 75

PINWHEEL STAR

STAR OF BETHLEHEM

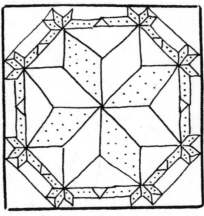

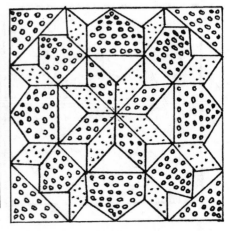

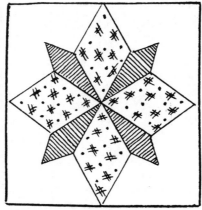

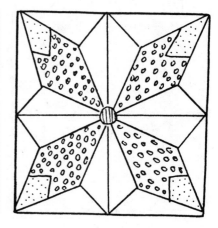

KING'S STAR

ORIENTAL STAR

ROSE POINT

The Romance of the Patch-work Quilt in America, page 56. No. 4
The Standard Book of Quilt Making and Collecting, page 246

Nancy Cabot

The Standard Book of Quilt Making and Collecting, page 249

The Romance of the Patch-work Quilt in America, page 60, No. 6

STAR AND CONE

NORTH CAROLINA STAR

MORNING STAR

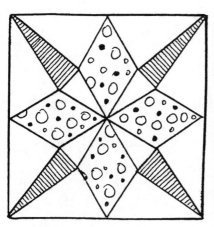

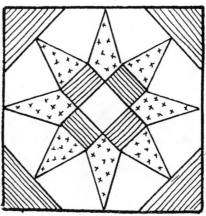

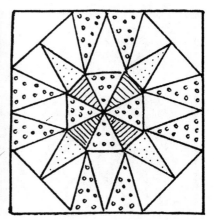

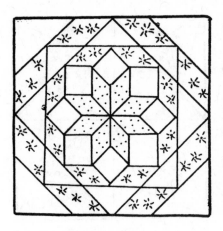

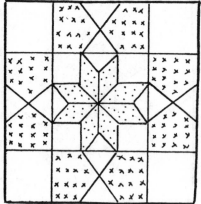

STAR AND CHAINS

Ladies Art Company, No. 6
Also **RING AROUND THE STAR**

ST LOUIS STAR

Ladies Art Company, No. 275
The Romance of the Patchwork Quilt in America, page 58, No. 6

POLARIS STAR

The Romance of the Patchwork Quilt in America, page 62, No. 16
Also **FLYING BAT**

Ladies Art Company, No. 44
Also **POLARIS STAR**

FLYING BAT

Also **FOUR-POINTED STAR**

BLAZING STAR

Also **CORONATION**

WASHINGTON'S QUILT

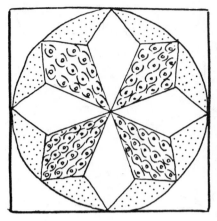

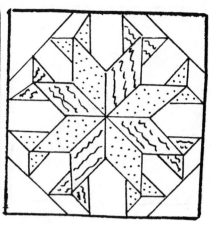

PURPLE CROSS

Kansas City Star, 1932

TWINKLING STARS

Ladies Art Company, No. 406

FISH BLOCK

One Hundred and One Patchwork Patterns, page 104
The Romance of the Patchwork Quilt in America, page 78, No. 2. Also **GOLD FISH.** Pattern is a nautical version of the 8-point star. In Colonial times, fish were a vital source of food and income along the Atlantic coast. This design has also been regarded as a Christian symbol since the early days of the Church.

The Romance of the Patchwork Quilt in America, page 78, No. 2
Also **FISH BLOCK**

GOLD FISH

Mrs. Danner's Quilts, Book 3, page 11

THE CROW FOOT

KALEIDOSCOPE

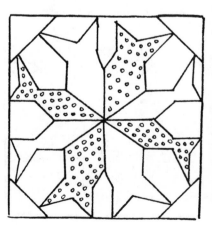

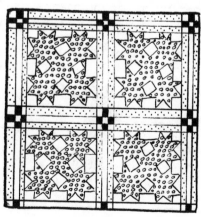

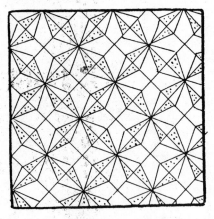

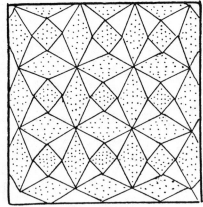

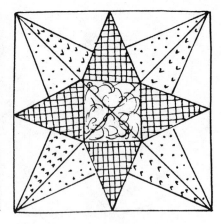

EVENING STARS

DIAMOND AND STAR

THE EXPLODING STAR

Ladies Art Company, No. 481

The Romance of the Patchwork Quilt in America, page 54, No. 1. Also **LEMON STAR.** Two brothers named Jean Baptiste and Pierre LeMoyne explored the Mississippi River and eventually founded, in 1718, the city of New Orleans where the French-speaking people named this 8-pointed star after them. However, in the North, the non-French-speaking quilters renamed it **LEMON STAR**, shortening the original name. All lily and tulip designs are based on this star.

STAR OF LEMOYNE

The Romance of the Patchwork Quilt in America, page 102, No. 15

FORMOSA TEA LEAF

Old Fashioned Quilts, page 13

STAR OF THE EAST

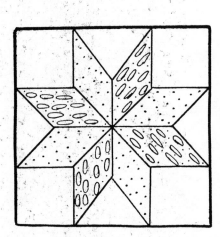

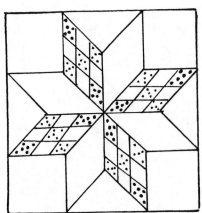

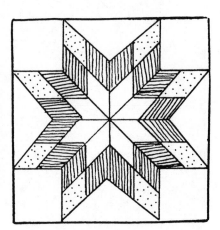

THE FISH QUILT

The Kansas City Star, 1930

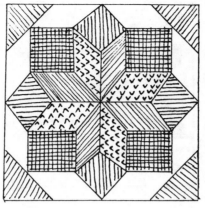

BRUNSWICK STAR

Old Patchwork Quilts and the Women Who Made Them, page 93

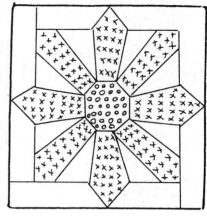

BROWN-EYED SUSAN

Needlecraft Magazine, February 1935, page 9

One Hundred and One Patchwork Patterns, page 20

Ladies Art Company, No. 371

SUNBURST

WATER LILY

NEW STAR

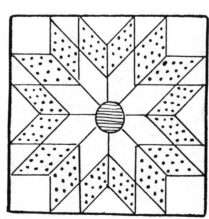

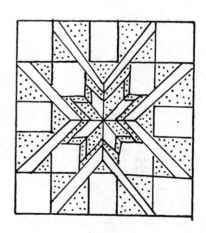

Diamond/195

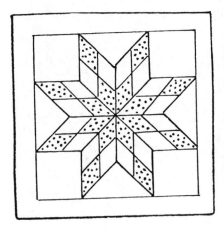

PATRIOTIC STAR

Kansas City Star, 1936

VIRGINIA STAR

One Hundred and One Patch-work Patterns, page 30
The Romance of the Patch-work Quilt in America, page 58, No. 1
Also **STAR-UPON-STARS**

THE LONE STAR QUILT

One Hundred and One Patch-work Patterns, page 72
Also **STAR OF BETHLEHM, STAR OF THE EAST**

One Hundred and One Patchwork Patterns, page 58
The Romance of the Patchwork Quilt in America, page 72, No. 3
Pattern named after windows con-structed near the rafters of old barns where the pigeons could fly in to roost. Pigeon pie was a familiar dish in the early days and an easy supply of the birds was thus ensured.

PLAID STAR

TEXAS LONE STAR

DOVE IN THE WINDOW

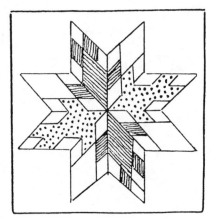

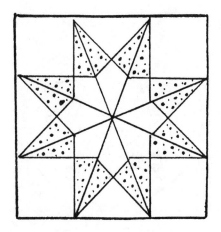

ST LOUIS BLOCK

Ladies Art Company, No. 491

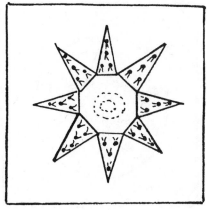

EVENING STAR

The Romance of the Patchwork Quilt in America, page 54, No. 3

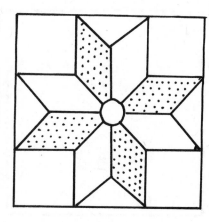

ALBUM BLOCKS

Ladies Art Company, No. 352

Kansas City Star, 1933

FRIENDSHIP STAR

Kansas City Star, 1933

FRIENDSHIP STAR

The Romance of the Patchwork Quilt in America, page 58, No. 19

TINY STAR

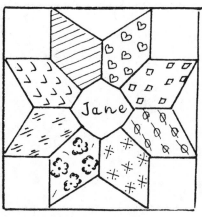

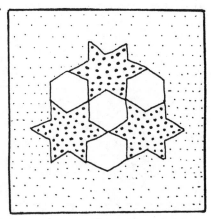

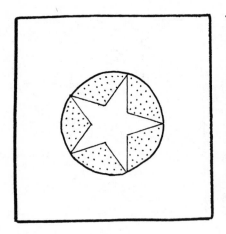

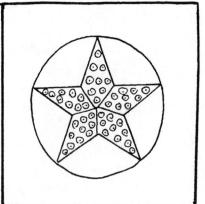

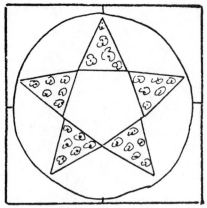

UNION STAR

Ladies Art Company, No. 381
The Romance of the Patch-
work Quilt in America, page
56, No. 13

STAR AND RING

STAR OF THE WEST

Ladies Art Company, No. 274
The Romance of the Patch-
work Quilt in America, page
54, No. 6
The Standard Book of Quilt
Making and Collecting, page
248

Ladies Art Company, No. 18

FIVE-POINTED STAR

The Standard Book of Quilt
Making and Collecting, page
248

FIVE-POINTED STAR

Kansas City Star, 1931

STAR IN A SQUARE

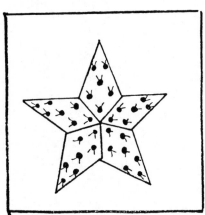

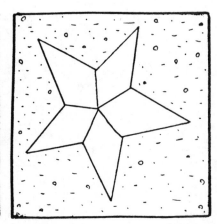

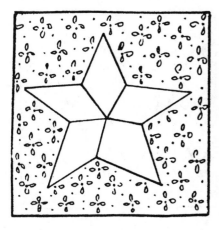

EVENING STAR

Woman's World, February 1928, page 30

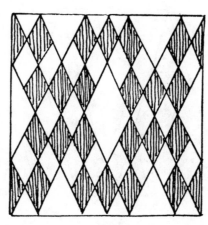

STARRY NIGHT

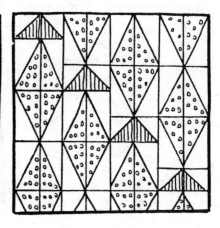

KITES IN AIR

Ladies Art Company, No. 312

DIAMOND DESIGN

GUIDE POST

Nancy Cabot

BOSTON CORNERS

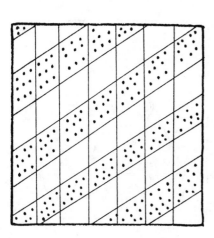

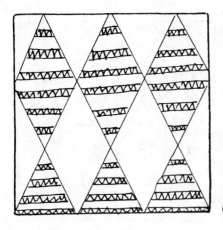

DIAMONDS

Grandmother Clark's Patchwork Quilt Designs, Book 21, 1931

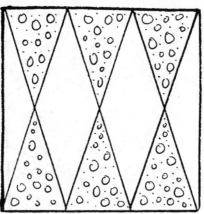

HERITAGE QUILT

NINE-PATCH DIAMOND

Ladies Art Company, No. 527 *The Romance of the Patchwork Quilt in America,* page 94, No. 6

Ladies Art Company, No. 370 *The Romance of the Patchwork Quilt in America,* page 82, No. 11

WALK AROUND

THE PYRAMID

SUGAR LOAF

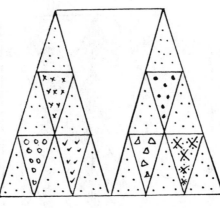

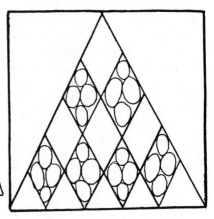

2'|8

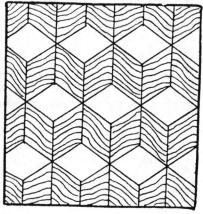

TRIANGULAR TRIANGLES

Ladies Art Company, No. 103
The Romance of the Patchwork Quilt in America, page 70, No. 23

VARIEGATED DIAMONDS

Ladies Art Company, No. 288

LIGHTNING STRIPS

The Perfect Patchwork Primer, page 73

2

Old Patchwork Quilts and the Women Who Made Them, page 51
The diamond cut crosswise forms the triangle.

STREAK OF LIGHTNING

One Hundred and One Patchwork Patterns, page 108
The Romance of the Patchwork Quilt in America, page 52, No. 13
Also **RAIL FENCE, STREAK-OF-LIGHTNING**

ZIG-ZAG

Everyday Life, 1930
Also **1000 PYRAMIDS**

JOSEPH'S COAT

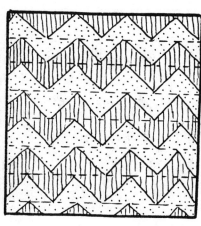

TRIANGLES

A THOUSAND PYRAMIDS

Nancy Cabot

THOUSAND PYRAMIDS

Old Patchwork Quilts and the Women Who Made Them, page 49

The Romance of the Patchwork Quilt in America, page 72, No. 9

Ladies Art Company, No. 6

Nancy Cabot

MOSAIC

MOSAIC NO. 4

BACHELOR'S PUZZLE

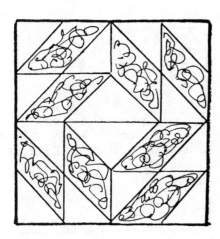

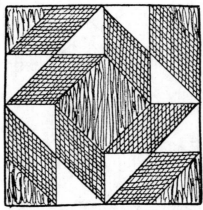

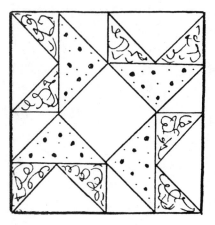

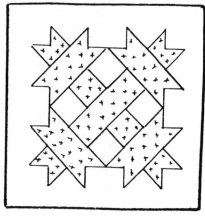

WINGED ARROW

Nancy Page

LILY QUILT PATTERN

Ladies Art Company, No. 365

OLD MAID'S PATIENCE

Nancy Cabot

The Romance of the Patch-work Quilt in America, page 58, No. 7
Also **FOUR STARS**

Nancy Cabot

CUBES AND TILE

JACKSON STAR

THE TRIPLE STAR QUILT

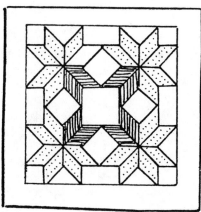

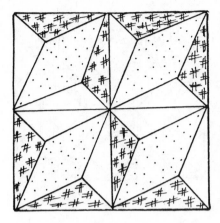

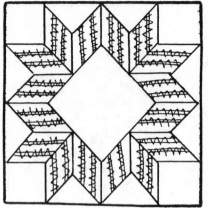

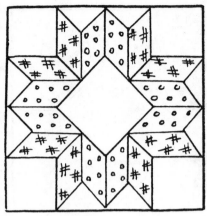

BLUE BOUTONNIERES

STAR OF MANY POINTS

THE LAUREL WREATH

Ladies Art Company, No. 2
Also **ARROWHEAD STAR**

*The Romance of the Patch-
work Quilt in America*, page
54, No. 16

*The Romance of the Patch-
work Quilt in America*, page
62, No. 18

Carlie Sexton

STAR OF BETHELEHEM

LUCINDA'S STAR

GOLD FISH

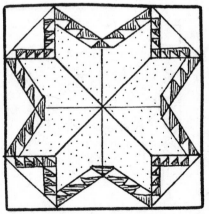

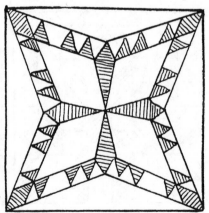

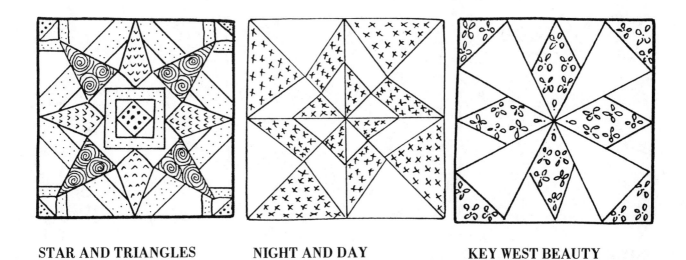

STAR AND TRIANGLES   **NIGHT AND DAY**   **KEY WEST BEAUTY**

Ladies Art Company, No. 482

JOSEPH'S COAT   **SILVER AND GOLD**   **PRAIRIE QUEEN**

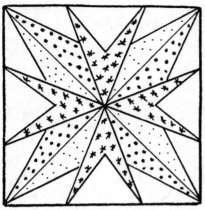

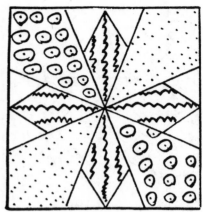

ROYAL STAR

The Romance of the Patchwork Quilt in America, page 76, No. 19

HATTIE'S CHOICE

Practical Needlework Quilt Patterns, Vol. 3

KEY WEST STAR

The Perfect Patchwork Primer, page 80

Nancy Cabot

TENNESSEE STAR

The Romance of the Patchwork Quilt in America, page 86, No. 2

SETTING SUN

Needlecraft Magazine, February 1934, page 8

WHITE HOUSE ROSE

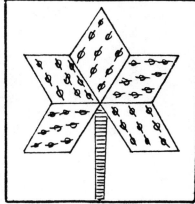

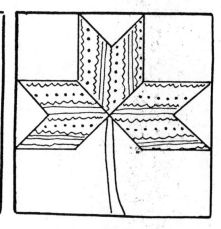

MISSOURI STAR

The Romance of the Patchwork Quilt in America, page 56, No. 6.
Also **SHINING STAR**
Kansas City Star
The Standard Book of Quilting and Collecting, page 235

MAPLE LEAF

SWEET GUM LEAF

The Romance of the Patchwork Quilt in America, page 102, No. 4
The Standard Book of Quilt Making and Collecting, page 234

Farm Journal and *Farmer's Wife,* 1942

SHOOTING STAR

Ladies Art Company, No. 222
The Romance of the Patchwork Quilt in America, page 102, No. 12

LIVE OAK TREE

Ladies Art Company, No. 308

PAEONY BLOCK

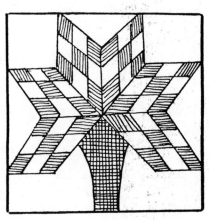

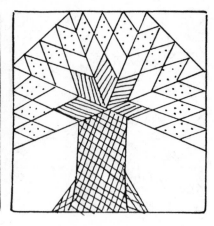

PEONY PATCH

The Romance of the Patchwork Quilt in America, page 110, No. 3
Also **PINEY**

LIVE OAK TREE

The Standard Book of Quilt Making and Collecting, page 43

FORBIDDEN FRUIT TREE

Ladies Art Company, No. 224
The Romance of the Patchwork Quilt in America, page 102, No. 7
The Standard Book of Quilt Making and Collecting, page 43

Old Patchwork Quilts and the Women Who Made Them, page 81
The Romance of the Patchwork Quilt in America, page 102, No. 5

Kansas City Star

Also **ARKANSAS TRAVELLER, COWBOY STAR**

THE CHRISTMAS TREE

TEA LEAF

TRAVEL STAR

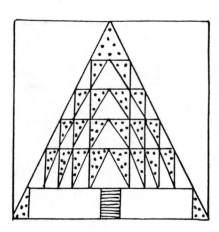

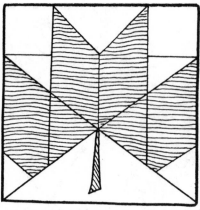

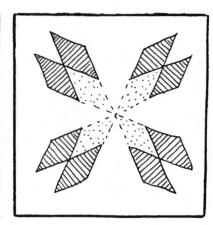

ROSE POINT

Nancy Cabot

STAR UPON STAR

The Standard Book of Quilt Making and Collecting, page 252

STAR

The Perfect Patchwork Primer, page 96

Old Patchwork Quilts and the Women Who Made Them, page 77
The Standard Book of Quilt Making and Collecting, page 241
Also **SUNFLOWER**

Grandmother Clark's Patchwork Quilt Designs, Book 21, 1931

TIME AND TIDE

BLAZING STAR

ROYAL STAR

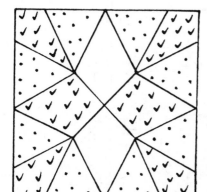

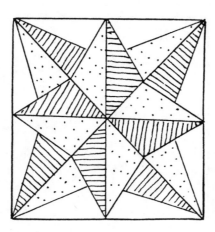

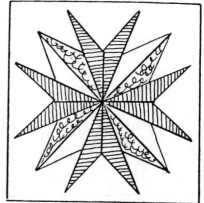

STARRY HEAVENS

GREEN MOUNTAIN STAR

Practical Needlework Quilt Patterns, Vol. 3

DOUBLE STAR

Kansas City Star, 1929
The Romance of the Patchwork Quilt in America, page 60, No. 13
Also **CARPENTER'S WHEEL, STAR-WITHIN-A-STAR**

Modern Patchwork, page 10

ROYAL STAR

SUNSHINY DAY

INDIAN ARROWHEAD

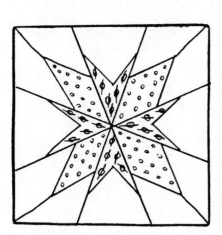

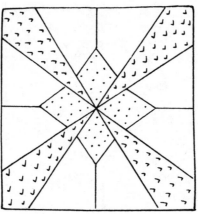

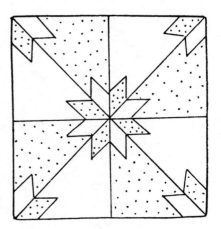

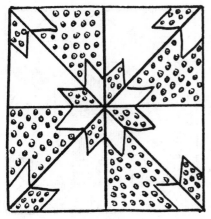

HUNTER'S STAR

The Romance of the Patchwork Quilt in America, page 60, No. 7

BLAZING STARS

American Quilts and Coverlets, page 61

THREE-IN-ONE QUILT

Kansas City Star

Woman's World, January 1930, page 20

PINWHEEL STAR

Modern Patchwork, page 27

MOSAIC

The Romance of the Patchwork Quilt in America, page 92, No. 3

SNOW CRYSTALS

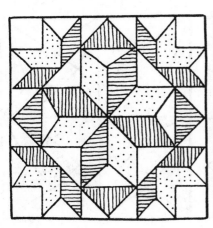

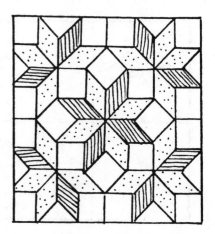

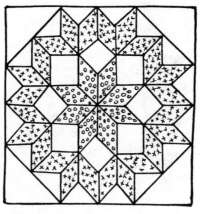

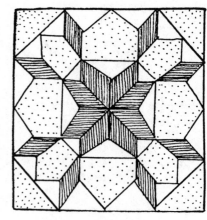

DIAMOND SOLITAIRE   **MORNING STAR**   **STAR OF MAGI**

Nancy Cabot

Grandmother Clark's Patch-work Quilt Designs, Book 20, 1931

Ladies Art Company, No. 306

Needlecraft Magazine, April 1929

FANCY STAR   **FOUR POINTS**   **STAR AND DIAMOND**

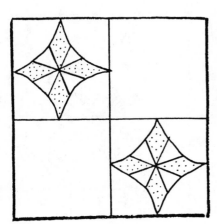

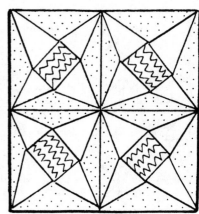

KALEIDOSCOPE

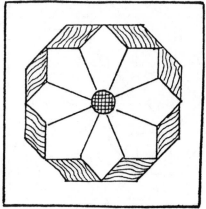

SNOWFLAKE CONTINUITY

Kansas City Star

THE KANSAS DUGOUT

The Romance of the Patchwork Quilt in America, page 100, No. 11

Ladies Art Company, No. 185
Old Fashioned Quilts, page 9
Also **OCTAGONAL STAR**

1938

THE KANSAS DUST STORM

Nancy Cabot

STAR OF NORTH CAROLINA

DUTCH ROSE

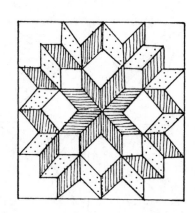

Diamond/213

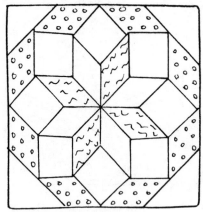

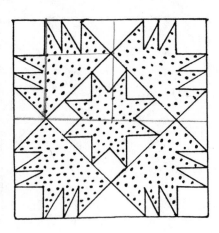

DIADEM-STAR

Hearth and Home, 1928

EIGHT-POINTED STAR

One Hundred and One Patchwork Patterns, page 56
Also **ROLLING STAR**

DELECTABLE MOUNTAINS

The Romance of the Patchwork Quilt in America, page 64, No. 10
The Standard Book of Quilt Making and Collecting, page 251
John Bunyan was born in England in 1628 during the period of religious persecution from which the founders of American freedom had fled 8 years before. While in prison he wrote *Pilgrim's Progress.* The pilgrims, after much travail, had just escaped from "Doubting Castle" which was kept by Giant Despair. "They went then till they came to the Delectable Mountains . . . behold the gardens and orchards, the vineyards and fountains of water . . ."

Ladies Art Company, No. 450

Ladies Art Company, No. 400
The Romance of the Patchwork Quilt in America, page 56, No. 11

EIGHT POINTED STAR

Nancy Cabot

ENIGMA

ENIGMA STAR

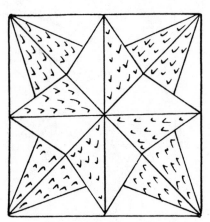

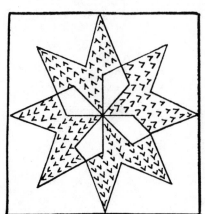

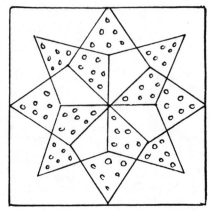

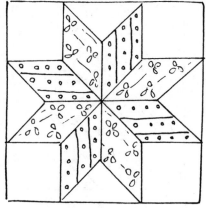

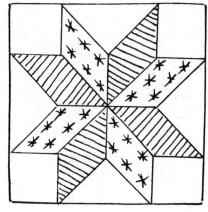

FRENCH STAR

EIGHT-POINTED STAR

DIAMOND STAR

The Romance of the Patchwork Quilt in America, page 58, No. 13
The Standard Book of Quilt Making and Collecting, page 248

Ladies Art Company, No. 261
The Standard Book of Quilt Making and Collecting, page 241

The Perfect Patchwork Primer, page 106

One Hundred and One Patchwork Patterns, page 56

Nancy Cabot

EASTERN STAR

EIGHT-POINTED STAR

CARPENTER'S WHEEL

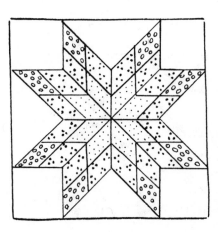

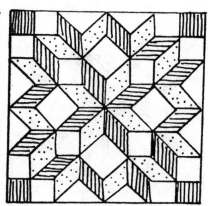

BROKEN STAR

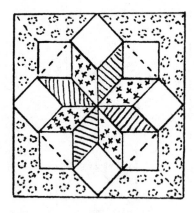

BRUNSWICK STAR

Laura Wheeler

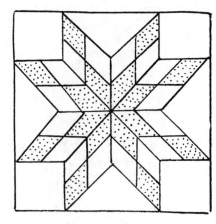

BLAZING STAR

Kansas City Star, 1929
Also **SAWTOOTH**

Ladies Art Company, No. 372
The Romance of the Patchwork Quilt in America, page 56, No. 14

BLAZING STAR

BLAZING STAR OF KENTUCKY

Needlecraft Magazine, February 1930, page 8

ALL HANDS AROUND

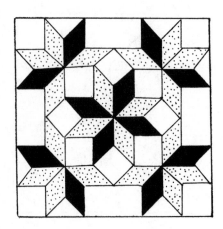

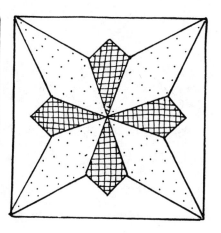

BLAZING STAR

The Romance of the Patch-work Quilt in America, page 56, No. 15

BEAUTIFUL STAR

One Hundred and One Patch-work Patterns, page 83
The Romance of the Patch-work Quilt in America, page 58, No. 14

GUIDING STAR

Kansas City Star, 1931
Also **WINDMILL STAR**
The Romance of the Patch-work Quilt in America, page 76, No. 16

The Romance of the Patch-work Quilt in America, page 62, No. 11

DIAMOND STAR

AMETHYST

MODERN STAR

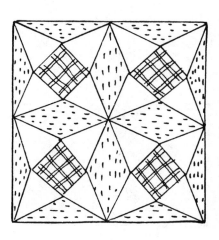

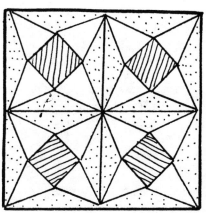

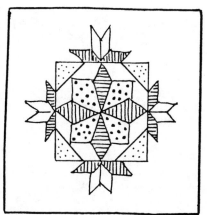

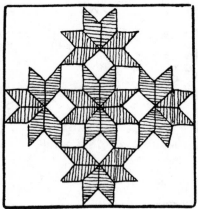

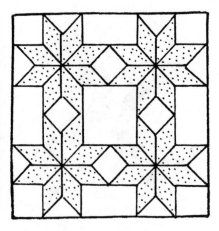

STARS AND CUBES

Ladies Art Company, No. 15

YANKEE PRIDE

Old Patchwork Quilts and the Women Who Made Them, page 95
The Romance of the Patchwork Quilt in America, page 84, No. 7.
Also **MAPLE LEAF**
The American colonists' pride in their new country and its destiny sustained them in their faith and determination to withstand dangers and setbacks and to look forward to a brighter future. All early Americans were called "Yankees" to distinguish them from the British. Later the Civil War gave the name a Northern meaning.

FOUR STARS PATCHWORK

Ladies Art Company, No. 311

Old Patchwork Quilts and the Women Who Made Them, page 93
Nancy Page, circa 1860
Also **TRAVEL STAR, ARKANSAS TRAVELER**
The Romance of the Patchwork Quilt in America, page 60, No. 9

The Standard Book of Quilt Making and Collecting, page 241

COWBOY'S STAR

COWBOY'S STAR

COWBOY'S STAR

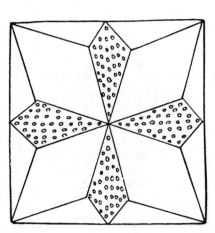

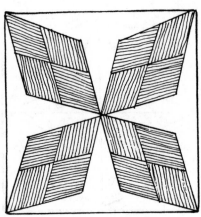

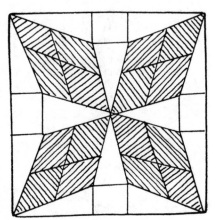

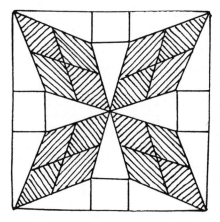

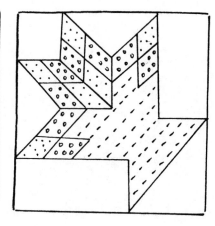

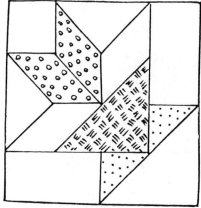

ARKANSAS TRAVELER

Old Patchwork Quilts and the Women Who Made Them, No. 61
Also **THE COWBOY'S STAR, TRAVEL STAR**

THE DISK

Ladies Art Company, No. 138

FLOWER POT

Needlecraft Magazine, April 1929, page 7
The Romance of the Patchwork Quilt in America, page 126, No. 19

One Hundred and One Patchwork Patterns, page 92

FLOWER POT

Ladies Art Company, No. 287

SOME PRETTY PATCHWORK

The Romance of the Patchwork Quilt in America, page 126, No. 6

BREAD BASKET

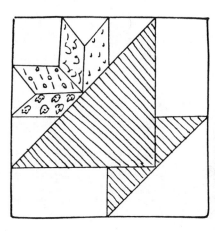

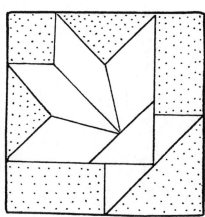

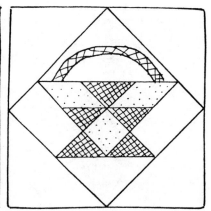

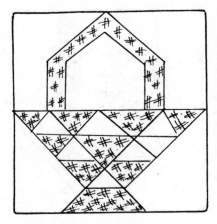

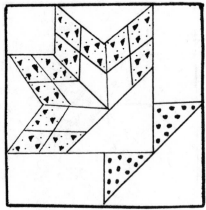

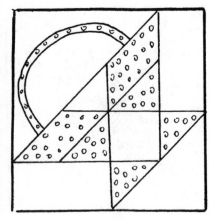

COLONIAL BASKET

The Romance of the Patchwork Quilt in America, page 126, No. 18

TULIP BASKET

Ladies Art Company, No. 518

BASKET QUILT

Ladies Art Company, No. 316

Ladies Art Company, No. 7
The Romance of the Patchwork Quilt in America, page 60, No. 4

MORNING STAR

Kansas City Star, 1932
The Romance of the Patchwork Quilt in America, page 98, No. 10
Also **THE LITTLE GIANT**

FLYING SAUCER

HEART'S DESIRE

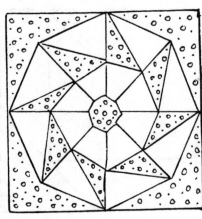

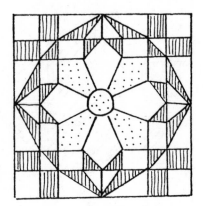

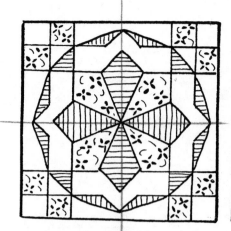

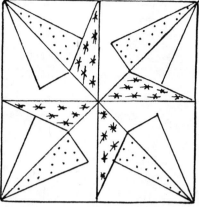

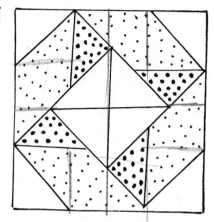

THE LITTLE GIANT

The Standard Book of Quilt Making and Collecting, page 252

FOUR-POINTED STAR

The Romance of the Patchwork Quilt in America, page 58, No. 3
Also **BLAZING STAR**

ROSE TRELLIS

Progressive Farmer

Ladies Art Company, No. 49

WHIRLING STAR

ARROWHEAD

DIAMONDS

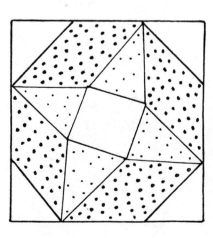

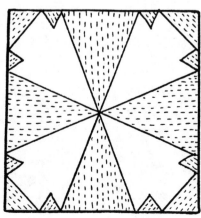

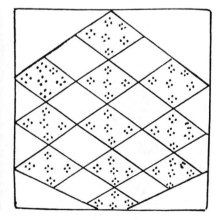

Diamond/221

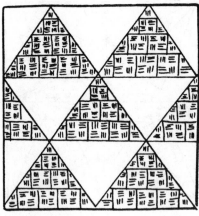

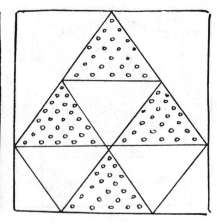

PIECED PYRAMIDS

The Romance of the Patchwork Quilt in America, page 100, No. 18

PYRAMIDS

Ladies Art Company, No. 411

CHARM

Ladies Art Company, No. 96

Kansas City Star, 1933
One of the popular designs used by quilters all over the country. The pattern was first published in 1859 in *Godey's Ladies Book,* which was among the earliest magazines issued for women and contained quilt designs.

LIGHT AND SHADOW

Ladies Art Company, No. 219

CRAZY QUILT

Nancy Page, 1930

ALLENTOWN

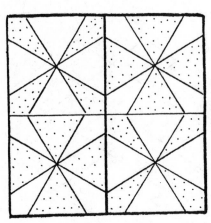

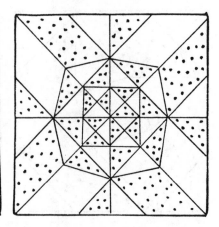

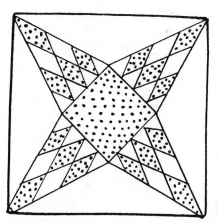

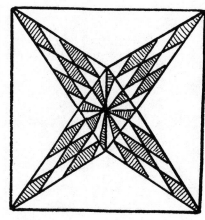

BUCKEYE BEAUTY

Nancy Cabot

STAR OF MANY POINTS

Nancy Cabot

HARLEQUIN STAR

American Quilts and Coverlets,
page 40

Kansas City Star, 1931
*The Romance of the Patch-
work Quilt in America,* page
96, No. 2
Also **SPRINGTIME
BLOSSOMS**

Ladies Art Company, No. 203

ROCKINGHAM'S BEAUTY

Laura Wheeler

COWBOY'S STAR

LAZY DAISY

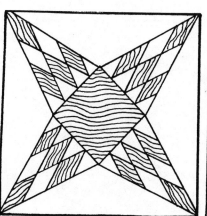

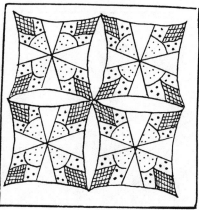

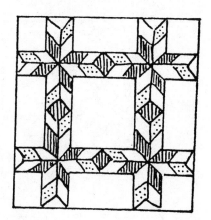

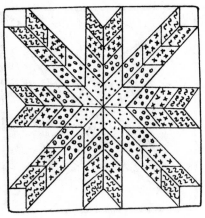

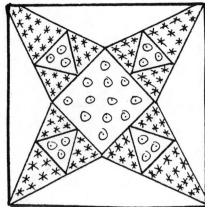

CHRISTMAS STAR

Kansas City Star, 1931
The Romance of the Patchwork Quilt in America, page 56, No. 7

IOWA STAR

Ladies Art Company, No. 468
The Romance of the Patchwork Quilt in America, page 60, No. 1
The Standard Book of Quilt Making and Collecting, page 242

THE PRISCILLA

Ladies Art Company, No. 199
Also **WORLD WITHOUT END**

Ladies Art Company, No. 8
One Hundred and One Patchwork Patterns, page 100
The Romance of the Patchwork Quilt in America, page 54, No. 15

SEVEN STARS

Ladies Art Company, No. 386

KALEIDOSCOPE

Nancy Cabot

CRAZY QUILT STAR

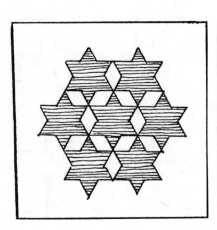

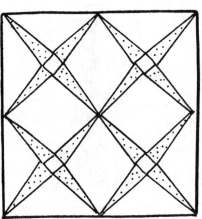

CRAZY STAR QUILT

Also **FOUR POINTS, KITE, PERIWINKLE, WORLD WITHOUT END**

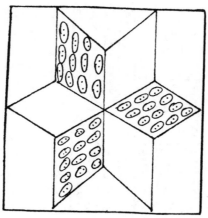

NOVEL STAR

Ladies Art Company, No. 366

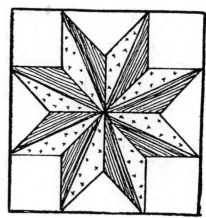

LE MOYNE STAR

The Standard Book of Quilt Making and Collecting, page 243

LIBERTY STAR

Nancy Page

FOLDED STARS

Also **STAR OF LEMOYNE**

LEMON STAR

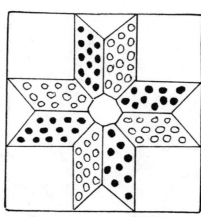

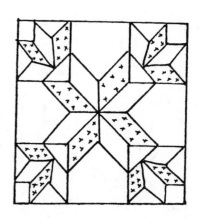

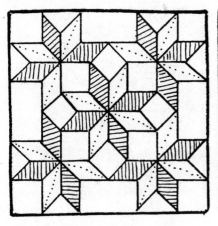

HEAVENLY STARS

American Quilts and Coverlets,
page 60

SUNLIGHT AND SHADOWS

Kansas City Star, 1942

SWING-IN-THE-CENTER

Ladies Art Company, No. 252
*Old Patchwork Quilts and the
Women Who Made Them,* page
112
*The Romance of the Patch-
work Quilt in America,* page
94, No. 15

Ladies Art Company, No. 37

SLASHED ALBUM

Nancy Cabot

PROSPERITY BLOCK

Nancy Cabot

DOVES IN THE WINDOW

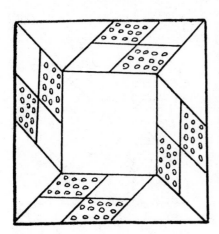

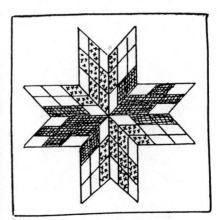

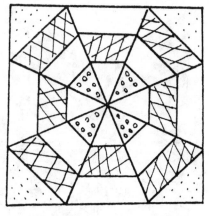

FLYING SWALLOWS

American Quilts and Coverlets,
page 26
Also **CIRCLING SWALLOWS,
FALLING STAR, FLYING
STAR**

SPIDER WEB

Laura Wheeler

SPIDER WEB

*Old Patchwork Quilts and the
Women Who Made Them,* page
115
*One Hundred and One Patch-
work Patterns,* page 118

Ladies Art Company, No. 191

SPIDER'S WEB

SPIDERWEB

LINKED DIAMONDS

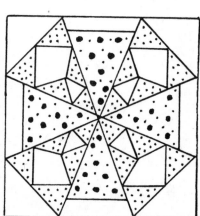

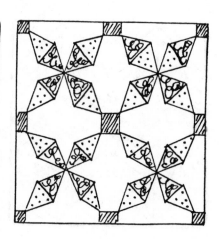

STAR OF THE EAST

Quilts: Their Story and How to Make Them, plate after page 64
Also **SILVER AND GOLD**

The Perfect Patchwork Primer, page 79

RIBBONS

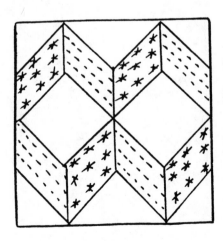

Ladies Art Company, No. 157

RIBBON BORDER

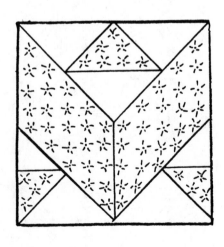

CROSSROADS See page 238.

Circle

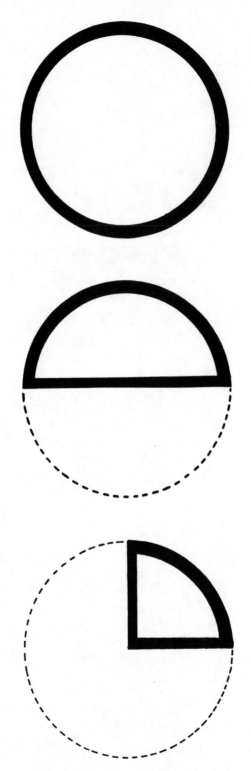

Circle: Circle patterns or parts thereof, such as arcs, will be considered circles. A Drunkard's Path quilt is obviously a circle pattern.

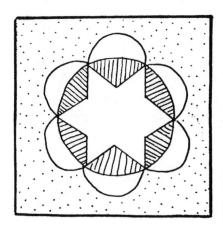

TWINKLING STAR

The Romance of the Patchwork Quilt in America, page 62, No. 12
Also **STAR AND CRESCENT**

STAR AND PLANETS

The Standard Book of Quilt Making and Collecting, page 247

STAR AND PLANETS

Grandmother Clark's Patchwork Quilt Designs, Book 21, 1931

Ladies Art Company, No. 494

WYOMING PATCH

Ladies Art Company, No. 505

COCKELBURR

FORE AND AFT

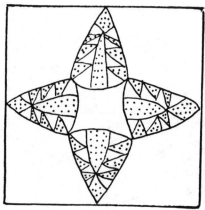

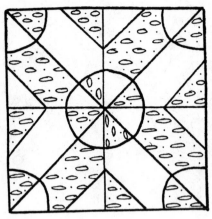

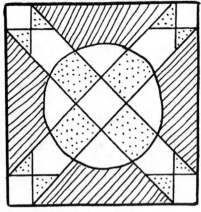

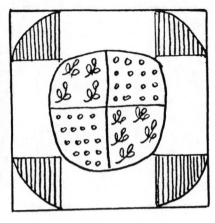

OLD MAID COMBINATION

Ladies Art Company, No. 214

HAZEL VALLEY CROSS ROADS

Kansas City Star, 1934

PILOT WHEEL

Grandmother Clark's Patchwork Quilt Designs, Book 21, 1931

Grandmother Clark's Patchwork Quilt Designs, Book 21, 1931

CART WHEEL

Woman's World, April 1907

QUARTER TURN

Ladies Art Company, No. 476

TRENTON QUILT BLOCK

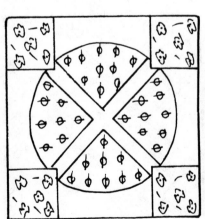

BASKET LATTICE

Ladies Art Company, No. 417

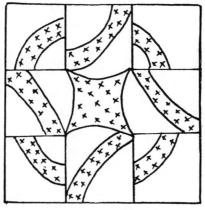

THE BROKEN CIRCLE

Kansas City Star, 1934

THE PINWHEEL

Needlecraft Magazine, March
1937, page 18

SUN, MOON AND STARS

Old Fashioned Quilts, page 12

ORANGE PEEL

Ladies Art Company, No. 183

MOON AND STARS

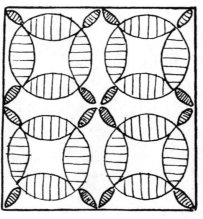

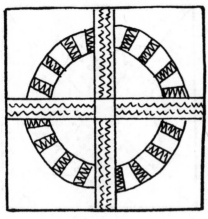

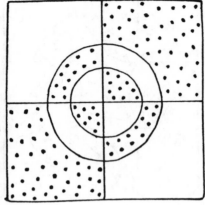

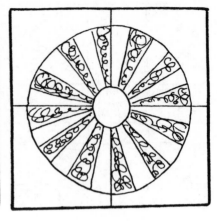

LADIES' FANCY

Ladies Art Company, No. 380

FAIR PLAY

Ladies Art Company, No. 454
Nancy Cabot

TRUE LOVERS BUGGY WHEEL

Kansas City Star, 1930
Also **WHEEL OF CHANCE**

The Romance of the Patchwork Quilt in America, page 96, No. 5
The Standard Book of Quilt Making and Collecting, page 52

KANSAS SUNFLOWER

Ladies Art Company, No. 99
The Romance of the Patchwork Quilt in America, page 76, No. 9

GEORGETOWN CIRCLE

Ladies Art Company, No. 487
The Romance of the Patchwork Quilt in America, page 60, No. 15

SAVANNAH BEAUTIFUL STAR

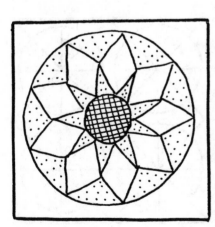

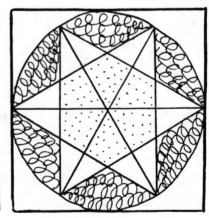

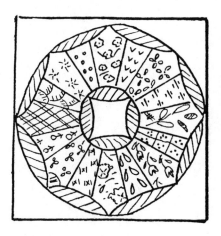

MY GRADUATION CLASS RING

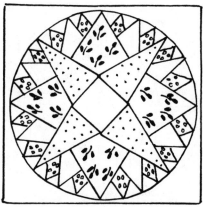

CHIPS AND WHETSTONES

The Romance of the Patchwork Quilt in America, page 76, No. 10
Nancy Page

FORTUNE'S WHEEL

Ladies Art Company, No. 521

Kansas City Star, 1940

THE CAR WHEEL QUILT

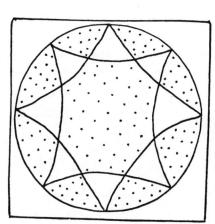

The Standard Book of Quilt Making and Collecting, page 252
Also **SUNFLOWER**

BLAZING SUN

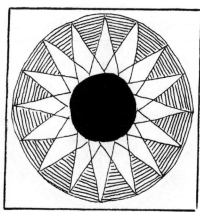

The Standard Book of Quilt Making and Collecting, page 247

ROLLING PIN WHEEL

HOUR GLASS

Early American Quilts, page 14

CIRCLE STAR

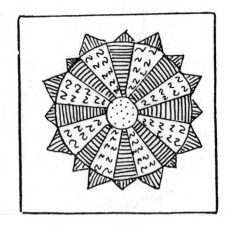

ORIENTAL STAR

The Romance of the Patchwork Quilt in America, page 62, No. 5

The Romance of the Patchwork Quilt in America, page 96, No. 8
Also **TRUE LOVERS BUGGY WHEEL**
The Standard Book of Quilt Making and Collecting, page 247

Woman's World, November 1926, page 38

WHEEL OF FORTUNE

Old Patchwork Quilts and the Women Who Made Them, page 62

WHEEL OF FORTUNE

WHEEL OF CHANCE

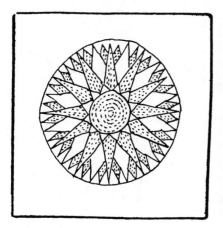

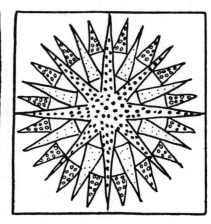

SLASHED STAR

Ladies Art Company, No. 266
The Romance of the Patch-
work Quilt in America, page
54, No. 7

SUNFLOWER

The Standard Book of Quilt
Making and Collecting, page
252

RISING SUN

One Hundred and One Patch-
work Patterns, page 78

The Romance of the Patch-
work Quilt in America, page
96, No. 4
Also **BLAZING STAR,**
BLAZING SUN

SUNFLOWER

The Romance of the Patch-
work Quilt in America, page
48, No. 9

NINE-PATCH

Laura Wheeler

MAGIC CIRCLE

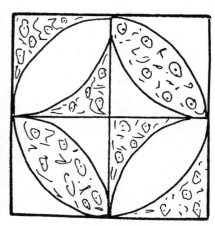

PEELED ORANGE

Nancy Cabot

WHITE ROSE

The Romance of the Patchwork Quilt in America, page 104, No. 1

FARMER'S WIFE

Old Fashioned Quilts, page 23

The Romance of the Patchwork Quilt in America, page 84, No. 11

FARMER'S WIFE

The Standard Book of Quilt Making and Collecting, page 244

COUNTRY CROSS ROADS

The Romance of the Patchwork Quilt in America, page 76, No. 7
Also **CROSSED ROADS TO TEXAS**

CROSS ROADS

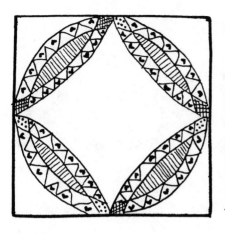

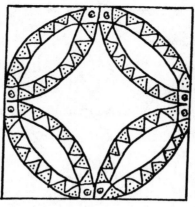

INDIAN WEDDING RING

Nancy Cabot

THE PICKLE DISH

Kansas City Star, 1931

PICKLE DISH

The Romance of the Patch-work Quilt in America, page 76, No. 24

Ladies Art Company, No. 81

PICKLE DISH

Ladies Art Company, No. 512
The Romance of the Patch-work Quilt in America, page 100, No. 12

DOUBLE WEDDING RING

WEDDING RING

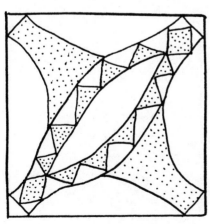

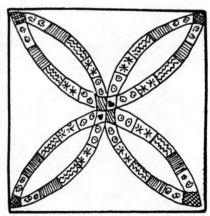

DOUBLE WEDDING RING **WEDDING RING BOUQUET** **GOLDEN WEDDING RING**

Needlecraft Magazine, June
1931, page 31
A popular pattern after the
Civil War.

*Old Patchwork Quilts and the
Women Who Made Them,* page
116

Also **WHIG DEFEAT** Also **BROKEN CIRCLE, SUN-
FLOWER**
GRANDMOTHER'S *Kansas City Star,* 1932
ENGAGEMENT RING **INDIAN SUMMER** **PINEAPPLE CACTUS**

 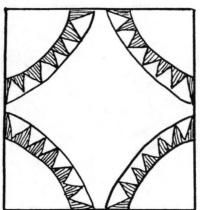 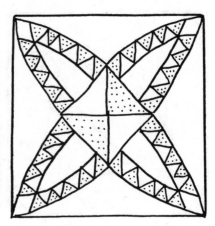

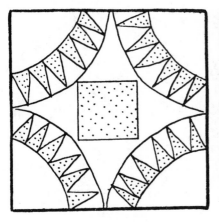

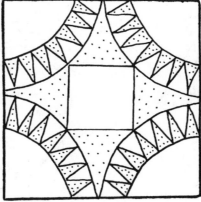

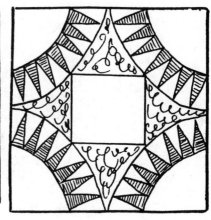

WHEEL OF FORTUNE

The Romance of the Patchwork Quilt in America, page 92, No. 9
Also **BUGGY WHEEL**
American Quilts, page 93

SUSPENSION BRIDGE

Ladies Art Company, No. 488

SUNFLOWER

The Romance of the Patchwork Quilt in America, page 96, No. 3
Also **INDIAN SUMMER, BROKEN CIRCLE**

The Romance of the Patchwork Quilt in America, page 80, No. 14

FANNY'S FAVORITE

Laura Wheeler

ROSE AND TRELLIS

Kansas City Star, 1942

CHAIN QUILT

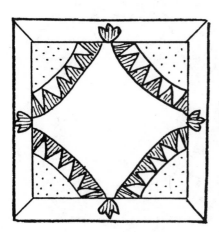

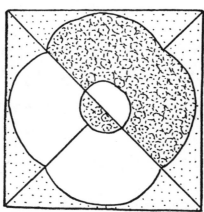

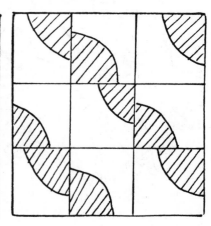

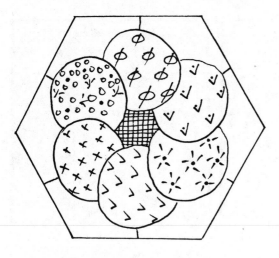

ROSES OF PICARDY

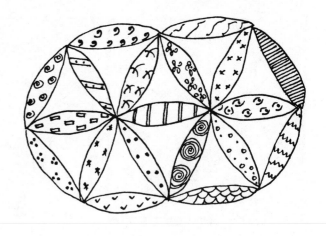

JOSEPH'S COAT

Kansas City Star, 1934

Ladies Art Company, No. 177
The Romance of the Patchwork Quilt in America, page 78, No. 16
Nancy Cabot

RISING SUN

Kansas City Star, 1939

THE ROLLING STONE

CHAINLINKS

Also **DRUNKARD'S PATH**

DIAGONAL STRIPES

Also **DRUNKARD'S PATH**

FOOL'S PUZZLE

Ladies Art Company, No. 29
The Romance of the Patchwork Quilt in America, page 90, No. 9 and 10

Ladies Art Company, No. 249

Ladies Art Company, No. 179
Also **PULLMAN PUZZLE**

Grandmother Clark's Patchwork Quilt Designs, Book 20, 1931

BOSTON PUZZLE

BASE BALL

CIRCLE DESIGN

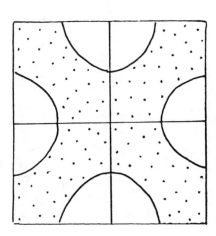

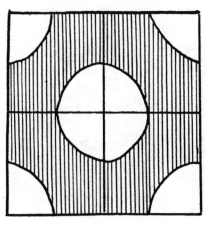

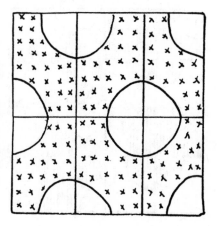

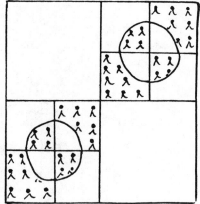

DRUNKARD'S TRAIL

SNOWBALL

DRUNKARD'S PATH
variation
Also **INDIANA PUZZLE,
ROB PETER TO PAY PAUL**

THE MILL WHEEL

One Hundred and One Patch-work Patterns, page 107

The Romance of the Patch-work Quilt in America, page 90, No. 13

MUSHROOMS

AROUND THE WORLD

OLD MILL WHEEL

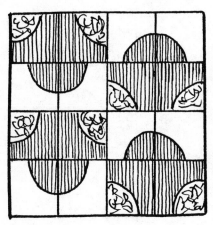

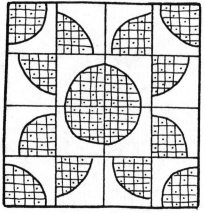

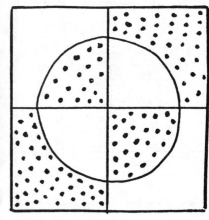

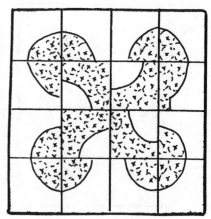

INDIANA PUZZLE

Early American Quilts, page 14

POLKA DOTS

ROB PETER TO PAY PAUL

The Romance of the Patchwork Quilt in America, page 90, No. 14

Kansas City Star, 1930

THE DOVE

DRUNKARD'S PATH
variation
Also **SNOWY WINDOWS**

DIRTY WINDOWS

The Romance of the Patchwork Quilt in America, page 90, No. 12

WONDER-OF-THE-WORLD

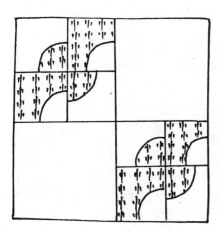

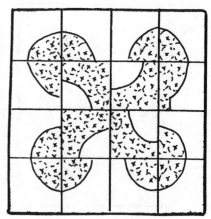

WISH-U-WELL

Hearth and Home, 1930

VINE OF FRIENDSHIP

The Romance of the Patch-work Quilt in America, page 90, No. 8

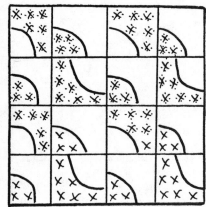

FALLING TIMBERS

The Romance of the Patch-work Quilt in America, page 64, No. 11

WONDER-OF-THE-WORLD

INDIAN PATCH

DRUNKARD'S PATH

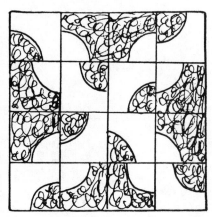

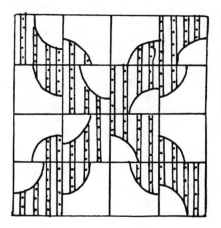

DRUNKARD'S PATH

ROCKY ROAD TO DUBLIN

Also **DRUNKARD'S PATH**

FALLING TIMBER

The Romance of the Patchwork Quilt in America, page 90, No. 11

Ladies Art Company, No. 220
Quilts: Their Story and How to Make Them, plate after page 64
One Hundred and One Patchwork Patterns, page 9
The Romance of the Patchwork Quilt in America, page 90, No. 7
Also **COUNTRY HUSBAND, ROBBING PETER TO PAY PAUL, ROCKY ROAD TO CALIFORNIA, ROCKY ROAD TO DUBLIN.**
Pattern dates from the early 19th century.

Needlecraft Magazine, February 1930, page 8
Also **DRUNKARD'S PATH**
Nancy Cabot

Nancy Cabot

SOLOMON'S PUZZLE

DRUNKARD'S PATH

CLEOPATRA'S PUZZLE

LOVE RING

The Romance of the Patch-work Quilt in America, page 90, No. 6
Also **NONESUCH**

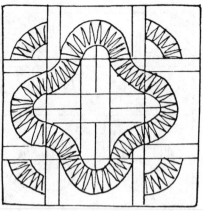

CHINESE FAN

MILL WHEEL

The Romance of the Patch-work Quilt in America, page 84, No. 22
The Standard Book of Quilt Making and Collecting, page 245

The Household Magazine, August 1934, page 23

SNOW BALL

Nancy Cabot

MOHAWK TRAIL

The Romance of the Patch-work Quilt in America, page 90, No. 6.
Also **LOVE RING**

NONESUCH

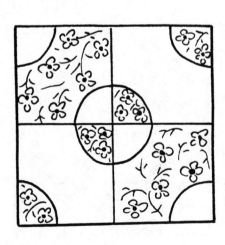

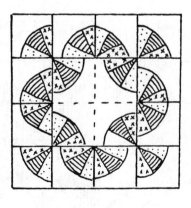

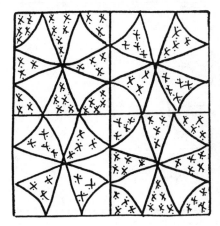

ROBBING PETER TO PAY PAUL

Also **DRUNKARD'S PATH**

WINDING WAYS

Ladies Art Company, No. 463
The Standard Book of Quilt Making and Collecting, page 249
Also **WHEEL OF MYSTERY**

WHEEL OF MYSTERY

The Romance of the Patchwork Quilt in America, page 86, No. 1
Also **WINDING WAYS**

Old Patchwork Quilts and the Women Who Made Them, plate 23

HEARTS AND GIZZARDS

The Romance of the Patchwork Quilt in America, page 74, No. 11
Also **LAZY DAISY, WHEEL OF FORTUNE, PETAL QUILT**

SPRINGTIME BLOSSOMS

The Standard Book of Quilt Making and Collecting, page 240
Also **SPRINGTIME BLOSSOMS**

WHEEL OF FORTUNE

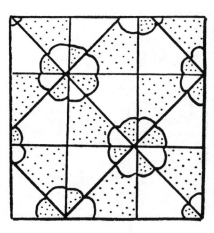
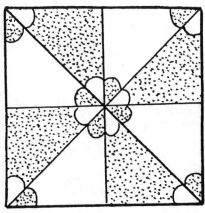

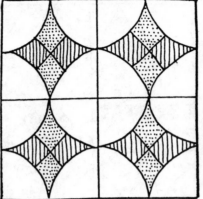
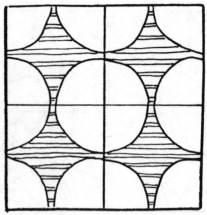

MARTHA'S CHOICE

Nancy Cabot

VIRGINIA SNOWBALL

Nancy Cabot

SNOW BALL

Ladies Art Company, No. 104
The Romance of the Patch-work Quilt in America, page 96, No. 1
Also **BASE BALL, PULLMAN PUZZLE**

Ladies Art Company, No. 23
The Romance of the Patch-work Quilt in America, page 70, No. 15
Also **BASEBALL, SNOW-BALL**

PULLMAN PUZZLE

Kansas City Star, 1934

THE SNOWBALL QUILT

Ladies Art Company, No. 176
The Romance of the Patch-work Quilt in America, page 82, No. 12

PYROTECHNICS

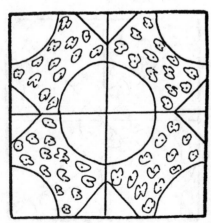
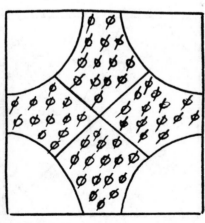

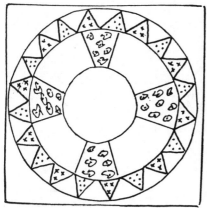

COGWHEEL

Grandmother Clark's Patchwork Quilt Designs, Book 20, 1931

FLYWHEEL

Grandmother Clark's Patchwork Quilt Designs, Book 20, 1931

FRIENDSHIP QUILT

The Romance of the Patchwork Quilt in America, page 94, No. 17
Also **ALWAYS FRIENDS**

PETAL CIRCLE IN A SQUARE

ALCAZAR

SPINNING WHEEL

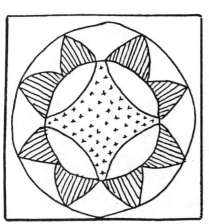

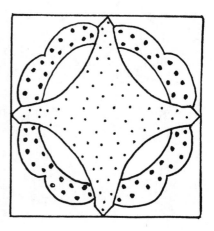

ALWAYS FRIENDS

Also known as **BADGE OF FRIENDSHIP, CHARM QUILT, FRIENDSHIP QUILT, JIGSAW, MOTHER'S ODDITY**

SHELL CHAIN

Ladies Art Company, No. 62

CLAMSHELL

The Romance of the Patchwork Quilt in America, page 72, No. 22
Also called **SUGAR SCOOP** on Long Island

Grandmother Clark's Patchwork Quilt Designs, Book 20, 1931

SEA SHELLS

Ladies Art Company, No. 107

ORANGE PEEL

Also **LAFAYETTE ORANGE PEEL**

JOSEPH'S COAT

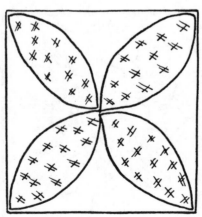

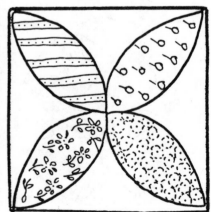

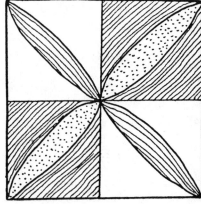

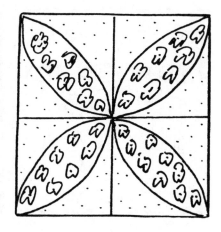

LAFAYETTE ORANGE PEEL

ORANGE PEEL

ORANGE PEEL

One Hundred and One Patch-work Patterns, page 12
The Romance of the Patch-work Quilt in America, page 96, No. 11
Also **JOSEPH'S COAT**

Nancy Cabot

The Romance of the Patch-work Quilt in America, page 96, No. 10

Mrs. Danner's Quilts, Book 2, page 19

Ladies Art Company, No. 69

MELON PATCH

CIRCLE UPON CIRCLE

TEA LEAF

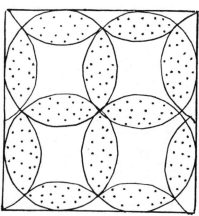

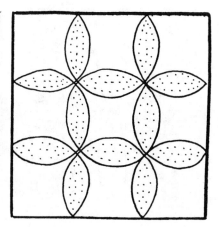

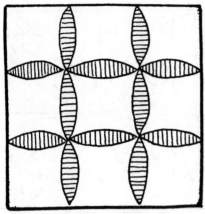 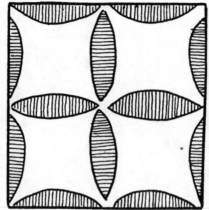 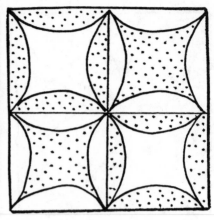

TRUE LOVER'S KNOT

Nancy Cabot

ROBBING PETER TO PAY PAUL

The Standard Book of Quilt Making and Collecting, page 246
The Romance of the Patchwork Quilt in America, page 64, No. 9

ROB PETER TO PAY PAUL

One Hundred and One Patchwork Patterns, page 59

Grandmother Clark's Patchwork Quilt Designs, Book 20, 1931

CUSHION DESIGN

Ladies Art Company, No. 133
American Quilts and Coverlets, page 36

PIN CUSHION

Old Fashioned Quilts, page 4

DOLLY MADISON'S WORK BOX

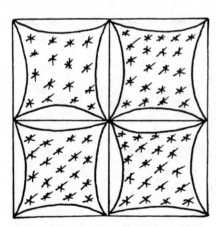 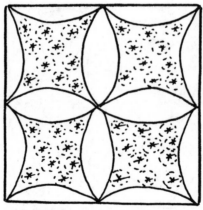 

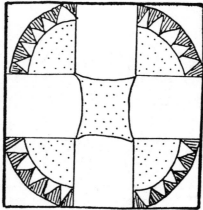

COMPASS

Ladies Art Company, No. 218

ORIOLE WINDOW

Also **CIRCULAR SAW, FOUR LITTLE FANS**

BROKEN CIRCLE

Nancy Page
Also **SUNFLOWER**

Ladies Art Company, No. 493
The Romance of the Patchwork Quilt in America, page 84, No. 14

BABY BUNTING

American Quilts and Coverlets, page 40

MARINER'S COMPASS

Laura Wheeler

FRIENDSHIP RING

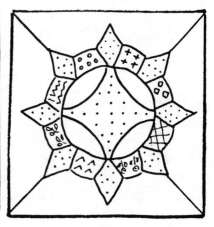

THE PILOT'S WHEEL

WHIRLING WHEEL

The Household Magazine, July 1933, page 29

THE SUNFLOWER

Ladies Art Company, No. 73

Grandmother Clark's Patchwork Quilt Designs, Book 20, 1931

GRECIAN STAR

BABY BUNTING

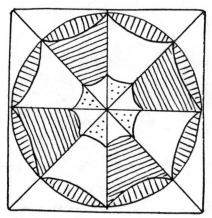

THE ELECTRIC FAN

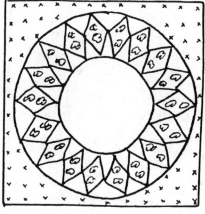

NOONDAY

Old Patchwork Quilts and the Women Who Made Them, plate 71

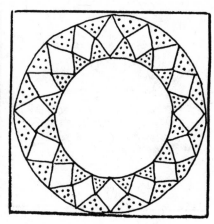

RISING SUN

Hearth and Home, 1927

CIRCLE AND STAR

Kansas City Star, 1936

THE STAR SAPPHIRE

Ladies Art Company, No. 42

CIRCLE WITHIN CIRCLE

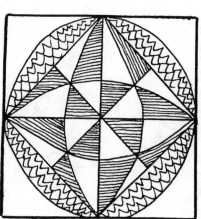

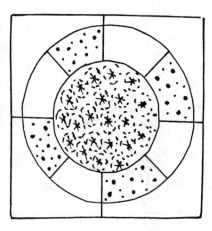

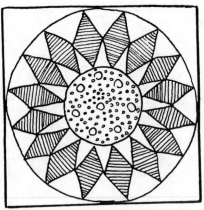

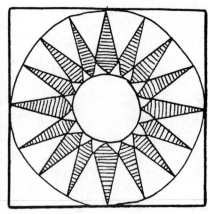

RUSSIAN SUNFLOWER

Kansas City Star

OKLAHOMA SUNBURST

Kansas City Star

SUNFLOWER

The Romance of the Patchwork Quilt in America, page 96, No. 6

The Romance of the Patchwork Quilt in America, page 78, No. 2

Ladies Art Company, No. 367

SUNFLOWER STAR

SUNBURST

SINGLE SUNFLOWER

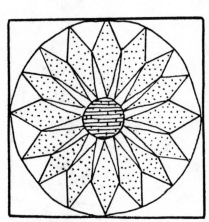

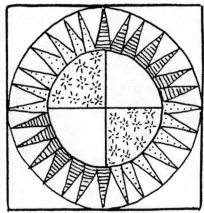

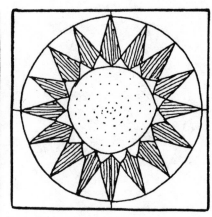

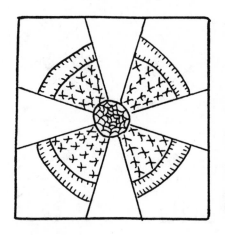

TEXAS TULIP

Nancy Cabot

THE YO-YO QUILT

Also called **BED OF ROSES, BONBON, PINWHEEL, POWDER PUFF, PUFF, ROSETTE**

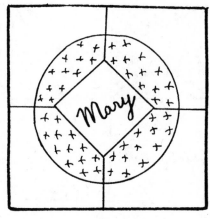

FRIENDSHIP RING

Kansas City Star, 1941

The Romance of the Patchwork Quilt in America, page 76, No. 6
The Standard Book of Quilt Making and Collecting, page 245

CHIPS AND WHETSTONES

The "spokes" were used for signatures of friends collected as a memento.

SIGNATURE

The Romance of the Patchwork Quilt in America, page 76, No. 21
Also **FOUR LITTLE FANS, ORIOLE WINDOW**
The Standard Book of Quilt Making and Collecting, page 244

CIRCULAR SAW

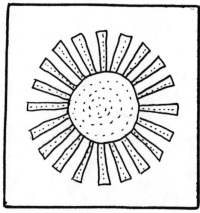

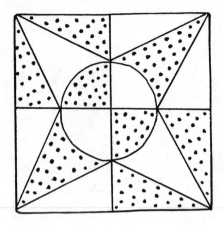

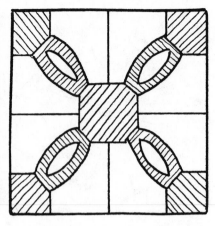

COMPASS

The Romance of the Patchwork Quilt in America, page 82, No. 20
The Standard Book of Quilt Making and Collecting, page 248

ALABAMA BEAUTY

Nancy Cabot

JOB'S TEARS

Old Patchwork Quilts and the Women Who Made Them, page 102
The Romance of the Patchwork Quilt in America, page 74. Also **ENDLESS CHAIN, KANSAS TROUBLES, SLAVE CHAIN, TEXAS TEARS**
About the beginning of the 19th century this pattern, without the intervening blocks, was known as **JOB'S TEARS.** However, events in history changed its name quite often. In the early 1800's, when Missouri was seeking admission into the Union, it was called **THE SLAVE CHAIN.** Then, there was a controversy about the state being a slave state or a free state. By 1840, in connection with the annexation of Texas to the Union, the name became **TEXAS TEARS.** When the prairie states were being settled after the Civil War, it became **THE ROCKY ROAD TO KANSAS,** and still later the **ENDLESS CHAIN** pattern.

Nancy Cabot

Ladies Art Company, No. 130
The Romance of the Patchwork Quilt in America, page 78, No. 19

RAINBOW

The Romance of the Patchwork Quilt in America, page 70, No. 6

FLO'S FAN

CHINESE GONGS

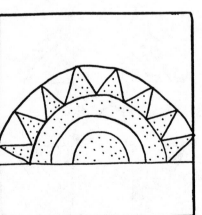

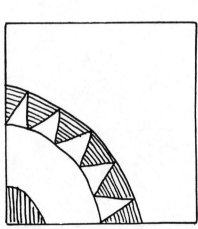

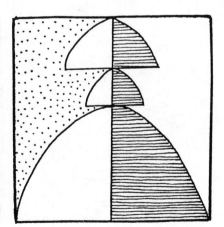

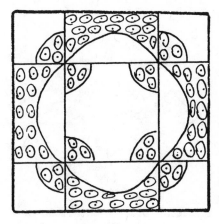

QUEEN'S CROWN

*Ladies Art Company, No. 456
The Romance of the Patchwork Quilt in America,* page
68, No. 8

IRISH CHAIN

Grandmother Clark's Patchwork Quilt Designs, Book
20, 1931

THE KANSAS BEAUTY

The Standard Book of Quilt Making and Collecting, page
247

Kansas City Star, 1939

THE OAK GROVE STAR

Kansas City Star, 1941

THE BUZZ SAW

QUEEN'S CROWN

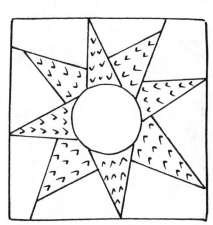

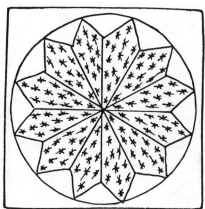

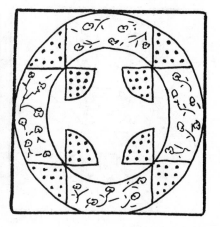

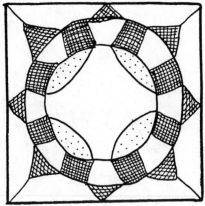

SUNFLOWER

Ladies Art Company, No. 448

STRAWBERRY

The Romance of the Patchwork Quilt in America, page 96, No. 19
Also **KENTUCKY BEAUTY**

SUNFLOWER

Needlecraft Magazine, June 1931, page 18

The Romance of the Patchwork Quilt in America, page 74, No. 1
Also **BOWS AND ARROWS**
Nancy Cabot

Ladies Art Company, No. 38

ROSE ALBUM

One Hundred and One Patchwork Patterns

ROSE ALBUM

STEEPLE CHASE

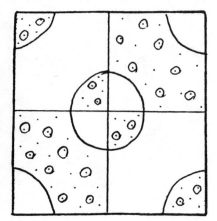

THE SUNBURST

Modern Priscilla, August 1928,
page 18

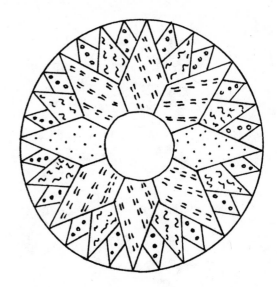

GEORGETOWN CIRCLE

*Grandmother Clark's Patch-
work Quilt Designs,* Book
21, 1931

SUNBURST

SNOW CRYSTALS   See page 270.

Hexagon

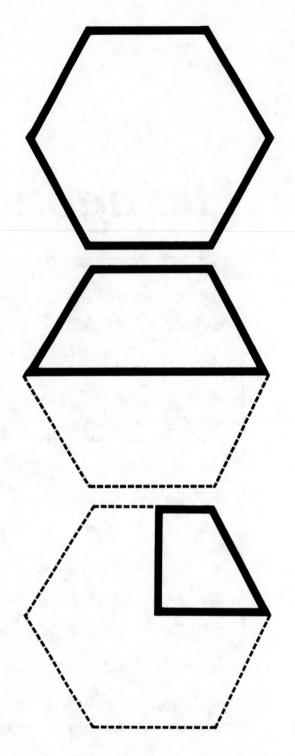

Hexagon: A six-sided pattern or parts thereof will be included in this category. The famous Grandmother's Flower Garden quilt or the Honeycomb quilts are typical examples.

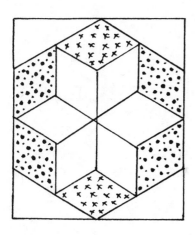

BUILDER'S BLOCKS

Kansas City Star, 1940

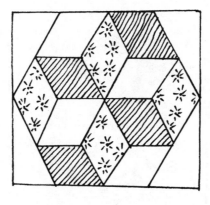

BLOCK PUZZLE

Grandmother Clark's Patchwork Quilt Designs, Book 21, 1931

ARABIAN STAR

The Romance of the Patchwork Quilt in America, page 62, No. 17
Also **DUTCH TILE**

Kansas City Star

DUTCH TILE

Kansas City Star, 1932

THE DIAMOND FIELD

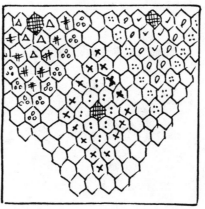

OCEAN WAVE

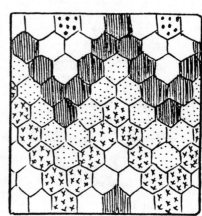

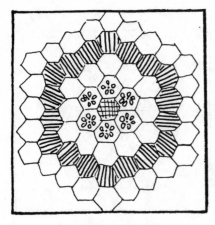 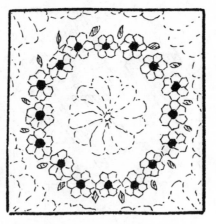 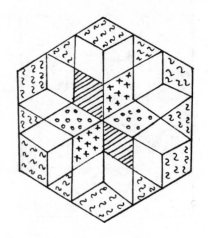

GRANDMOTHER'S FLOWER GARDEN Also **FRENCH BOUQUET, HONEYCOMB, MOSAIC**	**HEXAGON WREATH**	**GLORY BLOCK**

Ladies Art Company, No. 477 *The Romance of the Patchwork Quilt in America,* page 98, No. 5

MADISON'S PATCH

Kansas City Star, 1936

WHIRLIGIG HEXAGON

The Romance of the Patchwork Quilt in America, page 92, No. 12

FLORIDA STAR

 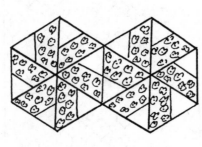 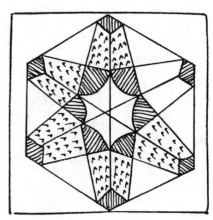

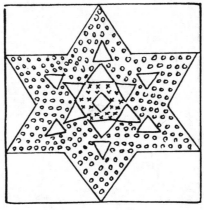

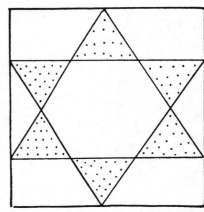

DOUBLE LINK

Nancy Cabot

DOUBLE STAR

The Romance of the Patchwork Quilt in America, page 72, No. 1

DIAMONDS AND ARROW POINTS

Kansas City Star, 1945

Woman's World, February 1928, page 30

The Perfect Patchwork Primer, page 28

SPIDER WEB

CABLE BLOCKS

STAINED GLASS

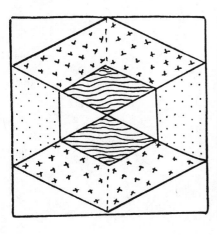

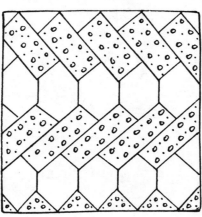

HONEYCOMB

The Perfect Patchwork Primer,
page 28
An English hexagon one-patch

HONEYCOMB PATCH

Ladies Art Company, No.
241

COLUMBIA STAR

*The Romance of the Patch-
work Quilt in America,* page
62, No. 7

Ladies Art Company, No.
109

THE COLUMBIA

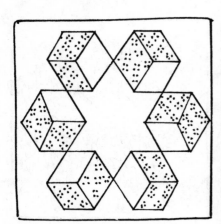

The Perfect Patchwork Primer,
page 110

STAR AND HEXAGON

Nancy Cabot

SNOW CRYSTALS

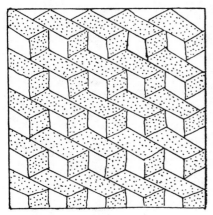

BRICK PILE

Ladies Art Company, No. 410
The Romance of the Patch-work Quilt in America, page 82, No. 23

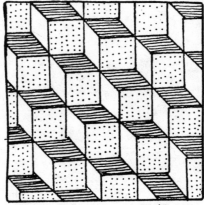

PANDORA'S BOX

Also **BABY BLOCK, BOX QUILT**

BOX QUILT

Also **BABY BLOCK, PAN-DORA'S BLOCK**

GRANDMA'S RED AND WHITE

Ladies Art Company, No. 228
The Romance of the Patch-work Quilt in America, page 52, No. 11

CUBE WORK

Also **PANDORA'S BOX, BOX QUILT**

BABY BLOCK

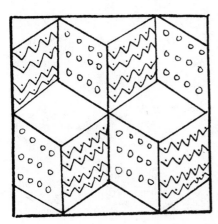

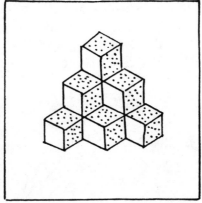

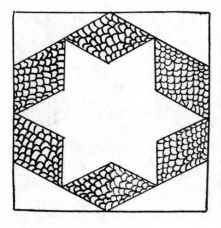

STAR QUILT

TEA BOX

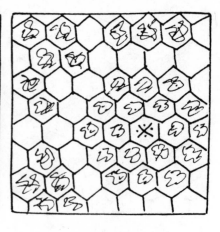

FLOWER GARDEN

The Romance of the Patch-work Quilt in America, page 52, No. 12
Also **BOX QUILT, CUBE WORK, TUMBLING BLOCKS**

BABY BLOCKS

Old Patchwork Quilts and the Women Who Made Them, page 49

HONEYCOMB

Also **FRENCH BOUQUET, GRANDMOTHER'S FLOWER GARDEN, HONEY-COMB**

MOSAIC

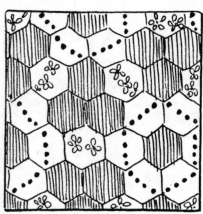

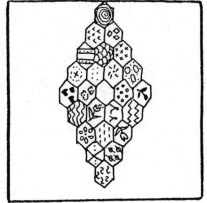

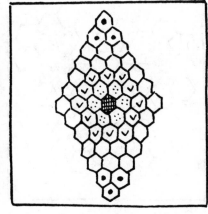

HEXAGON

RAINBOW TILE

The Romance of the Patchwork Quilt in America, page 86, No. 14
Also **DIAMOND FIELD**

MARTHA WASHINGTON'S FLOWER GARDEN

The Romance of the Patchwork Quilt in America, page 86, No. 17
Also **FRENCH BOUQUET, GRANDMOTHER'S FLOWER GARDEN, MOSAIC**

A variation of **GRANDMOTHER'S FLOWER GARDEN**

STAR HEXAGON

HEXAGON STAR

HONEYCOMB

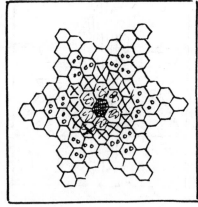

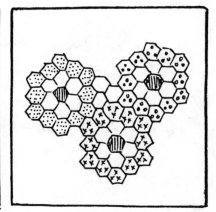

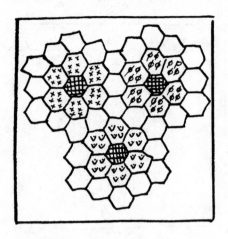

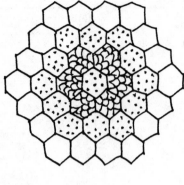

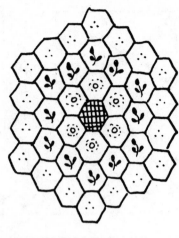

FRENCH BOUQUET

The Romance of the Patch-work Quilt in America, page 86. No. 17
Also **GRANDMOTHER'S FLOWER GARDEN, HONEY-COMB, MOSAIC**

BRIDE'S BOUQUET

Farmer's Wife Magazine

GARDEN WALK

Also **MARTHA WASHINGTON'S FLOWER GARDEN, OLD FASHIONED FLOWER GARDEN**

Ladies Art Company, No. 21
The Romance of the Patch-work Quilt in America, page 54, No. 14
Also **ROLLING STAR, CHAINED STAR**

BRUNSWICK STAR

Joseph Doyle & Company, N.J.

MORNING STAR

Also **BRUNSWICK STAR, ROLLING STAR**

CHAINED STAR

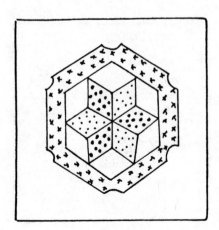

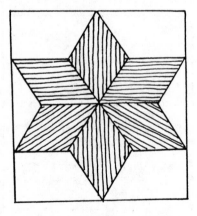

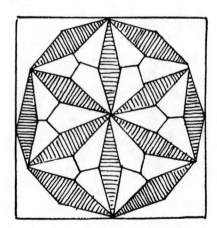

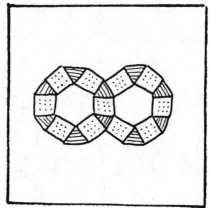

BOUTONNIERE

The Romance of the Patchwork Quilt in America, page 86, No. 18

FERRIS WHEEL

The Romance of the Patchwork Quilt in America, page 86, No. 5

JOSEPH'S COAT

Laura Wheeler
Also **ROLLING STONE**

The Perfect Patchwork Primer, page 110

STAR AND BLOCKS

Kansas City Star, 1942

FOUR O'CLOCK QUILT

Ladies Art Company, No. 91

DIAMOND CUBE

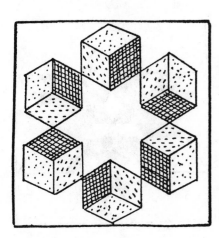

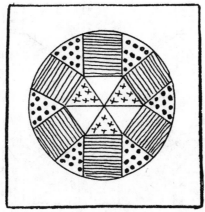

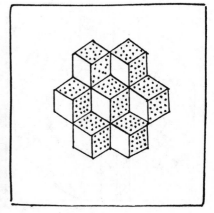

CRAZY TILE

Kansas City Star, 1939

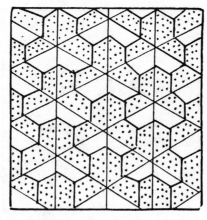

ECCLESIASTICAL

Ladies Art Company, No. 295
The Romance of the Patchwork Quilt in America, page 64, No. 12

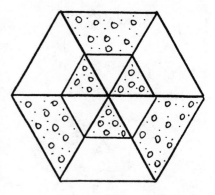

HEXAGON

Ladies Art Company, No. 353
The Romance of the Patchwork Quilt in America, page 72, No. 12
Pattern probably dates from the early 18th century.

Kansas City Star, 1939

ROSALIA FLOWER GARDEN

Ladies Art Company, No. 361

BLOCK PATCHWORK

The Household Magazine, August 1931, page 30
The Romance of the Patchwork Quilt in America, page 72, No. 11

BLUE BIRDS

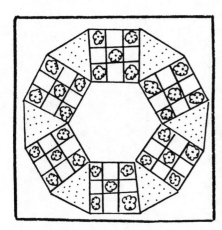

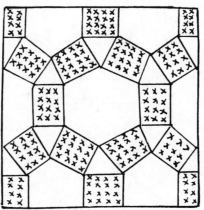

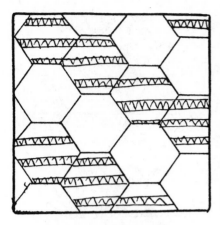

VARIEGATED HEXAGONS

Ladies Art Company, No. 292

OZARK DIAMOND

The Romance of the Patchwork Quilt in America, page 76, No. 12
Also **OZARK STAR**

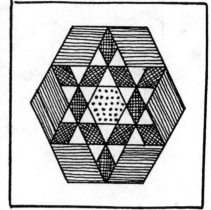

OZARK DIAMOND

Kansas City Star

Kansas City Star, 1945

THE OKLAHOMA STAR

Ladies Art Company, No. 47
Nancy Cabot

HEXAGONAL

The Standard Book of Quilt Making and Collecting, page 243
Also **HEXAGONAL STAR**

RISING STAR

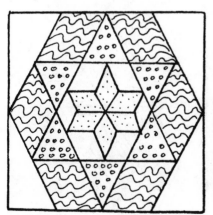

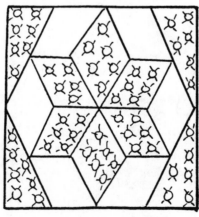

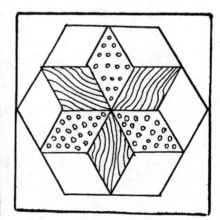

WHIRLING TRIANGLES

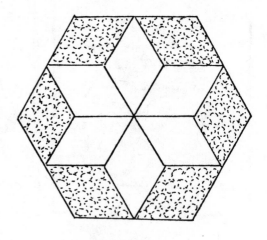

TEXAS STAR

The Romance of the Patch-work Quilt in America, page 54, No. 9
Also **LONE STAR**

Ladies Art Company, No. 466
Nancy Cabot

TEXAS STAR

The Romance of the Patch-work Quilt in America, page 56, No. 12
Also **RISING STAR**

HEXAGONAL STAR

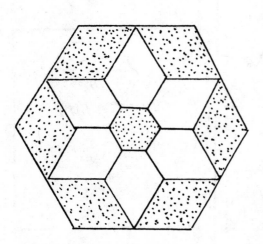

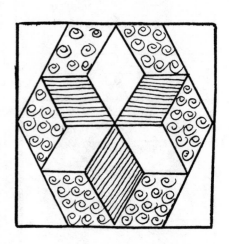

ROSE AND TULIPS   See page 281.

Applique

ROSE AND TULIPS

Nancy Cabot

KENTUCKY ROSE

WHIG ROSE

The Romance of the Patchwork Quilt in America, page 114, No. 3
In Pennsylvania in 1845 it was called the **DEMOCRAT ROSE**, the pattern being claimed by both the Democrats and the Whigs.

Nancy Cabot

ROSE OF SMARKAND

The Romance of the Patchwork Quilt in America, page 108, No. 4

OHIO ROSE

The Romance of the Patchwork Quilt in America, page 108, No. 9

ENGLISH ROSE

ORIGINAL ROSE

The Romance of the Patchwork Quilt in America, page 112, No. 1

ORIGINAL ROSE DESIGN

Quilts: Their Story and How to Make Them, plate after page 128

AUNT MARTHA'S WILD ROSE

The Romance of the Patchwork Quilt in America, page 110, No. 6

The Household Magazine, August 1931, page 30

Ladies Art Company, No. 447

AMERICAN BEAUTY ROSE

WILD ROSE

WILD ROSE

ROSE OF SHARON

The Romance of the Patch-work Quilt in America, page 112, No. 6

ROSE OF SHARON

The Romance of the Patch-work Quilt in America, page 112, No. 7

ROSE OF SHARON

The Romance of the Patch-work Quilt in America, page 112, No. 8

American Quilts and Coverlets, page 14

ROSE OF SHARON

Needlecraft Magazine, August 1933, page 9

THE ROSE OF THE FIELD

Nancy Cabot

FRENCH ROSE

ROSE OF SHARON

INDIANA ROSE

Nancy Cabot

THE WILD ROSE

Quilts: Their Story and How to Make Them, plate after page 104

Old Fashioned Quilts, page 8

THE ROSE SPRIG

Nancy Cabot

MARTHA WASHINGTON ROSE

One Hundred and One Patchwork Patterns, page 10
The Romance of the Patchwork Quilt in America, page 114, No. 6

ROSE APPLIQUE

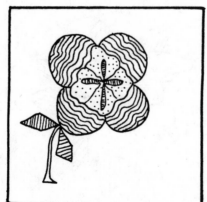

ROSE BUD WREATH

Ladies Art Company, No. 498

WILD ROSE

The Romance of the Patchwork Quilt in America, page 116, No. 6

COVENTIONAL ROSE

Quilts: Their Story and How to Make Them, plate after page 96
The Romance of the Patchwork Quilt in America, page 108, No. 10

American Quilts and Coverlets, page 36
Pieced in eight sections, each section being itself pieced three times in shaded colors. The buds are appliqued.

WHIG ROSE

Nancy Cabot

HARRISON ROSE

Nancy Cabot
GOLDEN ROSE OF VIRGINIA

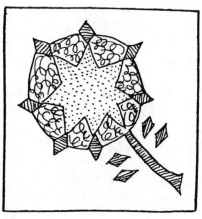

ROSE OF SHARON

The Romance of the Patchwork Quilt in America, page 112, No. 3

ROSE OF SHARON

The Romance of the Patchwork Quilt in America, page 112, No. 4

COMBINATION ROSE

Woman's World, January 1930, page 20
The Romance of the Patchwork Quilt in America, page 114, No. 5
Also **CALIFORNIA ROSE**
When the rose is appliqued in yellow it is called **TEXAS YELLOW ROSE.**

Also **CALIFORNIA ROSE, ROSE OF SHARON**

OHIO ROSE

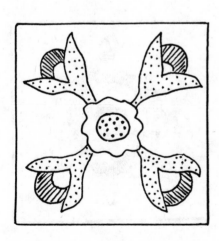

Quilts: Their Story and How to Make Them, plate after page 96
Old Fashioned Quilts, page 22

OHIO ROSE

Nancy Cabot

PENNSYLVANIA DUTCH ROSE

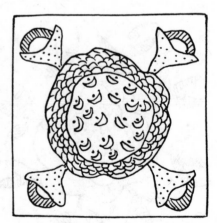

MAHONING ROSE

Nancy Cabot

KENTUCKY ROSE

Nancy Cabot

ORIGINAL ROSE NO. 3

The Romance of the Patchwork Quilt in America, page 112, No. 2

Nancy Cabot

FULL BLOWN ROSE

Quilts: Their Story and How to Make Them, plate after page 128
The Romance of the Patchwork Quilt in America, page 114, No. 8

VIRGINIA ROSE

The Romance of the Patchwork Quilt in America, page 108, No. 6

WIND BLOWN ROSE

OHIO ROSE

The Romance of the Patchwork Quilt in America, page 116, No. 2

OHIO ROSE

The Romance of the Patchwork Quilt in America, page 116, No. 10

PENNSYLVANIA ROSE

The Romance of the Patchwork Quilt in America, page 114, No. 11

ROSE CROSS

The Romance of the Patchwork Quilt in America, page 114, No. 11

PINK ROSE

Quilts: Their Story and How to Make Them, color plate after page 72

PINK ROSE DESIGN

TALLULAH ROSE

Nancy Cabot

MRS. KRETSINGER'S ROSE

The Romance of the Patchwork Quilt in America, page 116, No. 9

ROSE OF TENNESSEE

American Quilts and Coverlets, page 15

Modern Priscilla, August 1928, page 18

THE ROSE OF SHARON

Old Fashioned Quilts, page 21

ROSE TREE BLOCK

Nancy Cabot

DEMOCRATIC ROSE

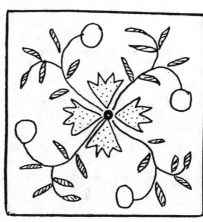

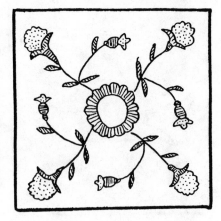

TEA ROSE

American Quilts and Coverlets,
page 15

THE WHIG ROSE

ROSE OF 1840

Nancy Cabot

The Romance of the Patch-work Quilt in America, page 112, No. 5

Quilts: Their Story and How to Make Them, plate after page 128

ROSE OF SHARON

DEMOCRAT ROSE

DEMOCRAT ROSE

TOPEKA ROSE

The Romance of the Patchwork Quilt in America, page 110, No. 10

CONVENTIONAL WILD ROSE

The Romance of the Patchwork Quilt in America, page 116, No. 5

TUDOR ROSE

The Romance of the Patchwork Quilt in America, page 112, No. 9

ROSE OF SHARON

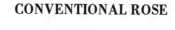

The Romance of the Patchwork Quilt in America, page 110, No. 7

OLD FASHIONED ROSE

CONVENTIONAL ROSE

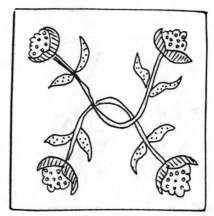

COMBINATION ROSE

Early American Quilts, page 11

WILD ROSE

Old Fashioned Quilts, page 13

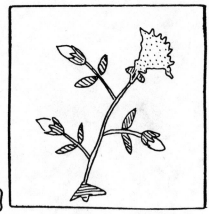

WHIG ROSE

Quilts: Their Story and How to Make Them, plate after page 97
The Romance of the Patchwork Quilt in America, page 114, No. 2

The Romance of the Patchwork Quilt in America, page 170, plate XXXVII

MOSS ROSE

The Romance of the Patchwork Quilt in America, page 114, No. 10

WILD ROSE

The Romance of the Patchwork Quilt in America, page 114, No. 4
Also **MISSOURI ROSE**

ROSE TREE

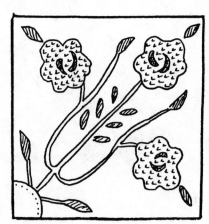

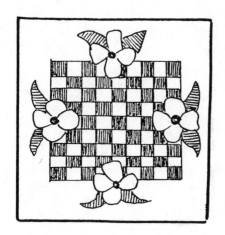

WILD ROSES AND SQUARES

Nancy Cabot

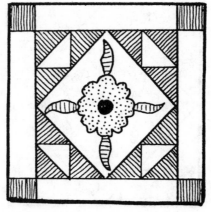

FRAMED ROSE

Nancy Cabot

FRAMED ROSES

Kansas City Star

ARKANSAS MEADOW ROSE

The Romance of the Patchwork Quilt in America, page 110, No. 8

ROSE OF SHARON

Nancy Cabot

ROSES AND PEONIES

THE ROSE AND TULIP

Needlecraft Magazine, June 1931, page 18

APPLIQUED ROSE

Nancy Cabot

THE ROSE OF LEMOYNE

The Romance of the Patch-work Quilt in America, page 114, No. 1

The Romance of the Patch-work Quilt in America, page 116, No. 4

LORETTA'S ROSE

Quilts: Their Story and How to Make Them, plate after page 126

ROSE OF LEMOINE

The Household Magazine, June 1933, page 21

PRAIRIE ROSE BLOCK

PRAIRIE ROSE

Nancy Cabot

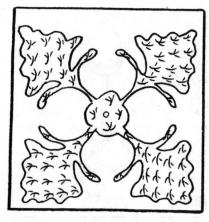

INDIANA ROSE

Early American Quilts, page 14
The Romance of the Patch-work Quilt in America, page 116, No. 3

RADICAL ROSE

The Romance of the Patch-work Quilt in America, page 116, No. 11
During the Civil War, the freeing of the slaves was a very controversial subject and there was talk of radicals and radicalism on all occasions. A famous quilt maker who wanted to show her radicalism, put a black circle in the center of the "Wild Rose" design and named it **RADICAL ROSE.**

The Romance of the Patch-work Quilt in America, page 110, No. 11

MRS. HARRIS' COLONIAL ROSE

Nancy Cabot

NASTURTIUMS

Nancy Cabot

TULIP BASKET

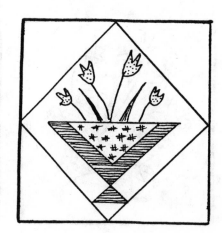

TULIPS IN BOWL

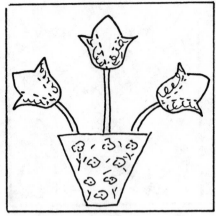

TULIP IN POT

Old Fashioned Quilts, page 22

BOWL OF FLOWERS

Nancy Cabot

Nancy Cabot

JONQUILS

Nancy Cabot

DEMOCRAT ROSE

Kansas City Star, 1929

SETH THOMAS ROSE

DAHLIA FLOWER POT

Nancy Cabot

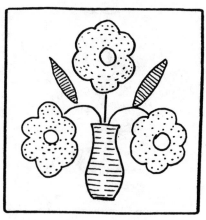

VASE OF ROSES

Nancy Cabot

ROSE BASKET

Nancy Cabot

The Romance of the Patchwork Quilt in America, page 106, No. 7

Woman's World, November 1926, page 38

VICTORIAN URN

CORNUCOPIA

CORNUCOPIA

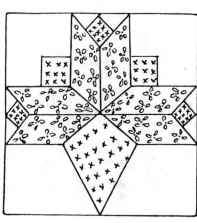

HORN OF PLENTY

Nancy Cabot

THE HORN OF PLENTY

Modern Priscilla, August 1928, page 18

GARDEN BOUNTY

Laura Wheeler

Nancy Cabot

The Romance of the Patchwork Quilt in America, page 106, No. 8

Nancy Cabot

GOLD AND YELLOW HORN

OLD FASHIONED NOSEGAY

WAX FLOWERS

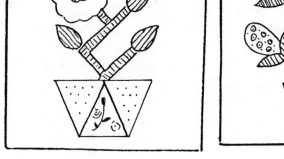

POT OF FLOWERS

Grandmother Clark's Patchwork Quilt Designs, Book 21, 1931

POT OF FLOWERS

Nancy Cabot

GRANDMOTHER'S TULIP

Grandmother Clark's Patchwork Quilt Designs, Book 21, 1931

The Romance of the Patchwork Quilt in America, page 126, No. 16

Kansas City Star, 1935

FLOWER TREE

TINY BASKET

BASKET APPLIQUE QUILT

BASKET OF DAISIES

The Romance of the Patchwork Quilt in America, page 126, No. 2

CARLIE SEXTON'S FLOWER BASKET

The Romance of the Patchwork Quilt in America, page 126, No. 9

FLOWER BASKET

Early American Quilts, page 9

The Romance of the Patchwork Quilt in America, page 126, No. 5

The Romance of the Patchwork Quilt in America, page 126, No. 8

Needlecraft Magazine, February 1935, page 9

MRS. HALL'S BASKET

MAUDE HARE'S BASKET

GARDEN GIFT

BASKET OF FLOWERS

The Romance of the Patchwork Quilt in America, page 126, No. 7

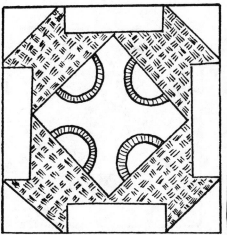

FLOWER BASKET

ENGLISH FLOWER POT

The Romance of the Patchwork Quilt in America, page 106, No. 4

The Standard Book of Quilt Making and Collecting, page 44

FLOWERS IN A POT DESIGN

The Romance of the Patchwork Quilt in America, page 82, No. 2

FENCE ROW

Woman's World, February 1928, page 30

COLONIAL BASKET

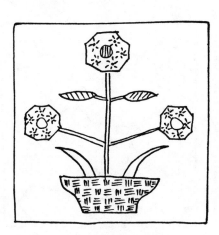

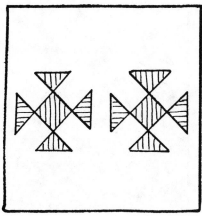

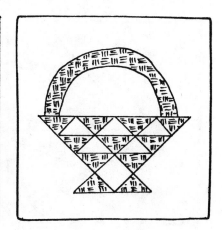

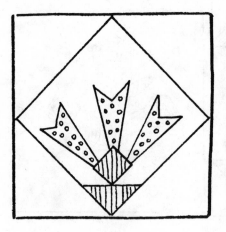

FLORAL BOUQUET

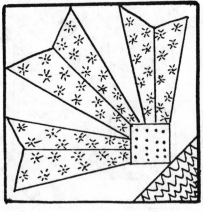

FLORAL BOUQUET

Nancy Cabot

FRIENDSHIP FAN

Nancy Cabot

Needlecraft Magazine, April 1929, No. 7

FRIENDSHIP FAN

One Hundred and One Patchwork Patterns, page 53
The Romance of the Patchwork Quilt in America, page 70, No. 7
The Standard Book of Quilt Making and Collecting, page 245

GRANDMOTHER'S FAN

Grandmother Clark's Patchwork Quilt Designs, Book 20, 1931

GRANDMOTHER'S FAN

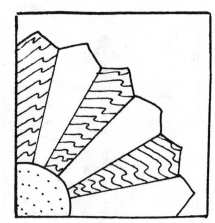

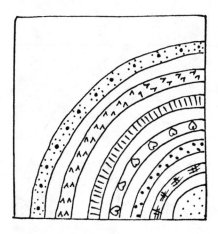

CAROLINE'S FAN

The Romance of the Patchwork Quilt in America, page 70, No. 5

FAN

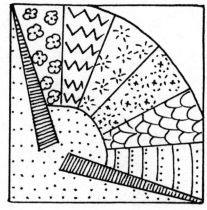

FLOWER OF AUTUMN

Kansas City Star

Kansas City Star

FANNY'S FAN

IMPERIAL FAN

IMPERIAL FAN

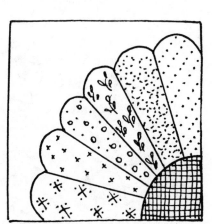

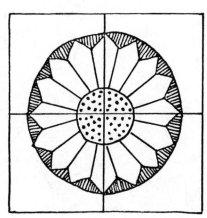

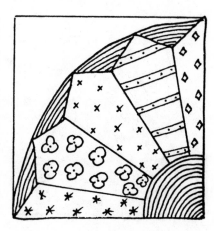

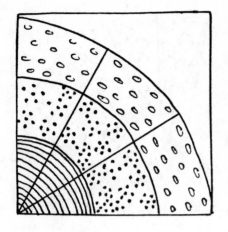

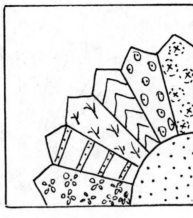

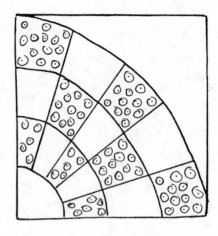

JAPANESE FAN   **JAPANESE FAN**   **LATTICE FAN QUILT**

Ladies Art Company, No. 296   *Ladies Art Company,* No. 143

FANNIE'S FAN   **FAN PATCHWORK**   **FAN**

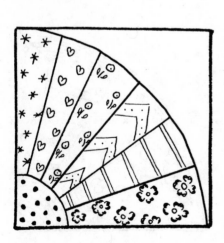

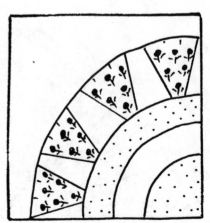

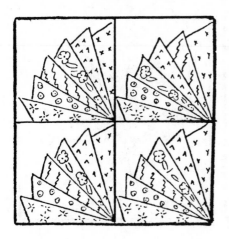

MILADY'S FAN

DRESDEN PLATE

Mrs. Danner's Quilts, Book 4, page 18

DRESDEN PLATE
Also **ASTER, FRIENDSHIP RING**

One Hundred and One Patchwork Patterns, page 76
The Romance of the Patchwork Quilt in America, page 94, No. 14

The Standard Book of Quilt Making and Collecting, page 248

DRESDEN PLATE

Grandmother Clark's Patchwork Quilt Designs, Book 20, 1931

SUN FLOWER

The Romance of the Patchwork Quilt in America, page 94, No. 14
Also **ASTER, DRESDEN PLATE**

FRIENDSHIP RING

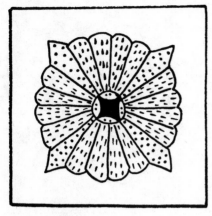

FRIENDSHIP CIRCLE

FRIENDSHIP DAHLIA

The Romance of the Patchwork Quilt in America, page 104, No. 14

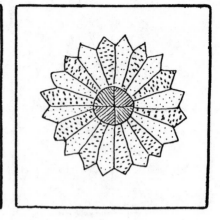

FRIENDSHIP DAISY

Nancy Cabot

Nancy Cabot
Also **FRIENDSHIP RING, DRESDEN PLATE**

The Romance of the Patchwork Quilt in America, page 62, No. 2

BABY ASTER

ASTER

CHINESE STAR

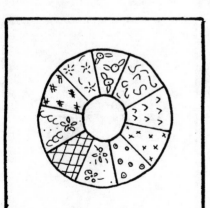

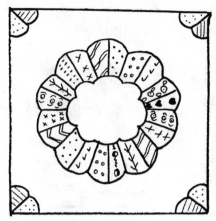

GOLD BLOOM

Kansas City Star, 1935

FERRIS WHEEL

FIELD FLOWER APPLIQUE

Kansas City Star, 1945

The Standard Book of Quilt Making and Collecting, page 247

The Romance of the Patchwork Quilt in America, page 120, No. 1

STAR FLOWER

IRIS

IRIS APPLIQUE

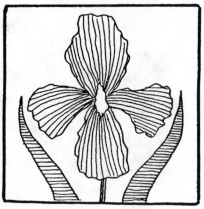

IRIS APPLIQUE

The Romance of the Patchwork Quilt in America, page 120, No. 4

PURPLE IRIS

Nancy Cabot

SHAMROCK

The Romance of the Patchwork Quilt in America, page 102, No. 10

Ladies Art Company, No. 499

Ladies Art Company, No. 500

SWEET CLOVER

CLOVER BLOCK

CUPID'S BLOCK

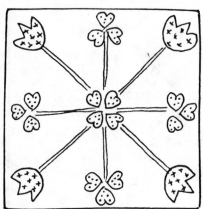

EIGHT OF HEARTS

Nancy Cabot

FOUR RED HEARTS QUILT

Kansas City Star, 1941

DOUBLE HEARTS

The Romance of the Patchwork Quilt in America, page 70, No. 10
Also **ST. VALENTINE'S PATCH**

Early American Quilts, page 11

GOOD LUCK

Ladies Art Company, No. 180

FRIENDSHIP QUILT

The Perfect Patchwork Primer, page 101

TRUE LOVER'S KNOT

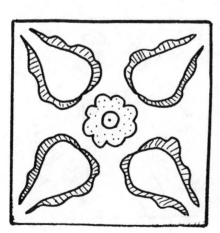

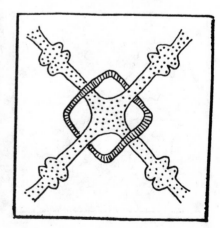

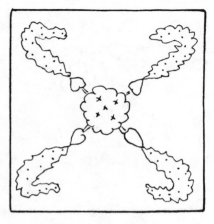

TRUE LOVER'S KNOT

Old Fashioned Quilts, page 4

FRIENDSHIP KNOT

Old Patchwork Quilts and the Women Who Made Them, page 94
The Romance of the Patchwork Quilt in America, page 94, No. 13
Also **STARRY CROWN**

CALIFORNIA PLUME

Ladies Art Company, No. 325
The Romance of the Patchwork Quilt in America, page 124, No. 11
Also **BEN HUR'S CHARIOT WHEEL, STAR AND PLUME**

PRINCESS FEATHER

The Romance of the Patchwork Quilt in America, page 124, No. 10
Also **PRINCESS FEATHER**

BEN HUR'S CHARIOT WHEEL

Old Fashioned Quilts, page 20

AUNT DINAH'S DELIGHT

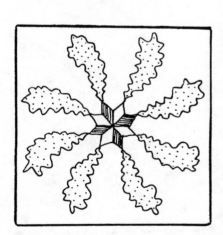

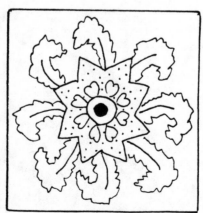

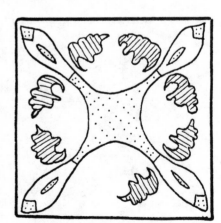

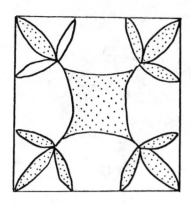 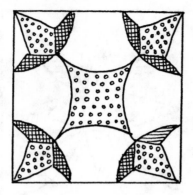 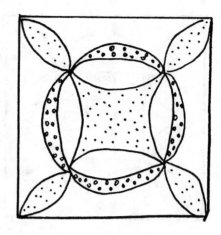

WANDERING FOOT

The Romance of the Patchwork Quilt in America, page 74, No. 15
Also **TURKEY TRACKS.**
Developed in green on a white background, it is also known as **IRIS LEAF.**

WANDERING FOOT

The Perfect Patchwork Primer, page 35

HICKORY LEAF

Ladies Art Company, No. 70
One Hundred and One Patchwork Patterns, 1931
The Romance of the Patchwork Quilt in America, page 118, No. 14
A favorite of the pioneer days—also known as **ORDER NO. 11.** A lady in her eighties brought up in Jackson City, Missouri, in the days of the Civil War is said to have reproduced it from memory. She remembered the pattern made by her mother, which was taken from the old homestead by marauders.

One Hundred and One Patchwork Patterns, page 70
Also **HICKORY LEAF**

ORDER NO. 11

The Romance of the Patchwork Quilt in America, page 102, No. 3
Also **WANDERING FOOT**

IRIS LEAF

Early American Quilts, page 14

TURKEY TRACK

 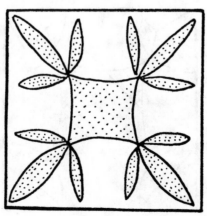 

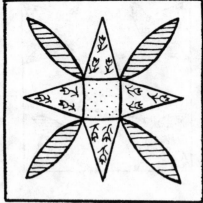

HONEY BEE

The Romance of the Patchwork Quilt in America, page 78, No. 6
Also **BLUE BLAZES**

MORNING STAR

The Standard Book of Quilt Making and Collecting, page 229

THE STRAWBERRY

One Hundred and One Patchwork Patterns, page 94
Also **FULL BLOWN TULIP**

Nancy Cabot

EIGHT HANDS AROUND

Ladies Art Company, No. 401

SWINGING CORNERS

Woman's World, February 1928, page 30

SQUARE AND SWALLOW

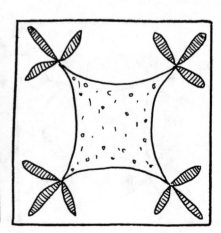

BIRD OF PARADISE

The Romance of the Patchwork Quilt in America, page 72, No. 18

The Standard Book of Quilt Making and Collecting, page 252

CALIFORNIA ROSE

Ladies Art Company, No. 184
Old Fashioned Quilts, page 5
Also **COMBINATION ROSE**

CAESAR'S CROWN

The Romance of the Patchwork Quilt in America, page 68, No. 9

The Standard Book of Quilt Making and Collecting, page 247

The Romance of the Patchwork Quilt in America, page 122, No. 1
Also **THE STRAWBERRY**

FULL BLOWN TULIP

Quilts: Their Story and How to Make Them, plate after page 128
The Romance of the Patchwork Quilt in America, page 114, No. 9

HARRISON ROSE

Ladies Art Company, No. 489

MILWAUKEE'S OWN

THE HAND

Ladies Art Company, No. 113

OAK LEAF

The Romance of the Patchwork Quilt in America, page 155, Plate XXIII

THE BEAR PAW

Mrs. Danner's Quilts, Book 2, page 15

Ladies Art Company, No. 187

HARRISON ROSE

Nancy Page

NANCY'S TULIP BLOCK

THE TULIP

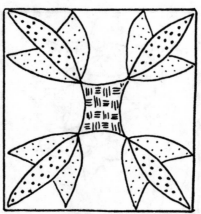

DUTCH TULIP

Old Patchwork Quilts and the Women Who Made Them, page 115
Kansas City Star, 1931
The Romance of the Patchwork Quilt in America, page 122, No. 9

THE FOUR WINDS

Kansas City Star, 1932
Also **STAR OF THE WEST, COMPASS**

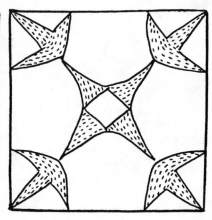

FLYING SWALLOWS

Nancy Cabot

Ladies Art Company, No. 501
The Romance of the Patchwork Quilt in America, page 106, No. 5

BLEEDING HEART

Kansas City Star, 1934

THE TEXAS POINTER

The Standard Book of Quilt Making and Collecting, page 249

STAR OF THE FOUR WINDS

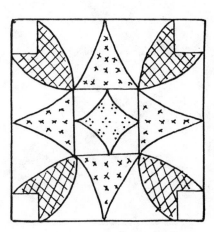

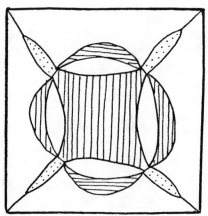

STAR OF THE WEST

STAR AND CRESCENT

STAR CRESCENT

The Romance of the Patch-work Quilt in America, page 56, No. 3
Also **COMPASS** and **THE FOUR WINDS**

Nancy Cabot

The Romance of the Patch-work Quilt in America, page 118, No. 18

The Standard Book of Quilt Making and Collecting, page 55

CROWN OF OAK

OAK LEAF AND CHERRIES

OAK LEAF WREATH

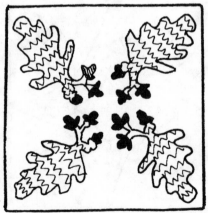

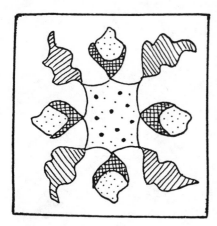

OAK LEAVES AND ACORN

Nancy Cabot

HERO'S CROWN

Old Patchwork Quilts and the Women Who Made Them, page 124
The Romance of the Patchwork Quilt in America, page 118, No. 13

OAK LEAF AND ACORN

The Romance of the Patchwork Quilt in America, page 118, No. 15

Old Patchwork Quilts and the Women Who Made Them, page 124

CHARTER OAK

Ladies Art Company, No. 72

MAPLE LEAF

Ladies Art Company, No. 302

OAK LEAF AND ACORN

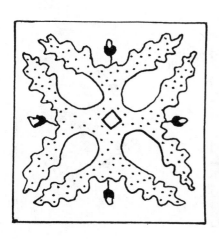

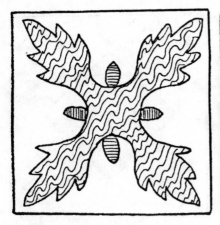

OAK LEAF

The Romance of the Patchwork Quilt in America, page 118, No. 16
American Quilts, page 128

OAK LEAF

The Perfect Patchwork Primer, page 101

CALIFORNIA OAK LEAF

Ladies Art Company, No. 497
Also **TRUE LOVER'S KNOT**

The Romance of the Patchwork Quilt in America, page 118, No. 17

CHARTER OAK

The Romance of the Patchwork Quilt in America, page 118, No. 10

CHARTER OAK

ACORN AND OAK LEAF

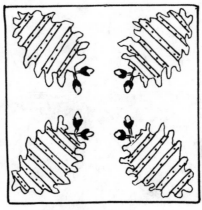

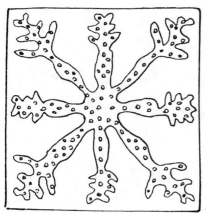

FOREST OAK

Woman's World, January 1930
page 21

PINEAPPLE

The Romance of the Patch-work Quilt in America, page 120, No. 9

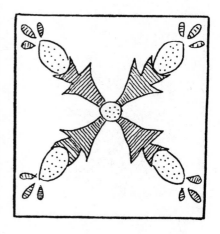

PINEAPPLE

American Quilts and Coverlets
page 60

Nancy Cabot

THE PINEAPPLE BLOCK

The Standard Book of Quilt Making and Collecting, page 125

MELON PATCH

Ladies Art Company, No. 93
The pineapple motif, traditional symbol of domestic hospitality, was also a favorite quilting design. It dates from the early 18th century.

PINEAPPLE

PINEAPPLE

The Romance of the Patch-work Quilt in America, page 120, No. 10
The Standard Book of Quilt Making and Collecting, page 82

PINEAPPLE

Quilts: Their Story and How to Make Them, plate after page 128

PINEAPPLE

The Romance of the Patch-work Quilt in America, page 108, No. 8

The Romance of the Patch-work Quilt in America, page 70, No. 2

Farm Journal and *Farmer's Wife,* 1942

DAINTY PETALS

Nancy Cabot

BEADS

STRING OF BEADS

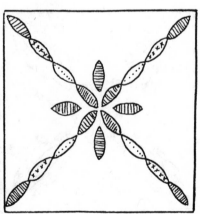

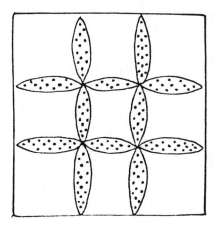

BAY LEAF

The Romance of the Patchwork Quilt in America, page 102, No. 1
Also **TEA LEAVES**

DAISY CHAIN

The Romance of the Patchwork Quilt in America, page 104, No. 2

DAISY

Woman's World, February 1928, page 30

The Romance of the Patchwork Quilt in America, page 104, No. 8

Nancy Page

DAISY APPLIQUE

DAISY BLOCK

POPPY

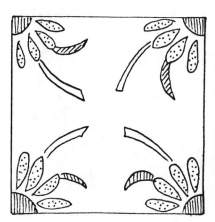

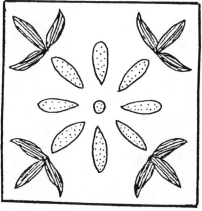

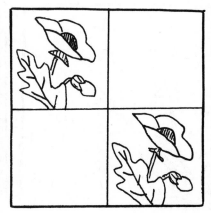

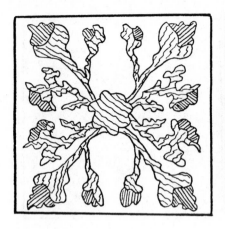

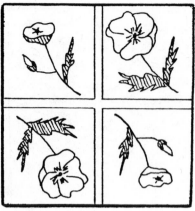

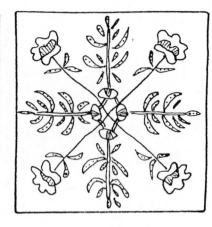

THE POPPY

Old Patchwork Quilts and the Women Who Made Them, page 65

POPPY GARDEN

Nancy Cabot

NODDING POPPIES

Modern Priscilla, December 1920, page 22

The Romance of the Patchwork Quilt in America, page 122, No. 4

TULIP GARDEN

Quilts: Their Story and How to Make Them, plate after page 96
The Romance of the Patchwork Quilt in America, page 122, No. 15

CONVENTIONAL TULIP

WREATH OF ROSES

The Romance of the Patchwork Quilt in America, page 124, No. 5
Also **GARDEN WREATH**

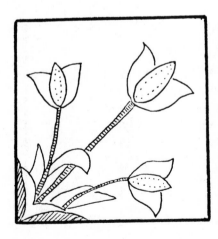

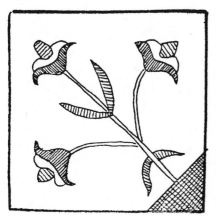

RARE OLD TULIP

Nancy Cabot

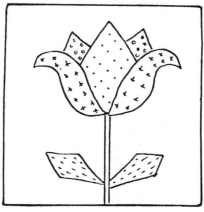

COLONIAL TULIP

The Romance of the Patchwork Quilt in America, page 122, No. 16

RARE OLD TULIP

Grandmother Clark's Patchwork Quilt Designs, Book 20, 1931

The Romance of the Patchwork Quilt in America, page 122, No. 10

ANNA BAUERFELD'S TULIP

The Romance of the Patchwork Quilt in America, page 122, No. 2

ANNA'S IRISH TULIP

The Romance of the Patchwork Quilt in America, page 122, No. 11

MRS. EWER'S TULIP

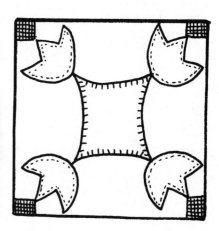

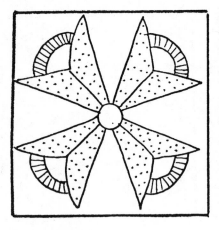

GRANDMA'S TULIPS

The Romance of the Patchwork Quilt in America, page 122, No. 7

OLIVE'S YELLOW TULIP

HEARTS AND FLOWERS

Nancy Cabot

The Romance of the Patchwork Quilt in America, page 122, No. 6

TULIP APPLIQUE

Quilts: Their Story and How to Make Them, plate after page 96

SINGLE TULIP

Old Fashioned Quilts, page 17

BED OF DOUBLE RED TULIPS

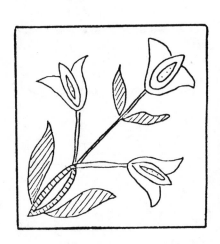

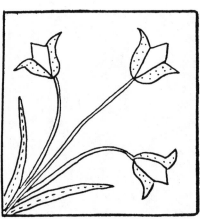

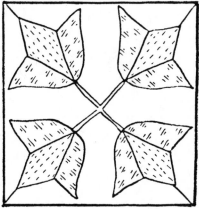

DOUBLE TULIP

Quilts: Their Story and How to Make Them, plate after page 64

FOUR TULIPS

Ladies Art Company, No. 453
The Romance of the Patchwork Quilt in America, page 122, No. 5

TULIP TREE LEAVES

Quilts: Their Story and How to Make Them, plate after page 96

Woman's World, February 1928, page 30

TENNESSEE TULIP

Ladies Art Company, No. 449

TULIP

Kansas City Star, 1942

TULIP

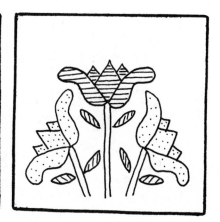

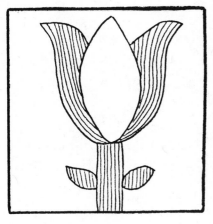

TULIP BLOCK

Ladies Art Company, No. 65

THE TULIP

American Quilts, page 128

TULIPS

Nancy Cabot

GARDEN TULIP

EGYPTIAN TULIP

SPRING TULIPS

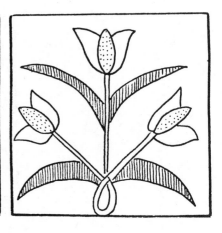

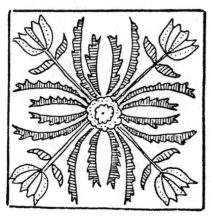

TULIP DESIGN

The Standard Book of Quilt Making and Collecting, page 109

WIND-BLOWN TULIPS

Quilts: Their Story and How to Make Them, color plate after page 72
The Romance of the Patchwork Quilt in America, page 120, No. 13
American Quilts and Coverlets, page 4

TULIP

The Romance of the Patchwork Quilt in America, page 122, No. 12

American Quilts and Coverlets, page 64

TULIP BASKETS

The Romance of the Patchwork Quilt in America, page 122, No. 8

COTTAGE TULIPS

Nancy Cabot

BABY CHRYSANTHEMUM

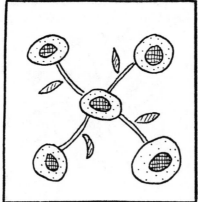

BABY ROSE

Nancy Cabot

BABY ROSE

Yesterday's Quilts in Homes of Today, page 10

BALM OF GILEAD

Nancy Cabot

Old Fashioned Quilts, page 21

The Perfect Patchwork Primer, page 103

NORTH CAROLINA ROSE

GRANDMOTHER'S DREAM

TRIANGLE FLOWER

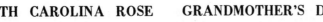

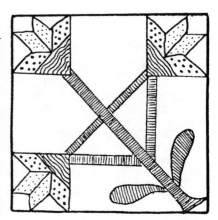

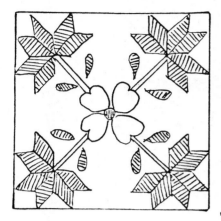

DOUBLE PEONY AND WILD ROSE

The Romance of the Patchwork Quilt in America, page 108, No. 2

MEXICAN ROSE

Ladies Art Company, No. 186

MEXICAN ROSE

The Romance of the Patchwork Quilt in America, page 108, No. 3

The Romance of the Patchwork Quilt in America, page 116, No. 7

MEXICAN ROSE

The Romance of the Patchwork Quilt in America, page 116, No. 8

MEXICAN ROSE

The Romance of the Patchwork Quilt in America, page 124, No. 6

WREATH OF WILD ROSES

TULIP APPLIQUE

One Hundred and One Patch-work Patterns, page 101

OVAL ROSE

Woman's World, November 1926

The Standard Book of Quilt Making and Collecting, page 138

BUD AND ROSE WREATH QUILT

Nancy Cabot

DOGWOOD BLOOMS

Nancy Cabot

SWEET PEA WREATH

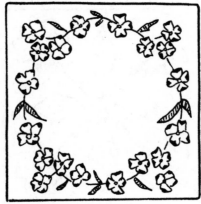

WILD ROSE WREATH

The Standard Book of Quilt Making and Collecting, page 67

WREATH OF ROSES

The Standard Book of Quilt Making and Collecting, page 59

Nancy Cabot

MOONFLOWER

Nancy Cabot

WREATH

COLUMBINE

Applique/331

DAHLIA WREATH

American Quilts and Coverlets, page 13

DAHLIA WREATH

BLUE BELL WREATH

Progressive Farmer

The Standard Book of Quilt Making and Collecting, page 61

FOLIAGE WREATH

Nancy Cabot

GARLAND OF LEAVES

Laura Wheeler

INDIAN SUMMER

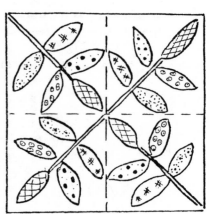

MOUNTAIN LAUREL

The Romance of the Patchwork Quilt in America, page 108, No. 5

PRESIDENT'S WREATH

The Romance of the Patchwork Quilt in America, page 124, No. 4

MT. VERNON WREATH

The Romance of the Patchwork Quilt in America, page 124, No. 8

MARTHA WASHINGTON'S WREATH

Nancy Cabot

CENTENNIAL WREATH

Grandmother's Authentic Early American Patchwork Quilts, Book No. 23

FLOWER WREATH

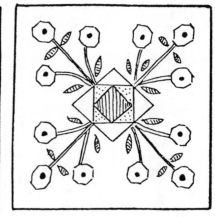

HOLLYHOCK WREATH

One Hundred and One Patchwork Patterns, page 77
The Romance of the Patchwork Quilt in America, page 124, No. 3
Nancy Cabot

WREATH OF ROSES

Ladies Art Company, No. 189

DAISY TILES

Nancy Cabot

American Quilts and Coverlets, page 5

Quilts: Their Story and How to Make Them, plate after page 152

Nancy Cabot

WREATH OF GRAPES

GRAPES AND VINES

CHERRIES

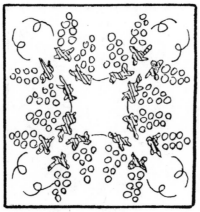

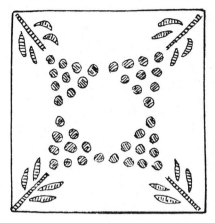

CHERRY

The Romance of the Patchwork Quilt in America, page 106, No. 15

IOWA ROSE WREATH

The Romance of the Patchwork Quilt in America, page 124, No. 9

IOWA ROSE

Early American Quilts, page 11

The Romance of the Patchwork Quilt in America, page 124

Nancy Cabot

Nancy Cabot

WREATH OF CARNATIONS

WREATH OF DAISIES

SWEETHEART GARDEN

PEONIES

Quilts: Their Story and How to Make Them, plate after page 96
The Romance of the Patchwork Quilt in America, page 110, No. 2

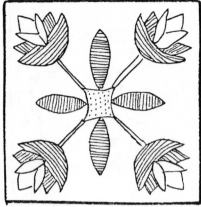

PEONY

Nancy Cabot

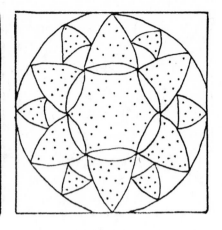

COG WHEELS

Ladies Art Company, No. 41

Old Fashioned Quilts, page 21
Also **MISSOURI ROSE**

The Romance of the Patchwork Quilt in America, page 114, No. 7
Also **PRAIRIE FLOWER, ROSE TREE**

TULIP TREE

PRAIRIE FLOWER

MISSOURI ROSE

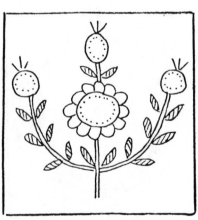

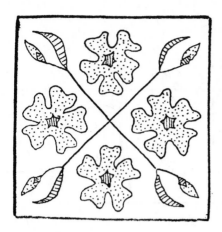

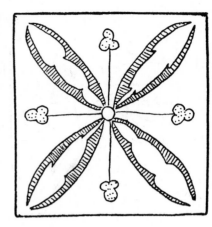

ANGEL'S BREATH

Nancy Cabot

OREGON DAISY

Nancy Cabot

BUDS AND LEAVES

Nancy Cabot

Nancy Cabot

HOLLY LEAVES

Kansas City Star, 1932

GOLDEN GLOW

Nancy Cabot

PANSY BLOCK

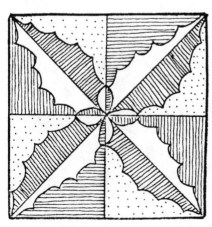

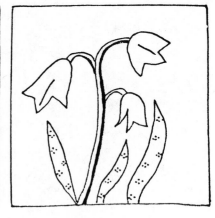

POPPIES

Nancy Cabot

FIELD FLOWERS

Nancy Cabot

BLUEBELLS

Nancy Cabot

Nancy Page

Nancy Cabot

Nancy Cabot

WREATH OF VIOLETS

LAVENDER LACE FLOWER

SIBERIAN WALLFLOWER

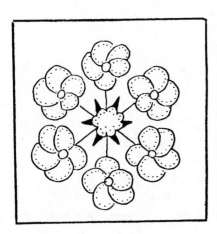

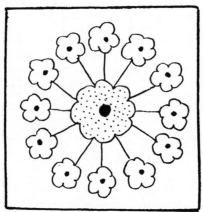

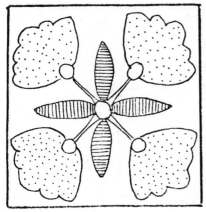

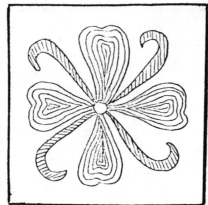

MEADOW DAISY

Nancy Cabot

VIRGINIA STOCK

Nancy Cabot

VISCARIA

Nancy Cabot

Nancy Cabot

DAHLIA

Nancy Cabot

CLEOME

Nancy Cabot

BURNING BUSH

YELLOW COSMOS

Nancy Page

CLEMATIS

Nancy Cabot

ROYAL WATERLILY

Nancy Cabot

Nancy Cabot

Nancy Cabot

AMARYLLIS

BUCKEYE BLOSSOMS

OLD SOLDIER'S ROSE

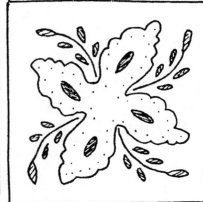

ANGEL'S TRUMPET

Nancy Cabot

OLD DUTCH TULIP

The Romance of the Patchwork Quilt in America, page 122, No. 13

OLD FASHIONED FLOWER GARDEN

The Romance of the Patchwork Quilt in America, page 106, No. 13

One Hundred and One Patchwork Patterns, page 119
Also **HONEY BEE**

Nancy Cabot

Nancy Cabot

ROSE AND PRIMROSE

FLANDER'S POPPY

BLUE BLAZES

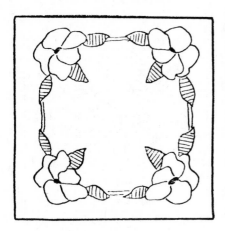

PANSY WREATH

Ladies Art Company, No. 509

WREATH OF PANSIES

The Romance of the Patchwork Quilt in America, page 124

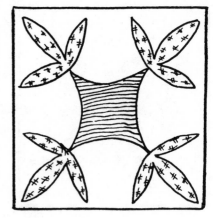

TURKEY TRACKS

The Standard Book of Quilt Making and Collecting, page 250
Also **WANDERING FOOT**

The Romance of the Patchwork Quilt in America, page 118, No. 11

TIGER LILY

Nancy Cabot

TIGER LILY

The Standard Book of Quilt Making and Collecting, page 72

COCK'S COMB PATTERN

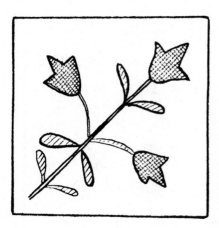

COXCOMB

The Romance of the Patchwork Quilt in America, page 120, No. 16

LOTUS BLOSSOMS

Nancy Cabot

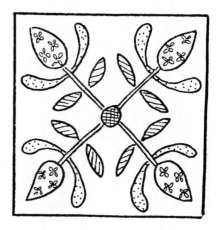

LOTUS BUD

The Romance of the Patchwork Quilt in America, page 120, No. 14

The Romance of the Patchwork Quilt in America, page 120, No. 15

LOTUS FLOWER

Nancy Cabot

LOTUS FLOWER

Nancy Cabot

LOTUS BLOCK

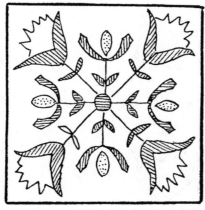

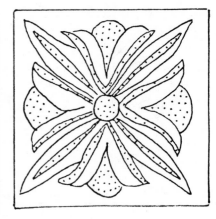

HONEYSUCKLE

Nancy Cabot

PERSIAN PALM LILY

Ladies Art Company, No. 52

EASTER LILY

The Romance of the Patch-work Quilt in America, page 118, No. 6

The Household Magazine, June 1933, page 21

Ladies Art Company, No. 418

MOUNTAIN LILY BLOCK

MORNING GLORY

MORNING GLORY

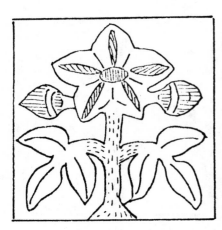

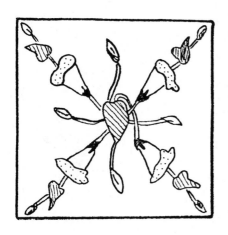

MORNING GLORIES

The Romance of the Patchwork Quilt in America, page 106, No. 2

PUMPKIN

Ladies Art Company, No. 508

PUMPKIN BLOSSOM

Ladies Art Company, No. 110

OLIVE BRANCH

Ladies Art Company, No. 188

THE LOVE ROSE

Nancy Cabot

VIOLETS

SUNFLOWER

BROWN-EYED SUSANS

Nancy Cabot

KANSAS BEAUTY

Nancy Cabot

Nancy Cabot

MODERN POINSETTIA

Nancy Cabot

POINSETTIA

Nancy Cabot

POINSETTIA SPRAY

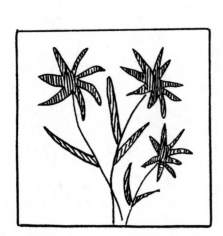

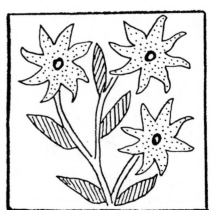

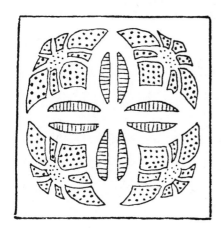

POINSETTIA

The Romance of the Patchwork Quilt in America, page 104, No. 11
Nancy Cabot

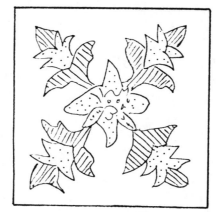

PERSIAN POINSETTIA

Nancy Cabot

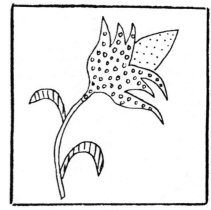

POINSETTIA

Quilts: Their Story and How to Make Them, plate after page 96
Woman's World, January 1930, page 20
The Romance of the Patchwork Quilt in America, page 104, No. 12

The Romance of the Patchwork Quilt in America, page 104, No. 10

POINSETTIA

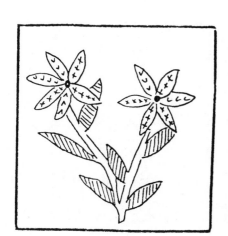

Home Art

POINSETTIA

Grandmother's Authentic Early American Patchwork Quilts, Book No. 23

WATERLILIES

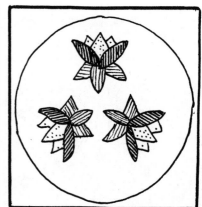

WATERLILY

The Romance of the Patch-work Quilt in America, page 118, No. 4

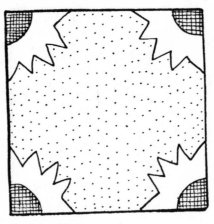

WATERLILY

The Romance of the Patch-work Quilt in America, page 118, No. 5

WHITE DAY LILY

Ladies Art Company, No. 56

The Romance of the Patch-work Quilt in America, page 110, No. 12

SADIE'S CHOICE ROSE

ELABORATE PATCH

Nancy Cabot

JERUSALEM CROSS

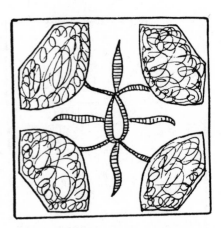

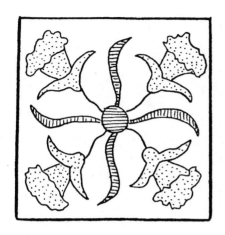

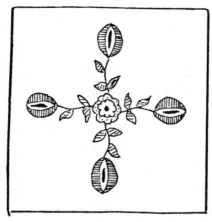

JONQUIL

Nancy Cabot

POMEGRANATE

Woman's World, January 1930, page 21

POMEGRANATE

The Romance of the Patchwork Quilt in America, page 110, No. 9

The Romance of the Patchwork Quilt in America, page 106, No. 14
Prior to 1850, the love apple or tomato was considered to be poisonous.

American Quilts and Coverlets, page 12

POMEGRANATE

Old Fashioned Quilts, page 15

TEMPERANCE BALL

LOVE APPLE

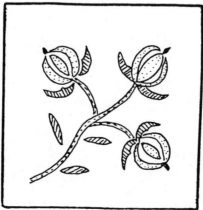

LOVE APPLE

Nancy Cabot

THE MAYAPPLE

The Household Magazine, March 1929, page 35

ST PETER'S PENNY

Nancy Cabot

The Romance of the Patchwork Quilt in America, page 104, No. 6

SPICE PINK

The Romance of the Patchwork Quilt in America, page 104, No. 7

SCOTCH THISTLE

American Quilts and Coverlets, page 63

THISTLES

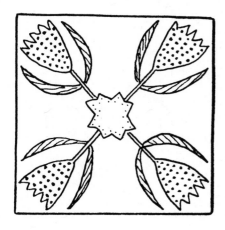

THISTLE

Early American Quilts, page 14

PRIMROSE

PRIMROSE

Nancy Cabot

Nancy Cabot

Nancy Cabot

Ladies Art Company, No. 450

NASTURTIUMS

VERBENA

CALIFORNIA SUNFLOWER

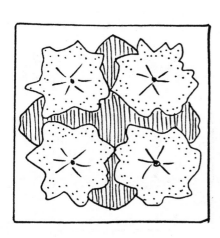

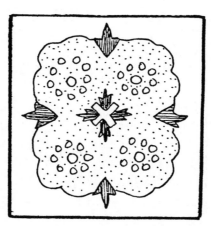

CACTUS BLOOM

Nancy Cabot

CACTUS BLOSSOM PATCH

Ladies Art Company, No. 300

CACTUS FLOWER

Needlecraft Magazine, February 1935, page 9

Nancy Cabot

FLOWERING BALSAM

Nancy Cabot

RED PEONY

Yesterday's Quilts in Homes of Today, page 5

RED "PINEY"

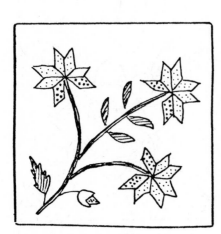

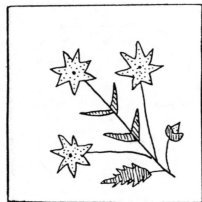

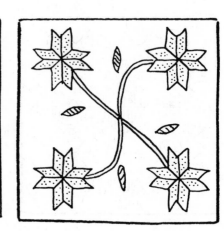

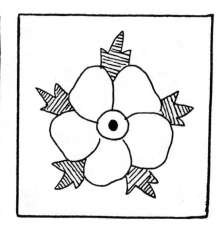

ROCK ROSES

Nancy Cabot

DIANTHUS

Nancy Cabot

ANEMONE

Nancy Cabot

Nancy Cabot

The Romance of the Patch-work Quilt in America, page 110, No. 1

ZINNIA

ZINNIA APPLIQUE

FOUR PEONIES

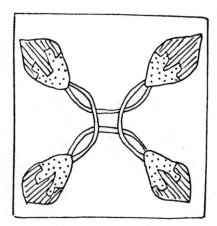

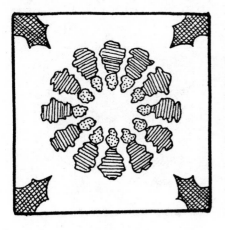

CONE FLOWER WREATH

Nancy Cabot

WHIRLING SWASTIKA

American Quilts and Coverlets,
page 20

FULL BLOWN ROSE

Nancy Cabot

Nancy Cabot

Nancy Cabot

SNOW ON THE MOUNTAIN

FLOWER SPEARS

ARROWROOT

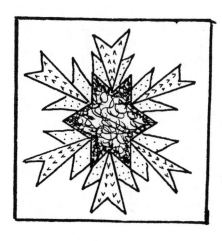

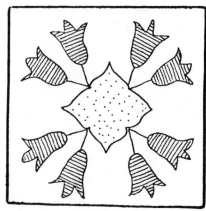

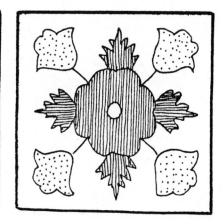

MODERNISTIC STAR

The Romance of the Patch-work Quilt in America, page 60, No. 2

HAREBELLS

Nancy Cabot

CALIFORNIA POPPY

Nancy Cabot

Nancy Cabot

LOVE IN THE MIST

CORNFLOWER

The Romance of the Patch-work Quilt in America, page 106, No. 6

MAUDE HARE'S FLOWER GARDEN

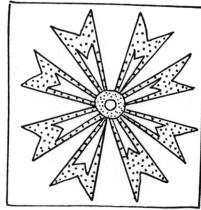

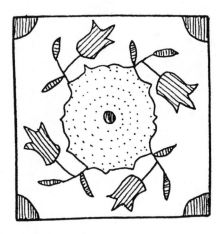

BLUEBELLS AND PETUNIA

Nancy Cabot

ORCHIDS

Nancy Cabot

ENGLISH POPPY

The Romance of the Patchwork Quilt in America, page 106, No. 11

Nancy Cabot

CATHEDRAL BELLS

Nancy Cabot

CALLA LILLY

Nancy Cabot

CARDINAL CLIMBER

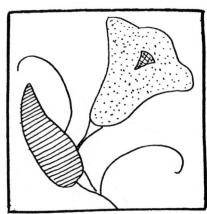

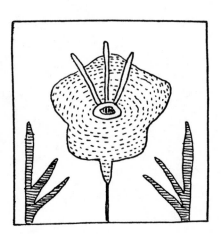

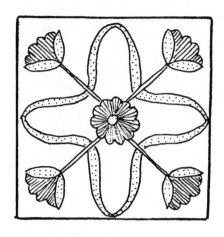

GERANIUM WREATH

Nancy Cabot

COTTON BOLL QUILT

Woman's World, January 1930, page 21

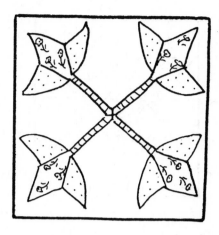

LILY OF THE VALLEY

Ladies Art Company, No. 391
*The Romance of the Patch-
work Quilt in America*, page 118, No. 2

Ladies Art Company, No. 54

The Perfect Patchwork Primer, page 104

CONVENTIONAL TULIPS

LILY OF THE VALLEY

NORTH CAROLINA LILY

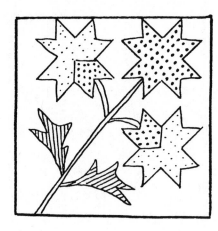

MISSISSIPPI PINK

Needlecraft Magazine, April 1929, page 7

PEONY

The Romance of the Patchwork Quilt in America, page 110, No. 4

THE URN

The Romance of the Patchwork Quilt in America, page 120, No. 19

Old Patchwork Quilts and the Women Who Made Them, page 125

The Romance of the Patchwork Quilt in America, page 104, No. 3

Also **BLACK-EYED SUSAN**

Nancy Cabot

The Romance of the Patchwork Quilt in America, page 120, No. 11

COLUMBINE

HYACINTHS

MEADOW DAISY

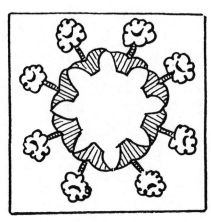

SWEET WILLIAM

Nancy Cabot

STARS AND PLANETS

The Romance of the Patchwork Quilt in America, page 76, No. 8

STAR FLOWER

The Romance of the Patchwork Quilt in America, page 76, No. 20
Also **GOLDEN GLOW**

Nancy Cabot

Grandmother Clark's Patchwork Quilt Designs, Book 21, 1931

Nancy Cabot

TULIP WREATH

STAR FLOWER

RED HOT POKER

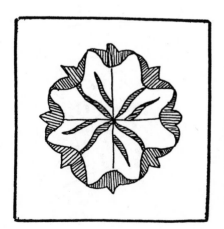

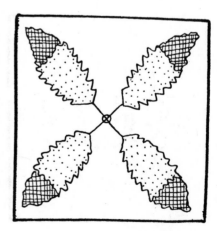

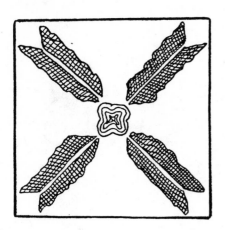

TOBACCO LEAF

The Romance of the Patch-work Quilt in America, page 118, No. 9

AN ODD PATTERN

Ladies Art Company, No. 217

THE FENCED-IN STAR

Kansas City Star, 1946

Kansas City Star

MISSOURI SUNFLOWER

Woman's World, February 1928, page 30

PANSY

Woman's World, February 1928, page 30

COSMOS

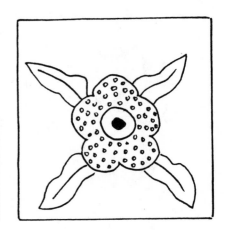

SUNFLOWER

Woman's World, February 1928, page 30

RAGGED ROBIN

THE REEL

The Romance of the Patchwork Quilt in America, page 100, No. 4
The Standard Book of Quilt Making and Collecting, page 246, No. 2

The Standard Book of Quilt Making and Collecting, page 246, No. 1

THE REEL

The Perfect Patchwork Primer, page 104

ROAD TO CALIFORNIA

Nancy Cabot

HUMMING BIRDS

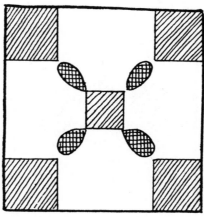

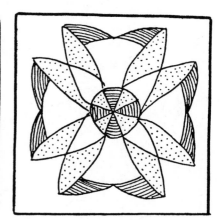

GOLDEN CORN

The Romance of the Patch-work Quilt in America, page 108, No. 7

PHILADELPHIA BEAUTY

Ladies Art Company, No. 116
Nancy Cabot

FOUR FROGS QUILT

Ladies Art Company, No. 283

**PENNSYLVANIA   DUTCH
DESIGN**

Ladies Art Company, No. 299

THE TWO DOVES

Ladies Art Company, No. 303

FOUR LITTLE BIRDS

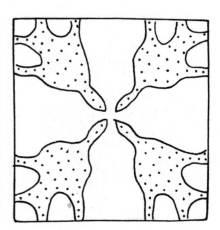

BLOO-JUN BIRD

Woman's World, November 1926, page 38
Design by Ruby Short McKim.

EAGLE

EAGLE APPLIQUE

American Quilts and Coverlets, page 42

Spinning Wheel, July-August 1968, page 16
The eagle, after it was adopted by Congress in 1782 for the Great Seal of the United States, was a popular motif used as applique on quilts and in quilting designs.

UNION QUILT

THE DOVE

Needlecraft Magazine, February 1935, page 9

SCOTTIE

LAMB

Nancy Cabot

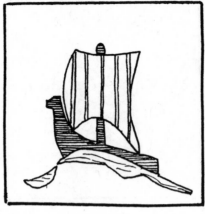

TREASURE SHIP

Needlecraft Magazine,
February 1935, page 9

PEACHES

Nancy Cabot

Nancy Cabot

CHATTERING GEESE

Progressive Farmer, Pattern
No. 1809

NOISY GEESE

Nancy Cabot

GEESE

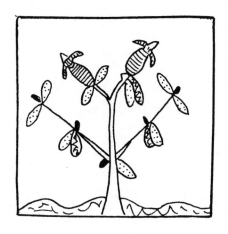

DESERT BELL FLOWER

Nancy Cabot

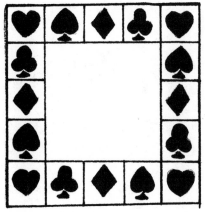

BRIDGE

Kansas City Star, 1931

SQUARE AND CIRCLE

The Romance of the Patchwork Quilt in America, page 100, No. 15

Nancy Cabot

BRIDE'S PRIZE

BRIDE'S QUILT

CHINESE LANTERNS

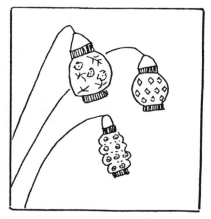

JAPANESE LANTERN

The Romance of the Patchwork Quilt in America, page 84, No. 20

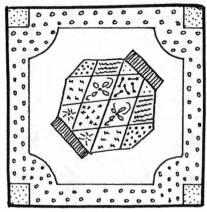

JAPANESE LANTERN

Nancy Cabot

INDIAN CHARM

Nancy Cabot

The Romance of the Patchwork Quilt in America, page 72, No. 13

BUTTERFLY

Nancy Cabot

BUTTERFLY

Kansas City Star, 1931

JUNE BUTTERFLY

EGYPTIAN BUTTERFLY

Grandmother Clark's Patchwork Quilt Designs, Book 20, 1931

FANCY BUTTERFLY

Grandmother Clark's Patchwork Quilt Designs, Book 21, 1931

PLAIN BUTTERFLY

Grandmother Clark's Patchwork Quilt Designs, Book 21, 1931

Ladies Art Company, No. 414

BUTTERFLIES

Ladies Art Company, No. 408

CHRYSANTHEMUM

Ladies Art Company, No. 495

SNOW FLAKE

Applique/367

OCTOBER FOLIAGE

Progressive Farmer

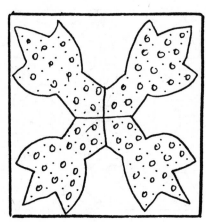

SNOWFLAKE

FOUR PETAL

Early American Quilts, page 14

The Romance of the Patch-work Quilt in America, page 118, No. 19

PRIDE OF THE FOREST

Ladies Art Company, No. 111

POPULAR LEAF PATCH-WORK

Ladies Art Company, No. 490

WHALE BLOCK

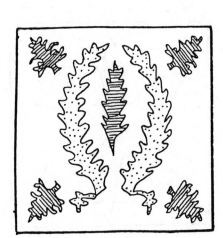

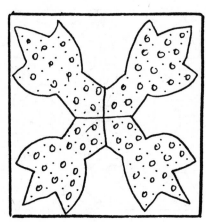

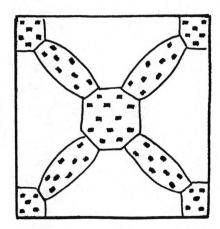

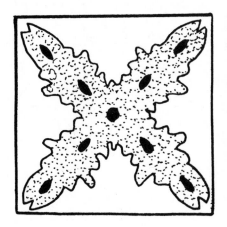

THE LOBSTER

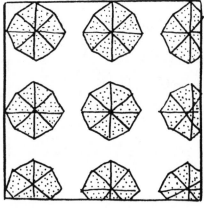

PATCHWORK SOFA QUILT

Ladies Art Company, No. 310

GRANDMA'S BROOCH

Kansas City Star, 1935

Pattern from Lockport Cotton
Batting Co.

WASHINGTON MERRY-GO-ROUND

Nancy Cabot

ANTIQUE FLEUR DE LIS

CENTENNIAL STAR

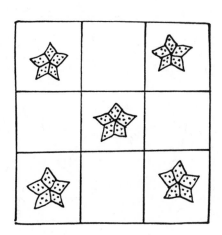

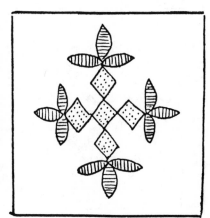

FLEUR DE LIS

Ladies Art Company, No. 416

FLEUR-DE-LIS

The Romance of the Patch-work Quilt in America, page 120, No. 8

DEMOCRATIC VICTORY

Early American Quilts, page 15

The Romance of the Patch-work Quilt in America, page 124, No. 2

Nancy Cabot

Old-Fashioned Quilts, page 6

FEATHER CROWN

FEATHER CROWN

PILOT'S WHEEL

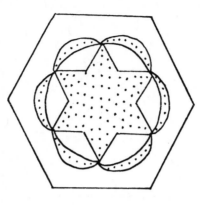

MOUNTAIN PINK

The Romance of the Patchwork Quilt in America, page 104, No. 9

FLOWER STAR

The Standard Book of Quilt Making and Collecting, page 246

FLOWER STAR

The Romance of the Patchwork Quilt in America, page 62, No. 10

Nancy Cabot

FLOWER STAR

Nancy Cabot

CALICO COMPASS

Kansas City Star

SUNBONNET SUE

SUNBONNET SUE

THE COLONIAL LADY

SUNBONNET GIRL

Bertha L. Corbett, author of *Sunbonnet Babies,* published about 1900, was creditted as the creator of these faceless figures.

OVERALL BILL

OVERALL BOY

OVERALL SAM

STRAW HAT BOY

COFFEE CUPS

The Hearth of the Home

CUP AND SAUCER

Kansas City Star, 1946

THE CUP AND THE SAUCER

The Romance of the Patchwork Quilt in America, page 82, No. 6

GOBLET

The Romance of the Patchwork Quilt in America, page 86, No. 21

OLD HOMESTEAD

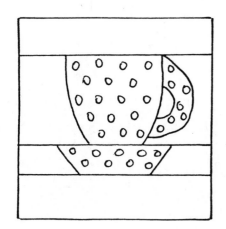

HOUSE

The Perfect Patchwork Primer,
page 77

SCHOOLHOUSE

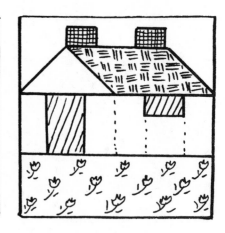

HOUSE ON THE HILL

*One Hundred and One Patch-
work Patterns,* page 117

Ladies Art Company, No. 108

THE OLD HOMESTEAD

Pattern originated in New
Jersey about 1870s.

**LITTLE RED SCHOOL
HOUSE**

Ladies Art Company, No. 373

LITTLE RED HOUSE

OLD KENTUCKY HOME

Needlecraft Magazine, April 1929, page 7

PEENY PEN'S COTTAGE

The Romance of the Patchwork Quilt in America, page 86, No. 20

JACK'S HOUSE

Ladies Art Company, No. 396

Ladies Art Company, No. 123

VILLAGE CHURCH

SCHOOLHOUSE

The Romance of the Patchwork Quilt in America, page 86, No. 19

HONEYMOON COTTAGE

Applique/375

LOG CABIN QUILT

Ladies Art Company, No. 307

DEMOCRATIC DONKEY

The Romance of the Patchwork Quilt in America, page 98, No. 6

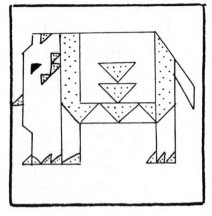

ELEPHANT

The Romance of the Patchwork Quilt in America, page 98, No. 7

Farm Journal, 1943

VICTORY

Kansas City Star, 1944

THE PRESIDENT ROOSEVELT QUILT

POINTS AND PETALS

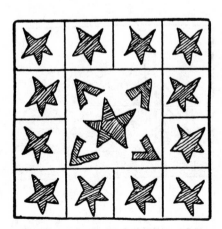

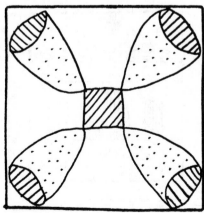

HALLOWE'EN BLOCK

Ladies Art Company, No. 496

OLD TOWN PUMP

American   Quilts,   page   43

GARFIELD'S MONUMENT

Ladies Art Company, No. 136

Kansas City Star

TURKEY TRACKS

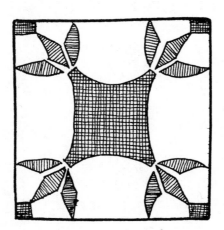

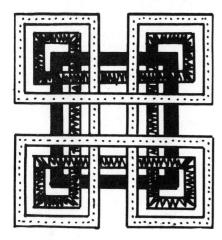

GORDIAN KNOT See page 436.

Miscellaneous

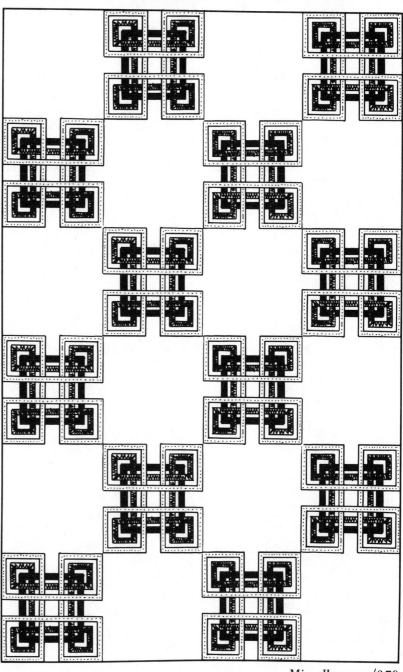

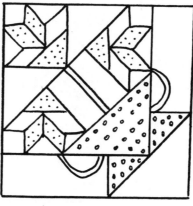

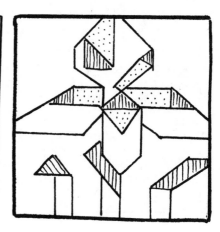

IRIS—PIECED

One Hundred and One Patchwork Patterns, 1931

ROYAL JAPANESE VASE

Ladies Art Company, No. 291

MODERNISTIC IRIS

The Romance of the Patchwork Quilt in America, page 120, No. 2

The Romance of the Patchwork Quilt in America, page 106, No. 9

One Hundred and One Patchwork Patterns, page 82

**MODERNISTIC
CALIFORNIA POPPY**

Circa 1930

PRIMROSE PATCH

ORIENTAL POPPY

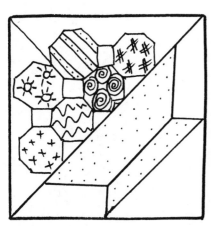

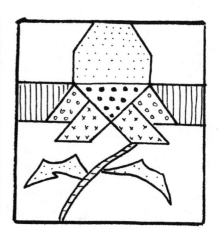

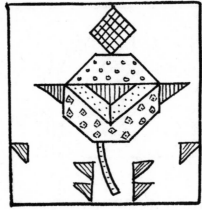

ORIENTAL ROSE

Nancy Cabot

MODERNISTIC ROSE

The Romance of the Patch-work Quilt in America, page 116, No. 1

POINSETTIA

Kansas City Star, 1931

The Romance of the Patch-work Quilt in America, page 104, No. 4

Kansas City Star, 1935

MODERNISTIC   TRUMPET VINE

TRUMPET FLOWER

MISSOURI DAISY

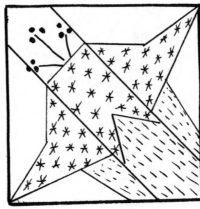

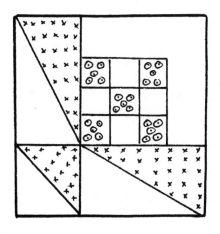

NOSE-GAY

The Romance of the Patch-work Quilt in America, page 120, No. 7
Nancy Cabot

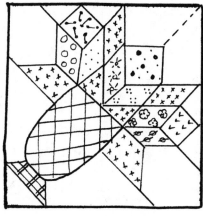

VASE OF FLOWERS

The Household Magazine, August 1934, page 23

HICK'S BASKET

Kansas City Star, 1940

The Romance of the Patch-work Quilt in America, page 96, No. 7

TRIPLE SUNFLOWER

Ladies Art Company, No. 74

THREE FLOWERED SUN-FLOWER

FLOWERS IN A BASKET

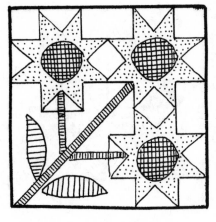

TRIPLE SUNFLOWER

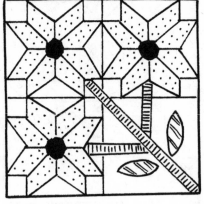

KANSAS SUNFLOWER

THE LILY

The Romance of the Patchwork Quilt in America, page 118, No. 7

LILY CORNERS

LILY FLOWER

MODERNISTIC ACORN

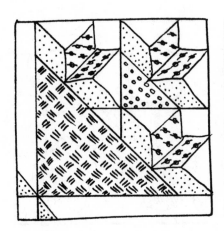

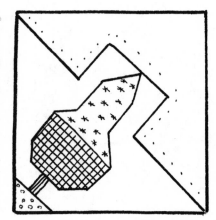

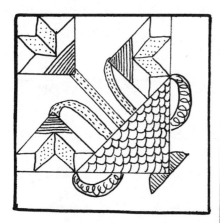

TULIPS IN VASE

The Romance of the Patch-work Quilt in America, page 122, No. 3
Also **ROYAL JAPANESE VASE**

TULIP IN VASE

Early American Quilts, page 12

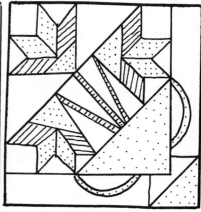

TULIP IN VASE

Ladies Art Company, No. 273

The Romance of the Patch-work Quilt in America, page 122, No. 17

CLEVELAND TULIP

The Romance of the Patch-work Quilt in America, page 122, No. 14

MODERNISTIC TULIP

Laura Wheeler

TULIP

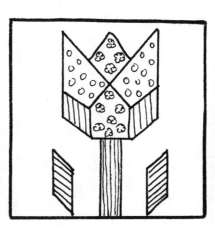

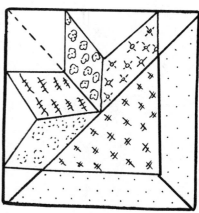

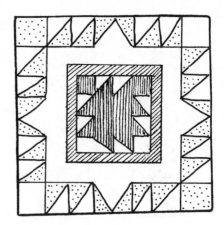

PRESIDENT'S QUILT

Ladies Art Company, No. 297
The Romance of the Patch-
work Quilt in America, page
98, No. 9
Also **CORONATION**

MEXICAN CROSS

The Perfect Patchwork Primer,
page 86

INDIAN HATCHET

The Romance of the Patch-
work Quilt in America, page
82, No. 10
Also **CRAZY ANN, FOLLOW**
THE LEADER, TREE EVER-
LASTING

One Hundred and One Patch-
work Patterns, page 103
The Romance of the Patch-
work Quilt in America, page
58, No. 11

Laura Wheeler

PRIMROSE PATH

MEXICAN STAR

The Romance of the Patch-
work Quilt in America, page
62, No. 8

PERSIAN STAR

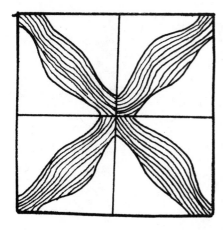

THE SNAIL'S TRAIL

Ladies Art Company, No. 356
*The Romance of the Patch-
work Quilt in America*, page
84, No. 16
*The Standard Book of Quilt
Making and Collecting*, page
250

SNAIL'S TRAIL

Nancy Cabot
Also **MONKEY WRENCH**

MONKEY WRENCH

*One Hundred and One Patch-
work Patterns*, page 116
*The Romance of the Patch-
work Quilt in America*, page
84, No. 17.   Also **SNAIL'S
TRAIL.**
Nancy Cabot
Also **CHINESE   COIN,
INDIAN PUZZLE**.

*The Romance of the Patch-
work Quilt in America*, page
80, No. 5
Pattern dates from the pioneer
days of Indiana.

INDIANA PUZZLE

Ladies Art Company, No. 193

SOLOMON'S TEMPLE

*The Romance of the Patch-
work Quilt in America*, page
68, No. 19

RED CROSS

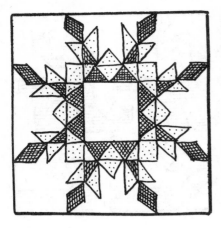

STAR OF CHAMBLIE

The Romance of the Patchwork Quilt in America, page 58, No. 2

THE PHILIPPINES

*Ladies Art Company, No. 404
The Romance of the Patchwork Quilt in America,* page 92, No. 10

MORNING STAR

The Romance of the Patchwork Quilt in America, page 60, No. 5

Old Patchwork Quilts and the Women Who Made Them, page 112
The Romance of the Patchwork Quilt in America, page 94, No. 20
American Quilts and Coverlets, page 17

The Romance of the Patchwork Quilt in America, page 98, No. 14
This pattern was designed at the time of the election of 1844 when the Whig presidential candidate, Henry Clay, was defeated by the Democrat, James K. Polk.

Nancy Cabot

NOONDAY

DUSTY MILLER

WHIG'S DEFEAT

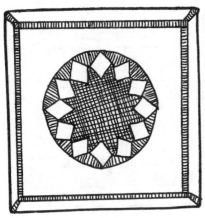

MORNING STAR

Laura Wheeler

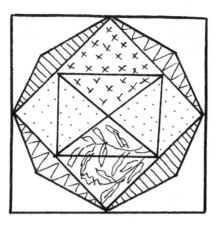

JEWEL

Grandmother Clark's Patch-work Quilt Designs, Book 20, 1931

KANSAS STAR

The Romance of the Patch-work Quilt in America, page 62, No. 14

Old Patchwork Quilts and the Women Who Made Them, page 109
The Romance of the Patch-work Quilt in America, page 98, No. 10. Also **HEART'S DESIRE.**
Stephen A. Douglas defeated Abraham Lincoln in 1858 for the Illinois senatorial seat. This pattern was nicknamed after him.

THE LITTLE GIANT

Ladies Art Company, No. 122
The Romance of the Patch-work Quilt in America, page 70, No. 21

LOVER'S LINKS

Kansas City Star, 1950

THE OKLAHOMA STRING QUILT

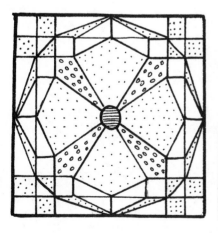

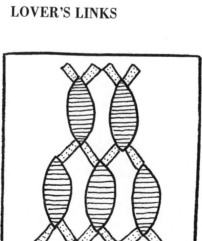

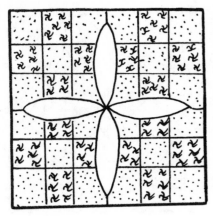

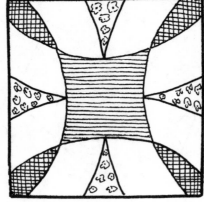

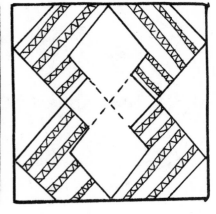

IMPROVED NINE-PATCH **RAINBOW BLOCK** **RAIL FENCE QUILT**

Nancy Cabot

Nancy Cabot *Ladies Art Company, No. 90* *Ladies Art Company, No. 33*

PATIENCE CORNERS **PATIENCE CORNERS** **THE   TRIANGLE   PUZZLE**

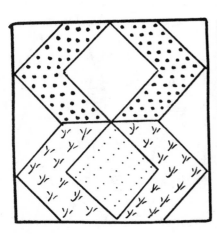

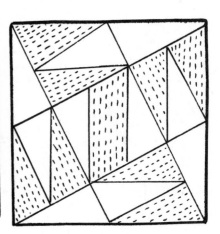

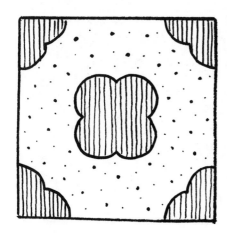

HEARTS AND GIZZARDS

Ladies Art Company, No. 125
The Romance of the Patchwork Quilt in America, page 84, No. 19
Also **PIERROT'S POM POM, DUTCH ROSE**
The Standard Book of Quilt Making and Collecting, page 245

HIDDEN FLOWER

Laura Wheeler

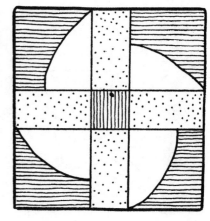

NOCTURNE

Nancy Cabot

The Standard Book of Quilt Making and Collecting, page 147

MOON OVER THE MOUNTAIN

Hearth & Home, 1923

PHARIEMIAS FAVORITE

Ladies Art Company, No. 403

STAR LANE

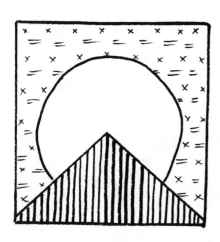

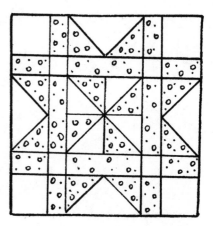

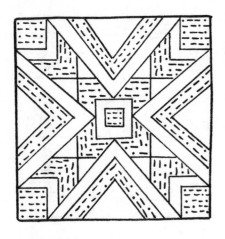

PERSIAN

Ladies Art Company, No. 525

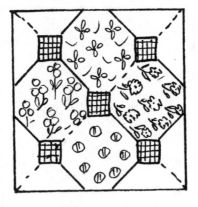

MEADOW FLOWER

Laura Wheeler

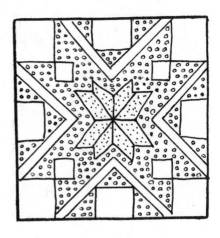

LEAVENWORTH STAR

The Romance of the Patchwork Quilt in America, page 62, No. 13

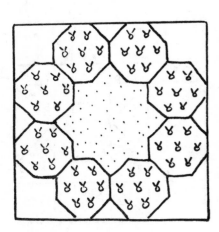

Nancy Cabot

OLD STAFFORDSHIRE

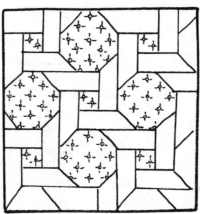

Ladies Art Company, No. 294

TWIST PATCHWORK

The Dictionary of Needlework: An Encyclopedia of Artistic, Plain and Fancy Needlework

TWIST PATCHWORK

STARRY CROWN

The Household Magazine, August 1934, page 23

THE MISSOURI DAISY

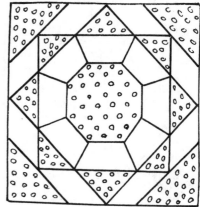

ORIENTAL STAR

Progressive Farmer

Needlecraft Magazine, February 1934, page 8

OMBRE

Laura Wheeler

MORNING GLORY

Ladies Art Company, No. 469

TALLAHASSEE QUILT BLOCK

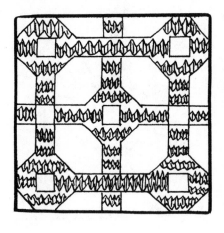

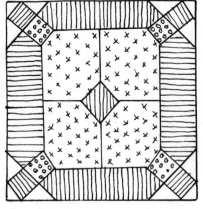

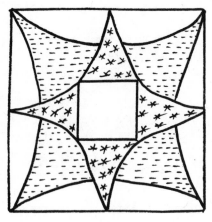

TILE PUZZLE

The Romance of the Patchwork Quilt in America, page 80, No. 8

FARMER'S FIELDS

Kansas City Star, 1939

HOME MAKER

Practical Needlework Quilt Patterns, Vol. III

The Romance of the Patchwork Quilt in America, page 96, No. 17
Also **SUN DIAL, TIRZAH'S TREASURE, TANGLED GARTER**

The Romance of the Patchwork Quilt in America, page 84, No. 23

Nancy Cabot

HONEYCOMB

GARDEN MAZE

GARDEN MAZE

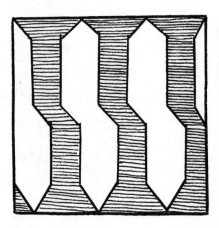

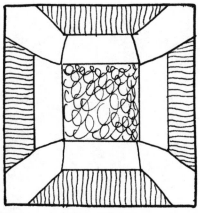

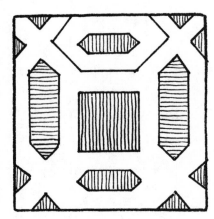

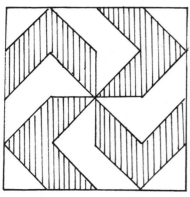

SWASTIKA

Joseph Doyle & Co., N.J.

SEESAW

The Perfect Patchwork Primer, page 79

WHIRLIGIG

Early American Quilts, page 14

Ladies Art Company, No. 213
Nancy Cabot

WALKING TRIANGLES

PINWHEEL

TWIN SISTERS

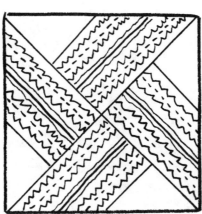

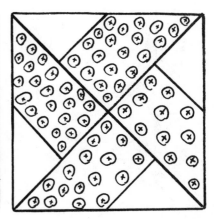

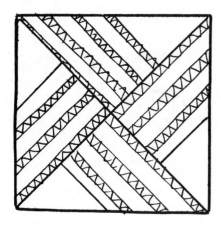

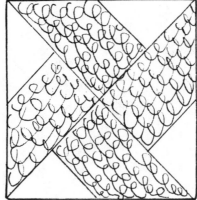

WATER WHEEL

The Standard Book of Quilt Making and Collecting, page 241

WHIRLWIND

One Hundred and One Patchwork Patterns, page 29

PALM LEAF

Ladies Art Company, No. 461
One Hundred and One Patchwork Patterns, page 36

American Quilts and Coverlets, page 17

PALM LEAVES HOSANNAH!

Old Patchwork Quilts and the Women Who Made Them, page 107
Also **PALM LEAVES**

HOSANNA

The Romance of the Patchwork Quilt in America, page 102, No. 14
Also **THE PALM**

HOZANNA

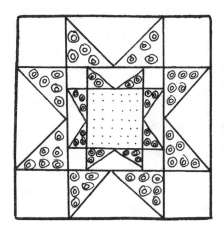 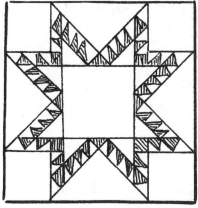 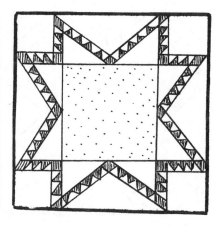

STARS AND SQUARES

Ladies Art Company, No. 11
The Romance of the Patch-work Quilt in America, page 54, No. 12
Also **RISING STAR**

SAWTOOTH

Kansas City Star, 1929
Also **BLAZING STAR, FEATHERED STAR**

TWINKLING STAR

Ladies Art Company, No. 301

The Romance of the Patch-work Quilt in America, page 80, No. 11
Old Patchwork Quilts and the Women Who Made Them, page 75
Also **DEVIL'S PUZZLE**
Nancy Cabot

Kansas City Star, 1930
Variations of the well known "swastika" and a motif on Indian pottery and blankets.

The Romance of the Patch-work Quilt in America, page 56, No. 5

RADIANT STAR

FLY FOOT

INDIAN EMBLEM QUILT

OCTAGONAL BLOCK

Nancy Cabot

OCTAGON

Ladies Art Company, No. 198
*The Romance of the Patch-
work Quilt in America,* page
52, No. 17

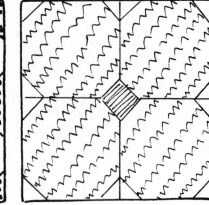

THE FOUR LEAF CLOVER

Kansas City Star, 1941
A symbol of good luck.

Early American Quilts, page 6
Nancy Cabot

ROB PETER TO PAY PAUL

Ladies Art Company, No. 480

MORNING PATCH

Nancy Cabot

LATTICE BLOCK

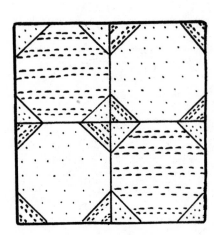

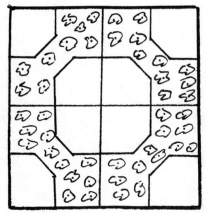

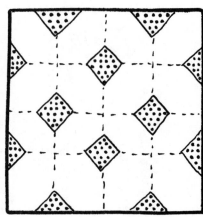

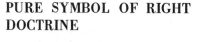

FLY FOOT

Laura Wheeler

SWASTIKA

One Hundred and One Patchwork Patterns, page 14
The Romance of the Patchwork Quilt in America, page 94, No. 8
The **SWASTIKA** symbolizes the movement and power of the sun, and it was used by the German Nazis as a flag of the Third Reich on the advice of astrologers. The swastika design appears in **CRAZY ANN, FOLLOW THE LEADER, FLY FOOT,** and **TWIST AND TURN.**

PURE SYMBOL OF RIGHT DOCTRINE

The Romance of the Patchwork Quilt in America, page 94, No. 21
Also **THE BATTLE AX OF THOR, CATCH-ME-IF-YOU-CAN, CHINESE 10,000 PERFECTIONS, FAVORITE OF THE PERUVIANS, HEART'S SEAL, MOUND BUILDERS, WIND POWER OF THE OSAGES**

Ladies Art Company, No. 132

OLD MAID'S RAMBLE

The Romance of the Patchwork Quilt in America, page 194, Plate LIX

FEATHER STAR

The Romance of the Patchwork Quilt in America, page 78, No. 10

OLD MAID'S RAMBLE

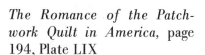

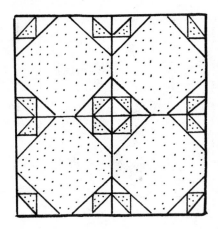

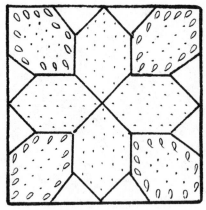

SIMPLE DESIGN

Ladies Art Company, No. 321

MAGIC CIRCLE

Ladies Art Company, No. 384

OUR EDITOR

Practical Needlework Quilt Patterns, Clara A. Stone, 1915

Ladies Art Company, No. 246
The Romance of the Patchwork Quilt in America, page 90, No. 20

SQUARE AND A HALF

Ladies Art Company, No. 13

MOSAIC

Nancy Cabot

MOSAIC NO. 1

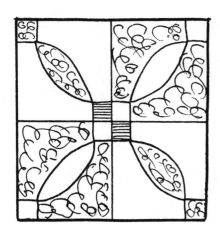

ROSE DREAM

The Romance of the Patchwork Quilt in America, page 100, No. 9

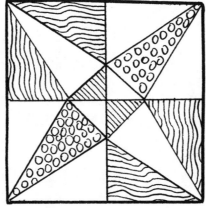

TIPPECANOE

The Perfect Patchwork Primer, page 32

GREEK SQUARE

Ladies Art Company, No. 328

One Hundred and One Patchwork Patterns, page 57
The Romance of the Patchwork Quilt in America, page 90, No. 5

SQUARE AND COMPASS

Progressive Farmer

FLAMING SUN

One Hundred and One Patchwork Patterns, page 13

FRENCH STAR

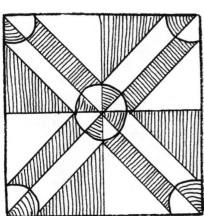

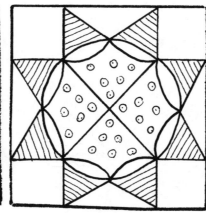

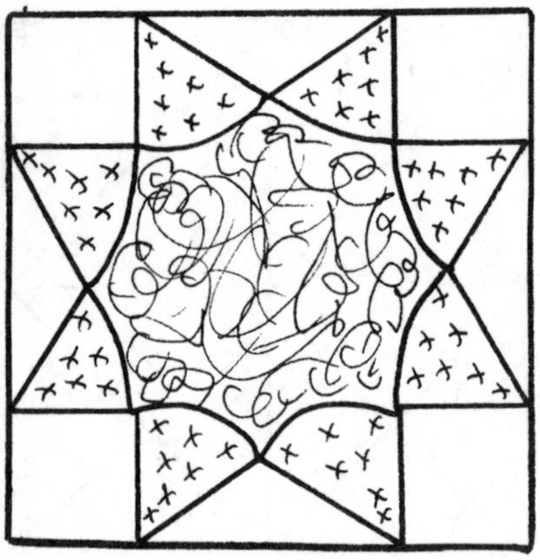

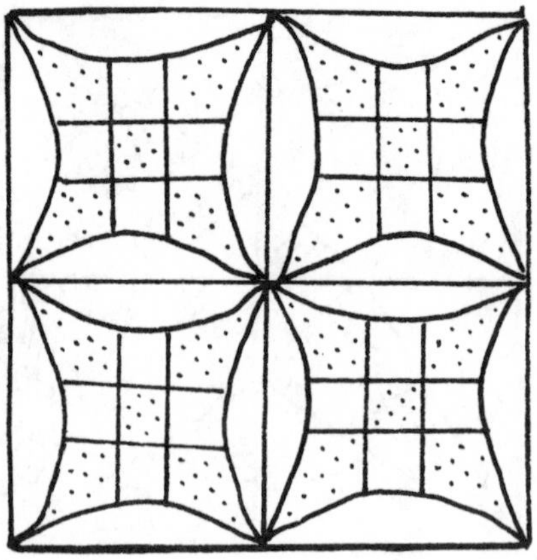

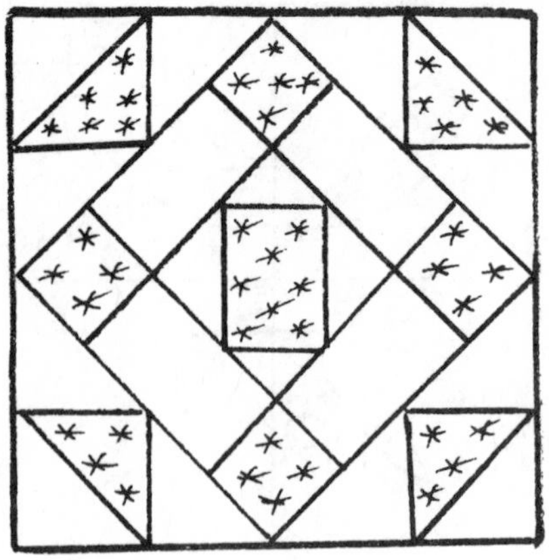

THE ARKANSAS STAR

Kansas City Star, 1933

GLORIFIED 9-PATCH

MOSAIC NO. 7

Ladies Art Company, No. 335

Ladies Art Company, No. 15

MOSAIC

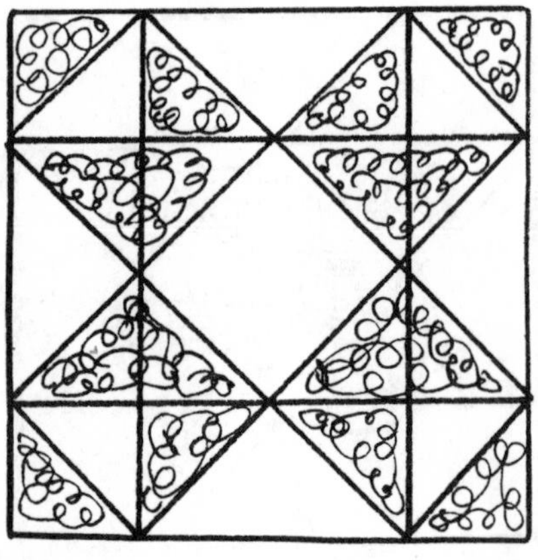

Nancy Page

HOUR GLASS

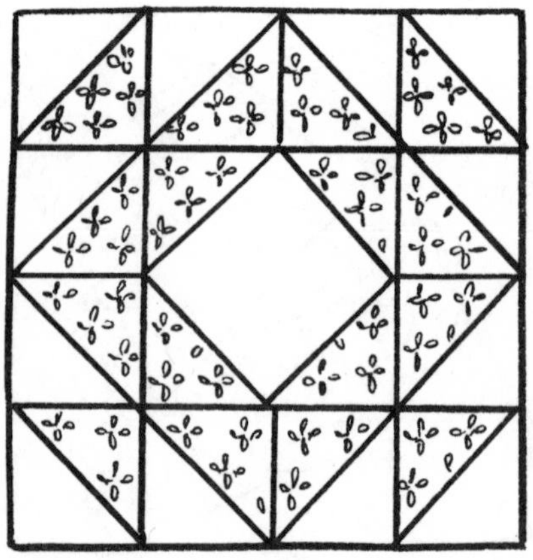

Ladies Art Company, No. 16

MOSAIC

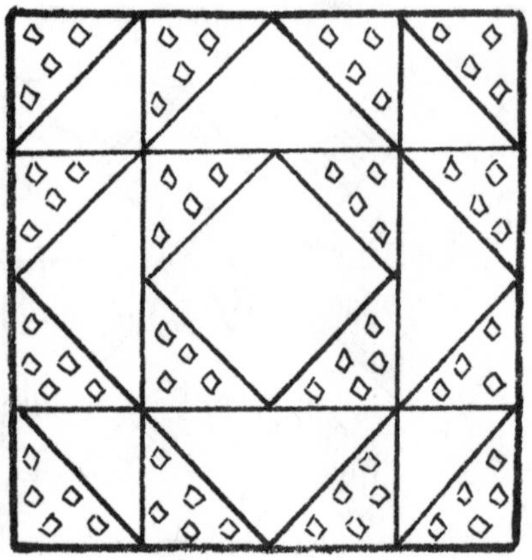

NORTHUMBERLAND STAR

The Perfect Patchwork Primer, page 81

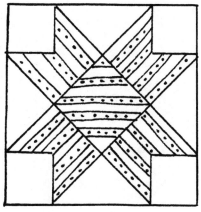

ODD FELLOW'S CROSS

The Standard Book of Quilt Making and Collecting, page 235

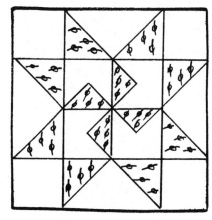

OCTAGONAL STAR

The Romance of the Patchwork Quilt in America, page 76, No. 23

The Romance of the Patchwork Quilt in America, page 68, No. 6

Ladies Art Company, No. 21

Nancy Cabot

ODD FELLOWS' CROSS

MOSAIC

MOSAIC NO. 6

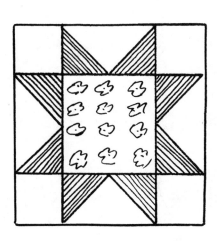

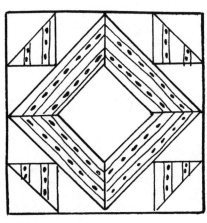

MOSAIC NO. 2

Nancy Cabot

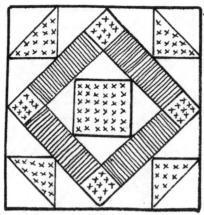

JACK-IN-THE-PULPIT

Old Patchwork Quilts and the Women Who Made Them, page 80
The Romance of the Patchwork Quilt in America, page 78, No. 17
Also **TOAD-IN-THE-PUDDLE**

THE HOUSE JACK BUILT

Ladies Art Company, No. 265

The Romance of the Patchwork Quilt in America, page 94, No. 16

AUTOGRAPH PATCH

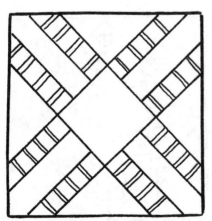

The Romance of the Patchwork Quilt in America, page 84, No. 8

FOUR H CLUB PATCH

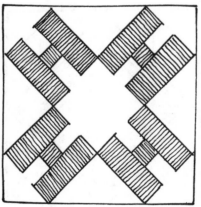

THE H SQUARE QUILT

MOSAIC

Ladies Art Company, No. 1

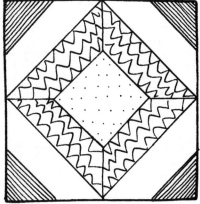

MOSAIC NO. 3

Nancy Page

MOSAIC

Ladies Art Company, No. 5

One Hundred and One Patchwork Patterns, page 22.
Also **CORONATION.**
The Romance of the Patchwork Quilt in America, page 68, No. 4
The Standard Book of Quilt Making and Collecting, page 237

Ladies Art Company, No. 2

MOSAIC

Practical Needlework Quilt Patterns, Vol. 3

HULL'S VICTORY

KING'S CROWN

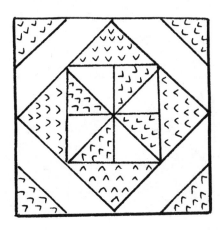

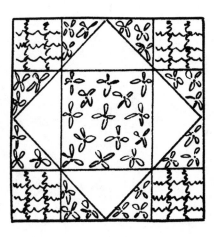

MOSAIC

Ladies Art Company, No. 10

MISSOURI STAR

Nancy Cabot

MOSAIC

Ladies Art Company, No. 12

Nancy Cabot

MOSAIC NO. 9

Ladies Art Company, No. 465

NEXT DOOR NEIGHBOR

Nancy Cabot

MOSAIC NO. 5

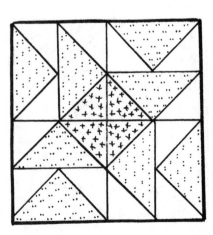

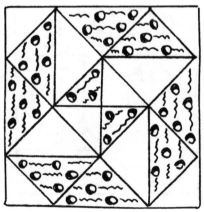

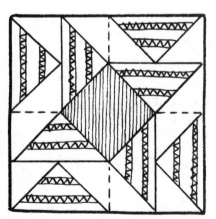

VENETIAN DESIGN

Ladies Art Company, No. 115

MOSAIC

Grandmother Clark's Patchwork Quilt Designs, Book 20, 1931

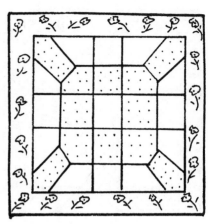

SUNBEAM

Woman's World, February 1928, page 31

Nancy Cabot

FLOWER BED

Ladies Art Company, No. 472

SPRINGFIELD PATCH

Ladies Art Company, No. 155
The Romance of the Patchwork Quilt in America, page 74, No. 2

TURKEY TRACKS

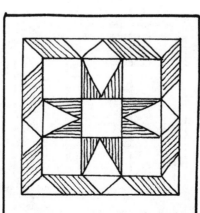

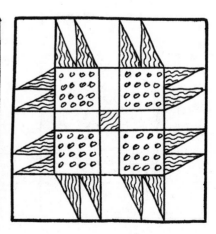

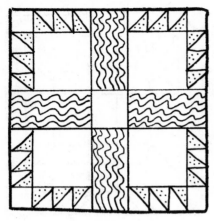

PREMIUM STAR

Ladies Art Company, No. 14

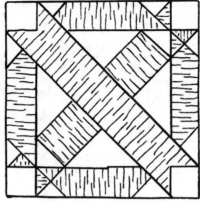

THE THREE CROSSES

The Standard Book of Quilt Making and Collecting, page 231

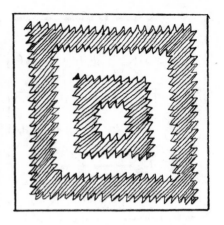

SAWTOOTH

Ladies Art Company, No. 221
The Romance of the Patchwork Quilt in America, page 98, No. 8
The Standard Book of Quilt Making and Collecting, page 231

Ladies Art Company, No. 21

FOX AND GEESE

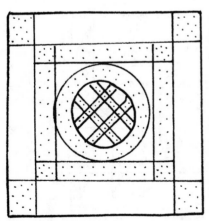

Ladies Art Company, No. 230

RIBBON SQUARE

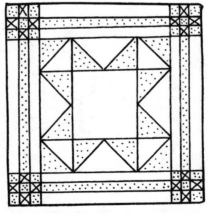

WHITE HOUSE STEPS

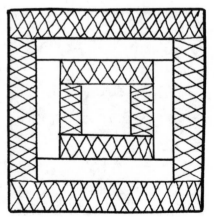

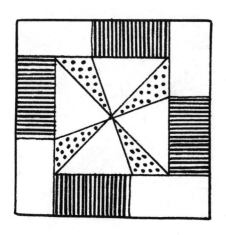

PINWHEEL SKEW

The Perfect Patchwork Primer, page 85

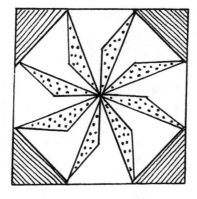

SILVER AND GOLD

Needlecraft Magazine, April 1929, page 7
The Romance of the Patchwork Quilt in America, page 84, No. 2
Also **STAR OF THE EAST**

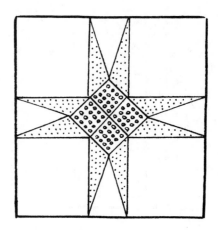

PINEAPPLE QUILT

Ladies Art Company, No. 94

The Perfect Patchwork Primer, page 73

SHADOW STAR

WILD GOOSE CHASE

TREE EVERLASTING

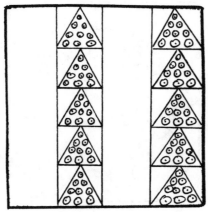

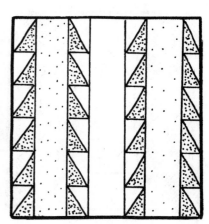

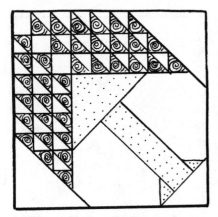

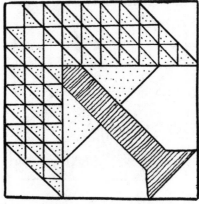

TREE OF PARADISE

Ladies Art Company, No. 260

TREE OF PARADISE

The Romance of the Patch-work Quilt in America, page 102, No. 17

THE ROYAL

Ladies Art Company, No. 282

Ladies Art Company, No. 471

ANNAPOLIS PATCH

Nancy Cabot

LADY OF THE LAKE

Ladies Art Company, No. 124
Also **GARDEN MAZE**

TANGLED GARTER

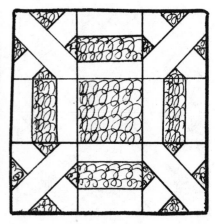

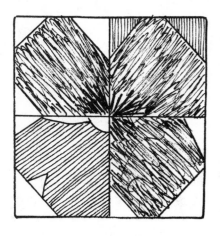

MODERNISTIC PANSY

Nancy Cabot

PANSY-PIECED

One Hundred and One Patch-work Patterns, 1931

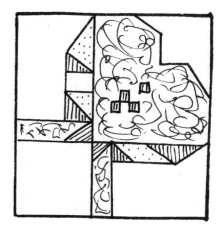

MODERNISTIC PANSY

The Romance of the Patch-work Quilt in America, page 104, No. 5

BOUQUET IN A FAN

THE PINWHEEL

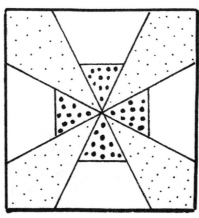

THE GUIDING STAR

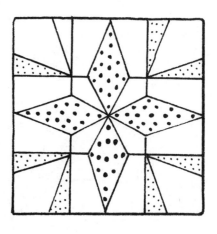

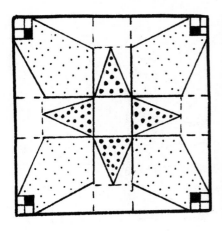

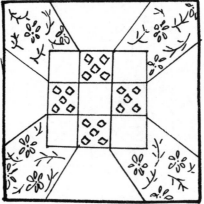

MAGNOLIA BUD

NINE-PATCH STAR

CHIMNEY SWALLOWS

The Romance of the Patchwork Quilt in America, page 120, No. 12
Nancy Cabot

Hearth and Home, 1928

Old Patchwork Quilts and the Women Who Made Them, page 93
The Romance of the Patchwork Quilt in America, page 74, No. 10

The Romance of the Patchwork Quilt in America, page 64, No. 19. Also **KING'S CROWN.**
The name **CORONATION** dates back to the days of Sir Walter Raleigh.
Also **POTOMAC PRIDE, PRESIDENT'S QUILT, WASHINGTON'S QUILT**

Nancy Cabot

Ladies Art Company, No. 355
The Romance of the Patchwork Quilt in America, page 74, No. 13

CORONATION

ARAB TENT

CHIMNEY SWALLOWS

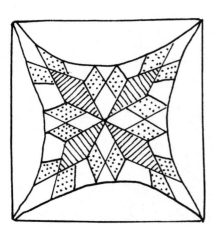

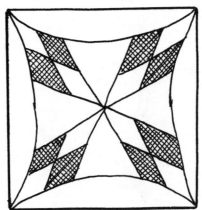

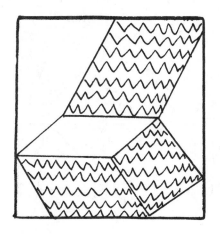

WORK BOX

Ladies Art Company, No. 358

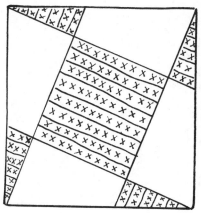

CHECKERBOARD SKEW

The Perfect Patchwork Primer,
page 83

TWIST AND TURN

Ladies Art Company, No. 98

The Perfect Patchwork Primer,
page 98

SHOOTING STAR

SPIDER WEB

MALTESE CROSS

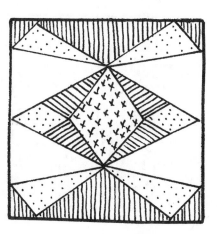

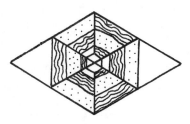

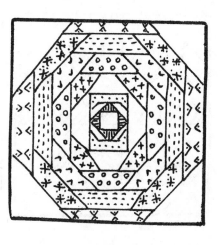

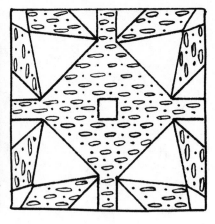

STRING QUILT

The Perfect Patchwork Primer,
page 77

THE STRING QUILT

One Hundred and One Patch-
work Patterns, page 37

NEW STAR

Old Patchwork Quilts and the
Women Who Made Them, page
106

The Household Magazine, July
1933, page 29

Kansas City Star, 1940

STAR AND CROSS

EASTER TIDE

THE E-Z QUILT

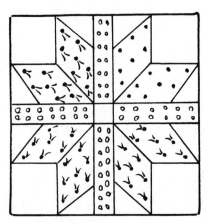

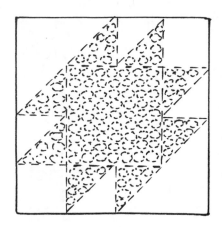

THE ANVIL

Old Patchwork Quilts and the Women Who Made Them, page 72

The Romance of the Patchwork Quilt in America, page 74, No. 9

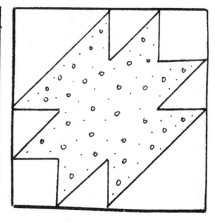

BUCKEYE BEAUTY

Kansas City Star, 1939

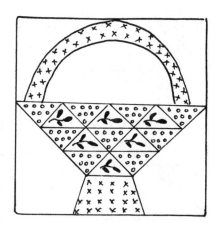

THE ANVIL

The Romance of the Patchwork Quilt in America, page 74, No. 14

The Standard Book of Quilt Making and Collecting, page 243

The Romance of the Patchwork Quilt in America, page 86, No. 9
Also **DOUBLE Z**

BROWN GOOSE

Old Patchwork Quilts and the Women Who Made Them, page 93

The Romance of the Patchwork Quilt in America, page 126, No. 15

CACTUS BASKET

Needlecraft Magazine, February 1930, page 8

HANGING BASKET

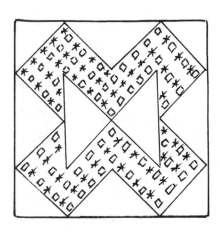

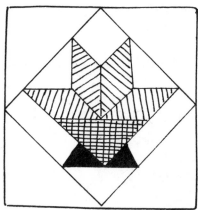

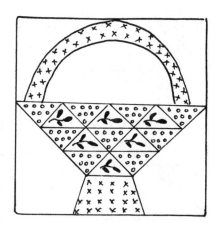

THE MAY BASKET

Kansas City Star, 1941

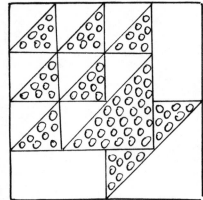

FLOWER BASKET

Ladies Art Company, No. 57

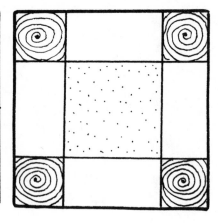

NINE PATCH

The Romance of the Patchwork Quilt in America, page 48, No. 15

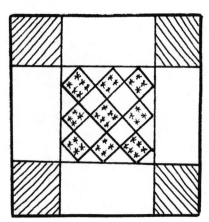

The Romance of the Patchwork Quilt in America, page 48, No. 13

NINE PATCH

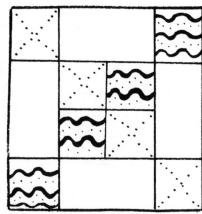

The Romance of the Patchwork Quilt in America, page 48, No. 5

FOUR-PATCH—Variation

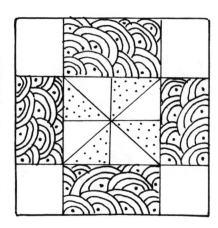

Modern Patchwork, page 38

FOREST PATHS

INDIAN TRAIL

Old Patchwork Quilts and the Women Who Made Them, page 102. Also **PRICKLY PEAR, RAMBLING ROAD, STORM AT SEA, WEATHER VANE, WINDING WALK.**
The Romance of the Patchwork Quilt in America, page 76, No. 11. Also **FOREST PATH, IRISH PUZZLE, OLD MAID'S RAMBLE, NORTH WIND** — according to the locality. When the early settlers were moving towards the West, they came in contact with the Indians who greatly influenced their daily lives. By then, the Indians were already using a swastika-like emblem in their native crafts. This pattern originated from it.

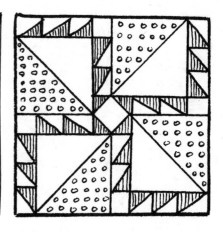

ETERNAL TRIANGLE

The Romance of the Patchwork Quilt in America, page 70, No. 22
Also **MERRY-GO-ROUND**

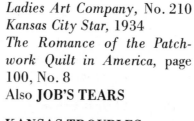

Ladies Art Company, No. 210
Kansas City Star, 1934
The Romance of the Patchwork Quilt in America, page 100, No. 8
Also **JOB'S TEARS**

KANSAS TROUBLES

OLD MAID'S RAMBLE

Also **INDIAN TRAILS**

Ladies Art Company, No. 149
The Romance of the Patchwork Quilt in America, page 94, No. 3
A dance figure familiar in Colonial times.

EIGHT HANDS AROUND

Ladies Art Company, No. 11

MOSAIC

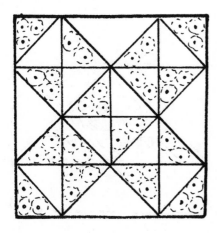

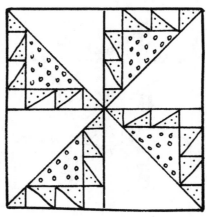

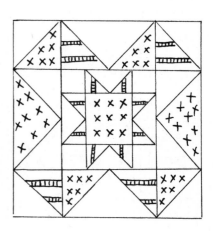

FLOWER POT

Grandmother's Authentic Early American Patchwork Quilts, Book 23

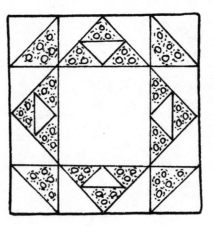

GRANDMOTHER'S FAVORITE
Kansas City Star, 1930
The Romance of the Patchwork Quilt in America, page 78, No. 14
The Standard Book of Quilt Making and Collecting, page 236

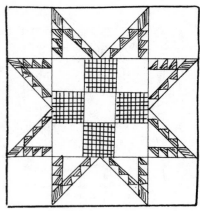

CALIFORNIA STAR

Ladies Art Company, No. 167

Ladies Art Company, No. 9
The Romance of the Patchwork Quilt in America, page 92, No. 11

FEATHER STAR

One Hundred and One Patchwork Patterns, page 88

THE FEATHER EDGED STAR

Kansas City Star, 1930

KALEIDOSCOPE

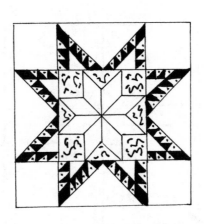

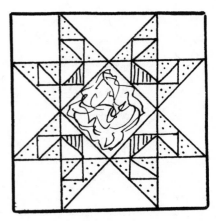

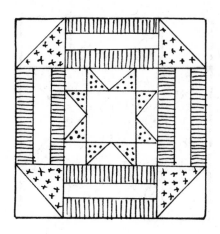

BURNHAM SQUARE

Ladies Art Company, No. 232
The Romance of the Patch-work Quilt in America, page 90, No. 4

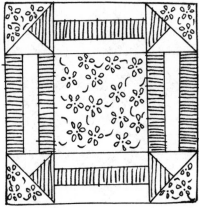

DOUBLE ARROW

Kansas City Star, 1933

GIRL'S JOY

Nancy Cabot

Ladies Art Company, No. 382

GIRL'S JOY

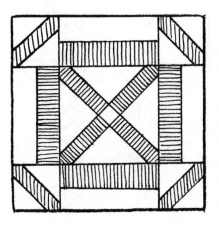

Nancy Page, 1920-30

BEACON LIGHTS

Nancy Page, 1920-30

NOON AND LIGHT

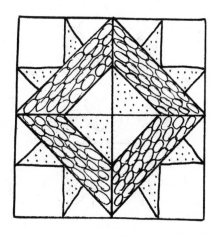

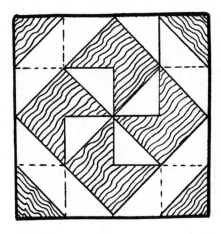

MOSAIC NO. 8

Nancy Cabot

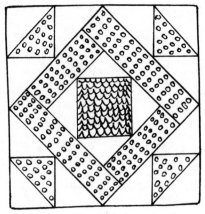

DOUBLE SQUARES

Ladies Art Company, No. 225
The Romance of the Patch-work Quilt in America, page 90, No. 15

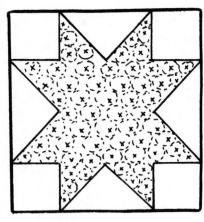

SIMPLE STAR

Old Fashioned Quilts, page 22

The Romance of the Patch-work Quilt in America, page 76, No. 14
The diamonds are first pieced of small strips, and then cut to form the star

Old Patchwork Quilts and the Women Who Made Them, page 84

NORTHUMBERLAND STAR

LOG CABIN STAR

Ladies Art Company, No. 50

COLUMBIAN STAR

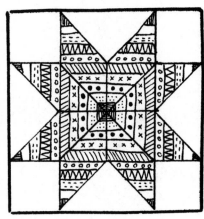

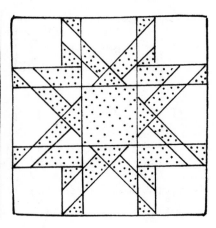

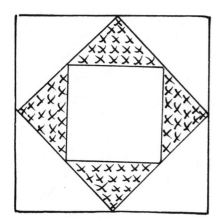

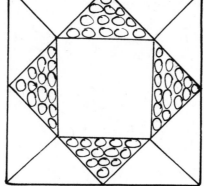

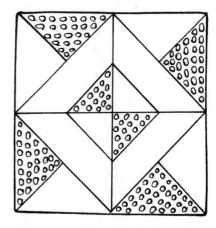

ECONOMY PATCH

The Romance of the Patchwork Quilt in America, page 52, No. 15

ECONOMY

Ladies Art Company, No. 264

THE BLOCKADE

Kansas City Star, 1938

Nancy Page, 1920-30

The Romance of the Patchwork Quilt in America, page 84, No. 5
Also **JACK IN THE BOX**

WHIRL POOL

WHIRLIGIG

DOUBLE PIN WHEEL

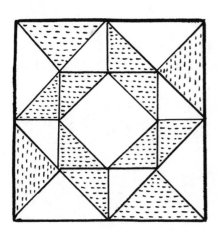

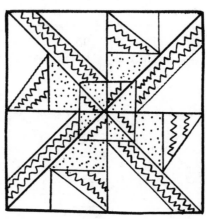

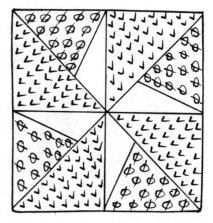

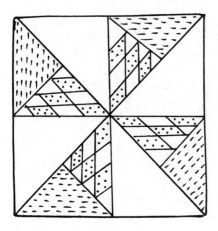

DUTCH WINDMILL

Ladies Art Company, No. 520

DUTCHMAN'S WINDMILL

One Hundred and One Patchwork Patterns, page 122

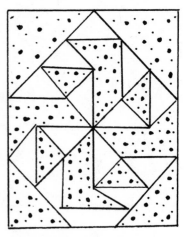

YANKEE PUZZLE

The Romance of the Patchwork Quilt in America, page 80, No. 3

Ladies Art Company, No. 28

YANKEE PUZZLE

Nancy Cabot

CRAZY ANN

Ladies Art Company, No. 165

CRAZY ANN

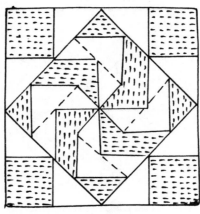

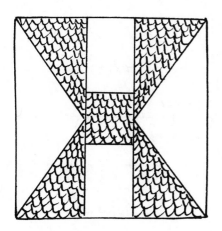

BAT'S WINGS

Ladies Art Company, No. 43
The Romance of the Patch-
work Quilt in America, page
78, No. 15

T BLOCKS

Old Patchwork Quilts and the
Women Who Made Them,
page 81

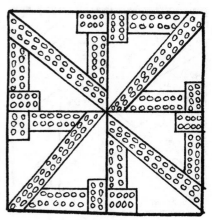

FOUR Z PATCH

Ladies Art Company, No. 375

The Romance of the Patch-
work Quilt in America, page
84, No. 4

WHIRLIGIG

Grandmother Clark's Patch-
work Quilt Designs, Book 21,
1931

CRAZY PATCH

Nancy Page, 1920-30

ENDLESS CHAIN

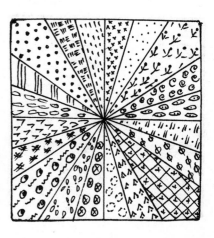

CRAZY TIES

CRAZY

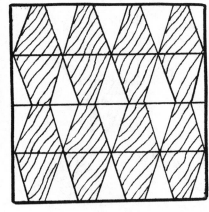

TUMBLER

Old Patchwork Quilts and the Women Who Made Them, page 76

The Romance of the Patchwork Quilt in America, page 52, No. 8
Also **FINE WOVEN**

Ladies Art Company, No. 368

THE TUMBLER

Ladies Art Company, No. 290

FANTASTIC PATCHWORK

COARSE WOVEN

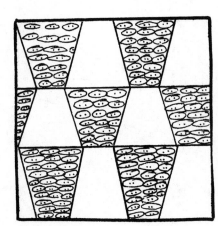

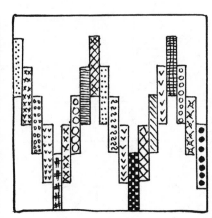

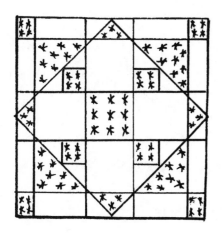

FANNY'S FAVORITE

Ladies Art Company, No. 464

MY FAVORITE

Nancy Cabot

ODDS AND ENDS

Ladies Art Company, No. 102

Ladies Art Company, No. 95

COXEY'S CAMP

Ladies Art Company, No. 150

TOAD IN A PUDDLE

One Hundred and One Patch-work Patterns, page 68

RAMBLER

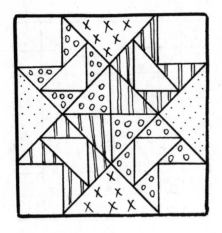

WILD GEESE

The Perfect Patchwork Primer,
page 78
Also **DOUBLE T**

STARRY PATH

Modern Patchwork, page 26

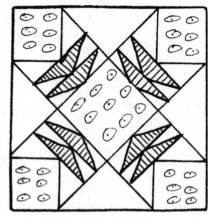

THE OZARK TRAIL

Kansas City Star, 1933

WILD GOOSE CHASE

Woman's World, November
1926, page 38

WILD GEESE

The Perfect Patchwork Primer,
page 82

WILD GOOSE CHASE

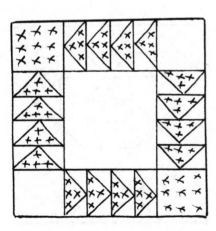

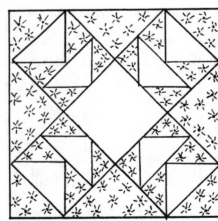

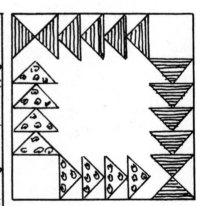

RAILROAD CROSSING

The Perfect Patchwork Primer, page 79

WILD GOOSE CHASE

One Hundred and One Patchwork Patterns, page 52
The Romance of the Patchwork Quilt in America, page 96, No. 8

RAILROAD CROSSING

Ladies Art Company, No. 67
Pattern designed after 1830 when the Baltimore and Ohio Company opened the first fourteen miles of track for commercial use in this country.

The Standard Book of Quilt Making and Collecting, page 235

Also **DOUBLE MONKEY WRENCH, KITTY CORNER, PUSS-IN-THE-CORNER**

Ladies Art Company, No. 235

CROSS ROADS TO TEXAS

Ladies Art Company, No. 137

PUSS IN THE CORNER

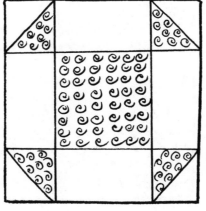

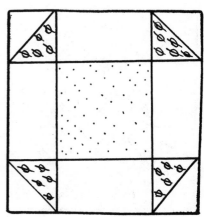

KITTY CORNER

The Romance of the Patchwork Quilt in America, page 72, No. 16
Also **PUSS-IN-THE-CORNER, TIC-TAC-TOE**

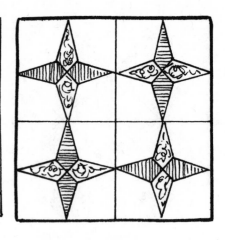

JOHNNIE AROUND THE CORNER

Ladies Art Company, No. 376
Also **ROLLING STONE**

JOB'S TROUBLES

The Romance of the Patchwork Quilt in America, page 64, No. 1
Also **FOUR-POINT, KITE, SNOWBALL**
The Standard Book of Quilt Making and Collecting, page 251

The Romance of the Patchwork Quilt in America, page 58, No. 15

The Standard Book of Quilt Making and Collecting, page 240
This phrase comes from the *Book of Common Prayer.*

PONTIAC STAR

SNOW BALL

WORLD WITHOUT END

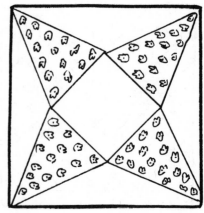

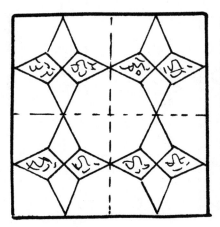

THE KITE QUILT

Kansas City Star, 1931

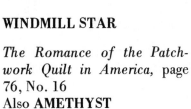

WINDMILL STAR

The Romance of the Patch-work Quilt in America, page 76, No. 16
Also **AMETHYST**

LADY FINGERS AND SUNFLOWERS

The Romance of the Patch-work Quilt in America, page 108, No. 1

Kansas City Star, 1939

WORLDS WITHOUT END   **BUZZARD'S ROOST**   **THE BROKEN PATH**

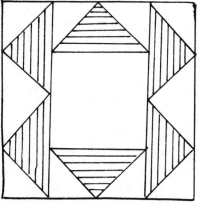

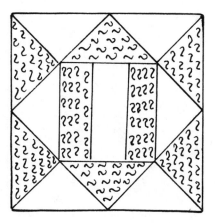

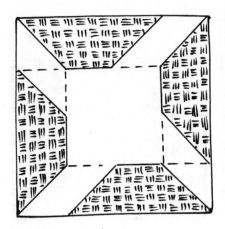

CAPTAIN'S WHEEL

The Perfect Patchwork Primer, page 87

FLYING BATS

Old Patchwork Quilts and the Women Who Made Them, page 113

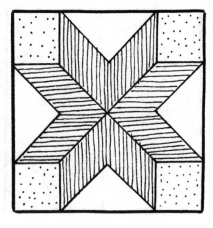

THE ARROW STAR

Kansas City Star, 1934

One Hundred and One Patchwork Patterns, page 14
The Romance of the Patchwork Quilt in America, page 54, No. 5
The Standard Book of Quilt Making and Collecting, page 235

Quilts and Coverlets, page 55
Barbara Fritchie, one of the most famous heroines in American literature, became immortalized at the age of 95 when she refused to lower her Union flag during the Confederate occupation of Frederick, Maryland. Her sympathies were for the Union, and neither threats nor cajolery could move her to yield her flag to the Confederates. Finally she was permitted to wave her flag without molestation. The poem on Barbara Fritchie by John Greenleaf Whittier is well known.

CONSTELI ATION

PIECED STAR

BARBARA FRITCHIE STAR

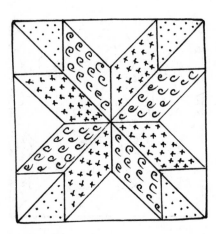

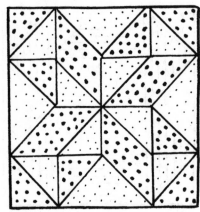

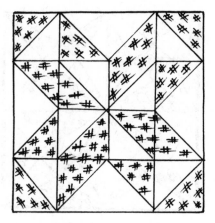

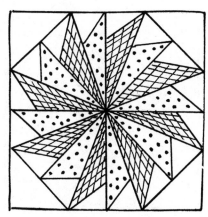

CALICO BOUQUETS

Progressive Farmer

ALBUM FLOWER

Laura Wheeler

NEW SHADED STAR

Ladies Art Company, No. 473
The Romance of the Patch-
work Quilt in America, page
54, No. 2

**STAR OF NORTH
CAROLINA**

Ladies Art Company, No. 529

WINGS

Ladies Art Company, No. 483

V BLOCK

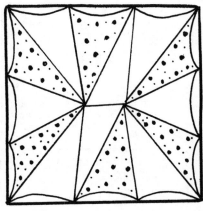

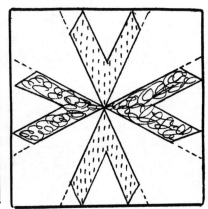

VIRGINIA REEL

Named after a popular dance.

DOUBLE PINWHEEL

Progressive Farmer

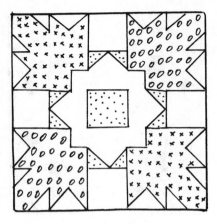

AUTUMN LEAVES

Needlecraft Magazine,
February 1934, page 8

One Hundred and One Patch-work Patterns, page 7
The Romance of the Patch-work Quilt in America, page 92, No. 4
The Standard Book of Quilt Making and Collecting, page 234
Also **INDIAN TRAIL, STORM AT SEA**

Kansas City Star, 1942

CHAIN OF DIAMONDS

THE CORNERSTONE

WEATHER VANE

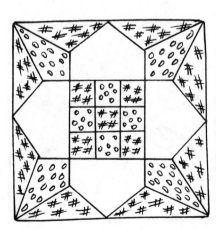

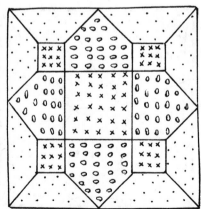

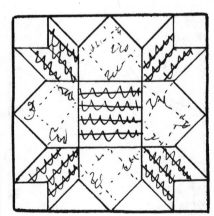

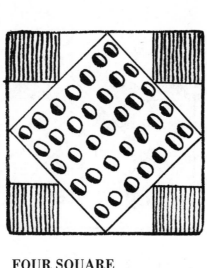

ALL TANGLED UP

Ladies Art Company, No. 309

FOUR SQUARE

8-POINTED STAR

Kansas City Star, 1934

The Romance of the Patchwork Quilt in America, page 64, No. 16
The Standard Book of Quilt Making and Collecting, page 251

The Perfect Patchwork Primer, page 93

DOUBLE SQUARE

CHILDREN OF ISRAEL

CROSS

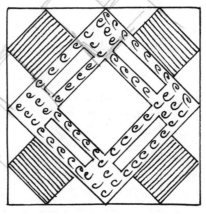

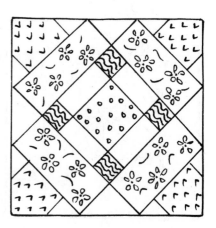

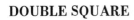

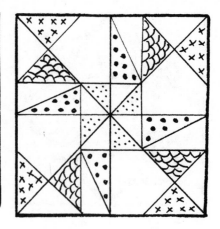

CAT AND MICE

The Perfect Patchwork Primer,
page 96
Also **BEGGAR'S BLOCKS**

HEATHER SQUARE

Nancy Cabot

PINWHEEL STAR

The Perfect Patchwork Primer,
page 98

*The Romance of the Patch-
work Quilt in America,* page
86, No. 3
Nancy Cabot

ROLLING PIN-WHEEL

Ladies Art Company, No. 253

ROLLING PINWHEEL

Ladies Art Company, No. 255
*The Romance of the Patch-
work Quilt in America,* page
80, No. 12

MRS. MORGAN'S CHOICE

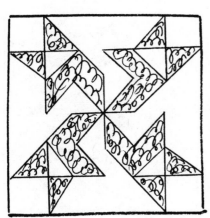

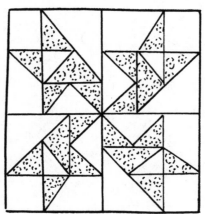

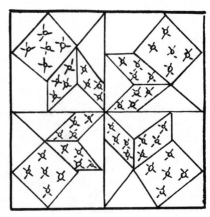

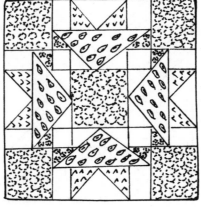

CROWN OF THORNS

CROW'S FOOT

Ladies Art Company, No. 118
Nancy Page
The Romance of the Patch-work Quilt in America, page 74, No. 17
Also **SUGAR BOWL**

COLUMNS

The Perfect Patchwork Primer, page 78

Old Patchwork Quilts and the Women Who Made Them, page 70
One Hundred and One Patchwork Patterns, page 93
The Romance of the Patchwork Quilt in America, page 70, No. 19
In 1845 the controversial question of the annexation of Texas wrecked the political hopes of Calhoun of South Carolina and Clay of Kentucky. James Knox Polk, a dark horse, became the 11th President of the United States. This quilt pattern was named for Henry Clay. It is also known as **HARRY'S STAR**, **HENRY OF THE WEST**, and **STAR OF THE WEST**.

Old Patchwork Quilts and the Women Who Made Them, page 107
The Romance of the Patchwork Quilt in America, page 68, No. 5
Also **CROSS AND CROWN**

The Standard Book of Quilt Making and Collecting, page 231

CLAY'S CHOICE

CROWN AND CROSS

CROWNED CROSS

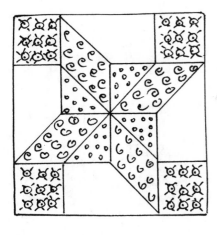

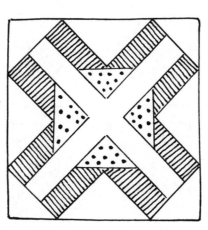

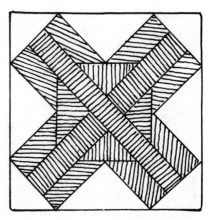

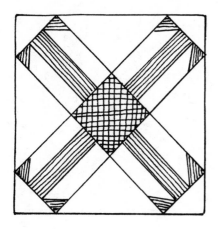

BOXED T'S

Ladies Art Company, No. 379

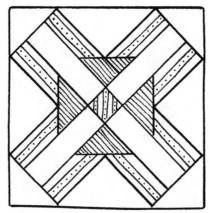

TEXAS TEARS

Ladies Art Company, No. 105
The Romance of the Patch-work Quilt in America, page 100, No. 16

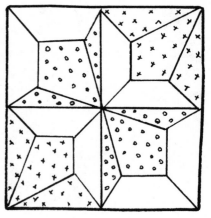

DOUBLE TULIP

From Greek mythology. Dates around 1870's. Gordius, King of Phrygia, was said to have tied an oxen to his chariot with a knot that had no beginning or end and dedicated the cart, oxen, and knot to Zeus. An oracle had promised the empire of Asia to anyone who could untie the knot. Alexander the Great, wanting to prove he was destined to conquer the world, tried to untie it. He then became impatient and slashed it in two with his sword. From that time the saying "to cut the Gordian knot" has meant to solve problems using drastic means.

Nancy Cabot

WEAVING PATHS

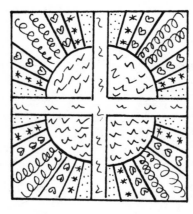

Kansas City Star, 1931
The Romance of the Patch-work Quilt in America, page 70, No. 3

REBECCA'S FAN

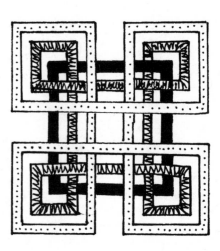

GORDIAN KNOT

GREEK CROSS

One Hundred and One Patchwork Patterns, page 61
The Romance of the Patchwork Quilt in America, page 68, No. 10
The Standard Book of Quilt Making and Collecting, page 233

VICE PRESIDENT'S QUILT

Ladies Art Company, No. 298

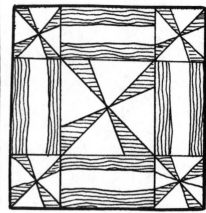

TANGLED LINES

Ladies Art Company, No. 22

Ladies Art Company, No. 522

MISSOURI PUZZLE

The Romance of the Patchwork Quilt in America, page 82, No. 7
Also **CATS AND MICE**

BEGGAR'S BLOCKS

Ladies Art Company, No. 377
The Romance of the Patchwork Quilt in America, page 82, No. 22

ALL KINDS

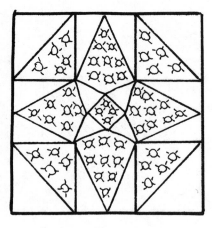

CHINESE SQUARE

Farm Journal and *Farmer's Wife,* 1942

ROYAL CROSS

The Romance of the Patchwork Quilt in America, page 68, No. 2
The Standard Book of Quilt Making and Collecting, page 251

LITTLE ROCK BLOCK

Ladies Art Company, No. 475

The Romance of the Patchwork Quilt in America, page 80, No. 10

The Romance of the Patchwork Quilt in America, page 82, No. 2

Ladies Art Company, No. 128

THELMA'S CHOICE

OCTAGON TILE

GRANDMOTHER'S DREAM

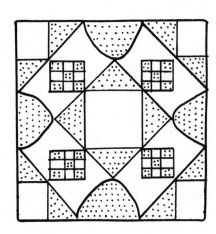

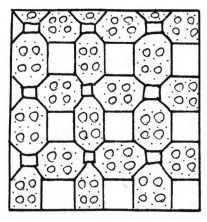

FISH

Old-Fashioned Quilts, page 6

FISH IN THE DISH

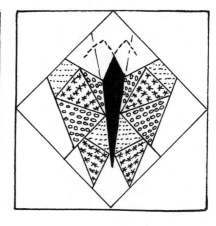

BUTTERFLY

The Household Magazine,
August 1934, page 23

**OLD FASHIONED
BUTTERFLY**

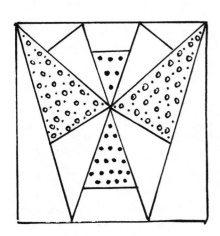

HERRINGBONE

Kansas City Star, 1941

CHEVRON

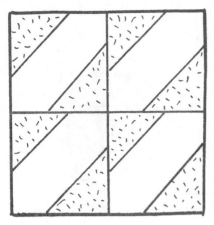

INDIAN HATCHET

Ladies Art Company, No. 20
One Hundred and One Patch-work Patterns, page 89
Nancy Page

 *(positioned under LETTER X)*

LETTER X

The Romance of the Patch-work Quilt in America, page 84, No. 13
The Standard Book of Quilt Making and Collecting, page 233

NEXT DOOR NEIGHBOR

The Perfect Patchwork Primer, page 79

Ladies Art Company, No. 26
The Romance of the .Patch-work Quilt in America, page 70, No. 4
One Hundred and One Patch-work Patterns, page 122
The Standard Book of Quilt Making and Collecting, page 237

DUTCHMAN'S PUZZLE

Ladies Art Company, No. 18

MOSAIC

Ladies Art Company, No. 239
One Hundred and One Patch-work Patterns, page 109
The Romance of the Patch-work Quilt in America, page 77, No. 4

ROAD TO OKLAHOMA

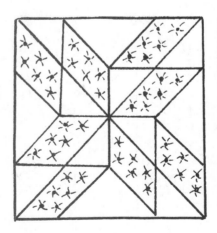

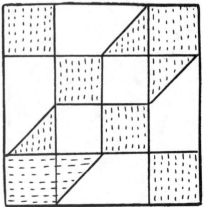

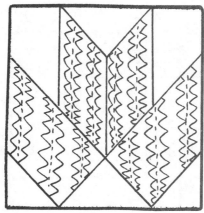

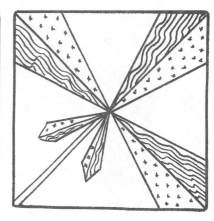

TEA LEAVES

Quilts: Their Story and How to Make Them, plate after page 64
Also **BAY LEAF**

TEA LEAF

The Perfect Patchwork Primer, page 88

STATE OF OHIO

The Romance of the Patchwork Quilt in America, page 100, No. 3
Also **BUCKEYE LEAF**

Laura Wheeler

Ladies Art Company, No. 412

ALICE'S FAVORITE

LOVER'S KNOT

CUBE LATTICE

CENTURY OF PROGRESS

SPIDER'S DEN

Ladies Art Company, No. 190

DUTCH WINDMILL

Old Fashioned Quilts, page 8
Kansas City Star
Also **DUTCH ROSE, HEARTS AND GIZZARDS**

Kansas City Star
Nancy Cabot
The original name for this pattern was **HEARTS AND GIZZARDS.** Also called **DUTCH WINDMILL.**

DUTCH ROSE

Ladies Art Company, No. 170

DOVER QUILT BLOCK

Grandmother Clark's Patchwork Quilt Designs, Book 21, 1931

BROKEN SQUARES

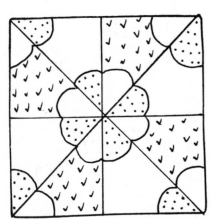

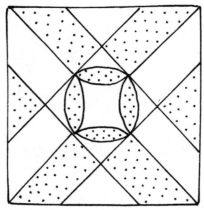

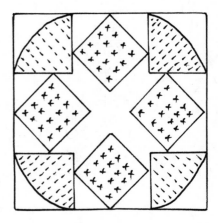

MISS JACKSON

Ladies Art Company, No. 479

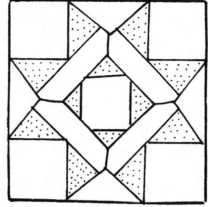

NO NAME QUILT

Ladies Art Company, No. 169

MANY POINTED STAR

Ladies Art Company, No. 451
The Romance of the Patch-work Quilt in America, page 72, No. 6
The Standard Book of Quilt Making and Collecting, page 242

DUTCH MILL

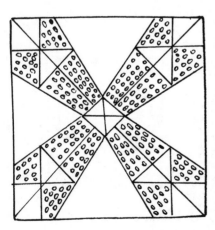

Ladies Art Company, No. 200

THE MAYFLOWER

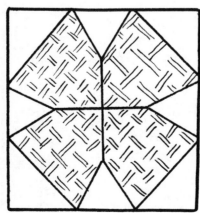

Ladies Art Company, No. 173

GREEK CROSS

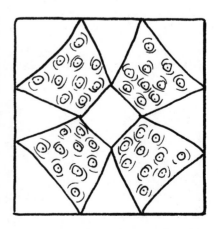

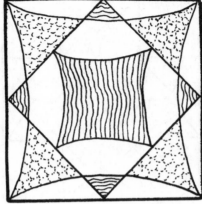

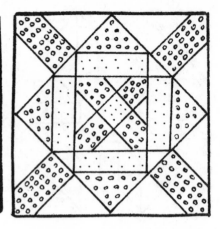

SECRET DRAWER

PENELOPE'S FAVORITE

CENTURY OF PROGRESS

The Romance of the Patch-work Quilt in America, page 84, No. 1. Also **SPOOLS.**

The Standard Book of Quilt Making and Collecting, page 250

Nancy Cabot

Ladies Art Company, No. 259

The Romance of the Patch-work Quilt in America, page 80, No. 6

CORNER POSTS

FOOL'S SQUARE

MISSOURI PUZZLE

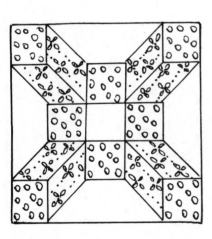

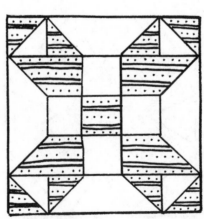

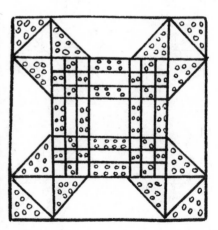

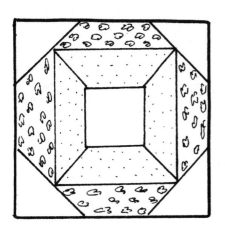

THE KITCHEN WOODBOX   **WIND BLOWN SQUARE**   **INTERLOCKED SQUARES**

Ond Hundred and One Patch-work Patterns, page 73
The Romance of the Patch-work Quilt in America, page 90, No. 18

Modern Patchwork, page 48
THIRTEEN SQUARES   **RIGHT ANGLES PATCHWORK**   **CRAZY QUILT**

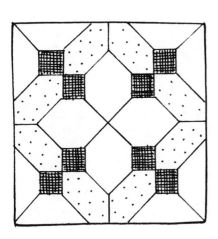

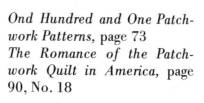

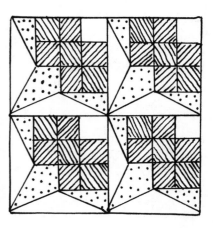

CRAZY QUILT BOUQUET

Nancy Cabot

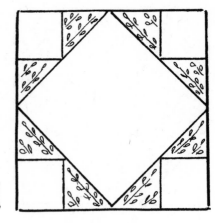

LINDY'S PLANE

ART SQUARE

Ladies Art Company, No. 324

Nancy Page, 1920-30

CASTLES IN SPAIN

Nancy Page, 1920-30

CONNECTICUT

CATHEDRAL WINDOW

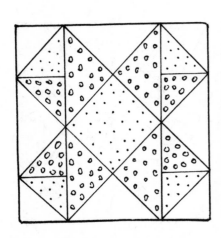

TARGET

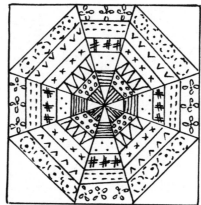

MYSTIC MAZE

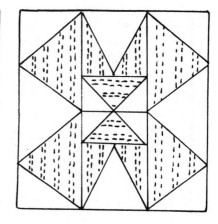

DOUBLE Z

Ladies Art Company, No. 192
*The Romance of the Patch-
work Quilt in America,* page
86, No. 10

The Perfect Patchwork Primer,
page 93

BOW

*One Hundred and One Patch-
work Patterns,* page 43

SPOOL

*The Romance of the Patch-
work Quilt in America,* page
68, No. 20

OLD KING'S CROWN

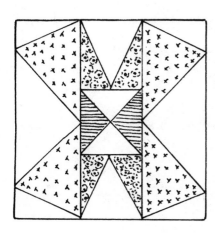

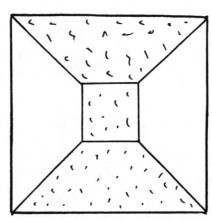

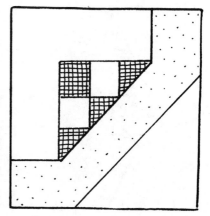

FRIENDSHIP NAME CHAIN

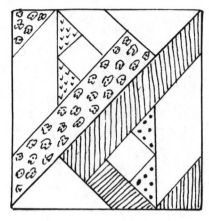

CHINESE PUZZLE

The Romance of the Patch-work Quilt in America, page 80, No. 1

STAR OF BETHLEHEM

Ladies Art Company, No. 3 *The Standard Book of Quilt Making and Collecting,* page 249

Kansas City Star, 1935

ARKANSAS SNOW FLAKE

Kansas City Star, 1941

STAR SPANGLED BANNER

Ladies Art Company, No. 528 Nancy Cabot

STARLIGHT

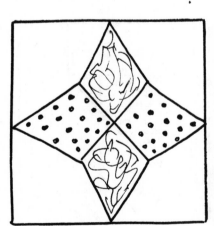

CUPID'S ARROW POINT

Kansas City Star, 1929

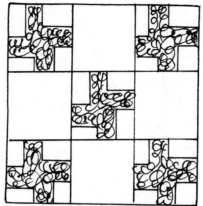

ILLINOIS ROAD

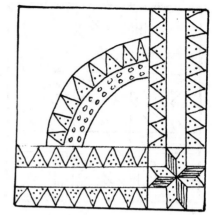

CROWN OF THORNS

The Romance of the Patchwork Quilt in America, page 82, No. 9
Also **NEW YORK BEAUTY, ROCKY MOUNTAIN ROAD**

Ladies Art Company, No. 134

THE WORLD'S FAIR

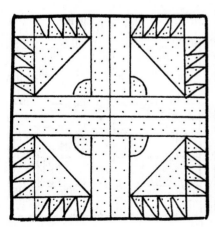

Ladies Art Company, No. 14

DRUNKARD'S PATCHWORK

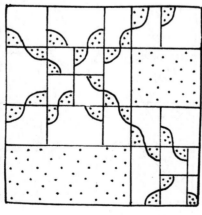

One Hundred and One Patchwork Patterns, page 71
The Romance of the Patchwork Quilt in America, page 72, No. 5

OCEAN WAVE

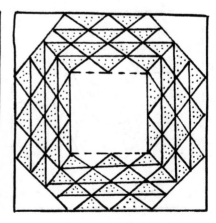

BRIGHT STAR

Nancy Cabot

SWASTIKA

Grandmother Clark's Patch-work Quilt Designs, Book 20, 1931

TENNESSEE CIRCLE

STAR OF THE SEA

FOX CHASE

NOSE GAY

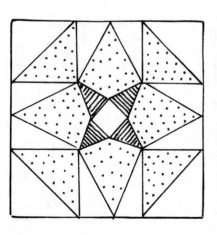

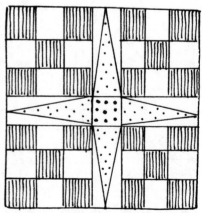

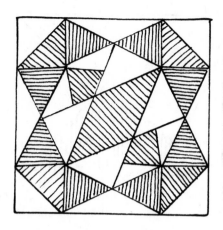

DOVE IN THE WINDOW

Old Patchwork Quilts and the Women Who Made Them, page 115

Ladies Art Company, No. 135

STORM AT SEA

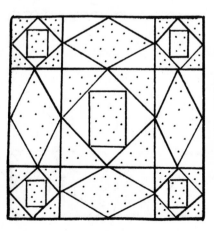

KING'S CROWN

Progressive Farmer

Quilts: Their Story and How to Make Them, page 96, plate. *The Romance of the Patchwork Quilt in America,* page 56, No. 5
Also **SAW TOOTH, STAR OF BETHLEHEM, TWINKLING STAR.** When it is pieced with a hexagon in the center it is known as **CALIFORNIA STAR.**

FEATHER STAR

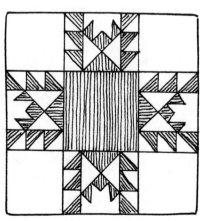

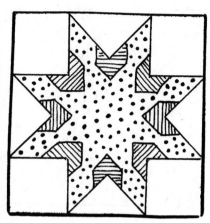

VIRGINIA'S STAR

The Standard Book of Quilt Making and Collecting, page 249

Ladies Art Company, No. 515
Nancy Cabot

MERRY KITE

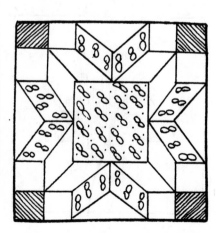

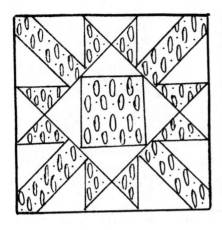

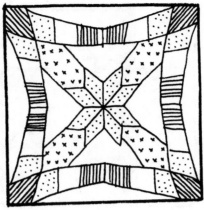

TURNABOUT T

PEGGY-ANNE'S SPECIAL

SWALLOWS FLIGHT

The Romance of the Patch-work Quilt in America, page 86, No. 11

1936

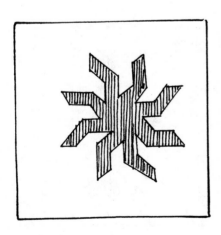

Ladies Art Company, No. 97
The Romance of the Patch-work Quilt in America, page 52, No. 14

Old Fashioned Quilts, page 14

SPIDER LEGS

ICE CREAM BOWL

WATER GLASS

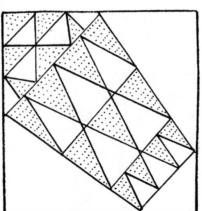

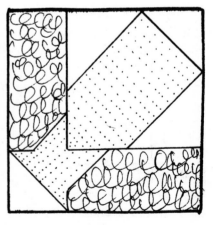

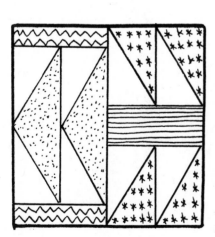

SHADOW TRAIL

EVERGREEN TREE

Progressive Farmer

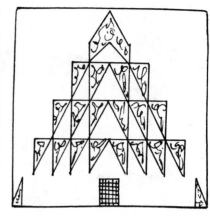

PINE TREE

Ladies Art Company, No. 405
The Romance of the Patch-work Quilt in America, page 100, No. 2
Nancy Cabot

The Romance of the Patch-work Quilt in America, page 102, No. 9

TALL PINE TREE

Ladies Art Company, No. 492

PHILADELPHIA PATCH

1937

THE KITE

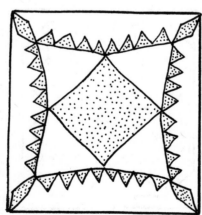

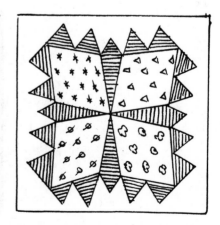

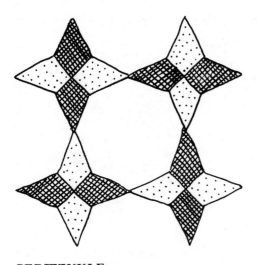

PERIWINKLE

Also **CRAZY STAR QUILT**

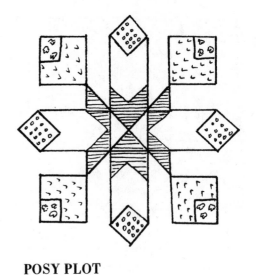

POSY PLOT

Needlecraft Magazine,
February 1934, page 8

Kansas City Star, 1936

MISSOURI WONDER

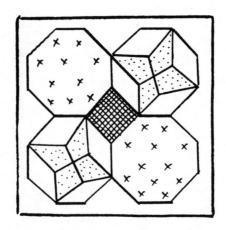

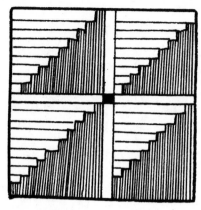

LOG CABIN — BARN RAISING

See page 173.

Index

S=Square   R=Rectangle   D=Diamond   C=Circle   H=Hexagon   A=Applique   M=Miscellaneous

S=Square   R=Rectangle   D=Diamond   C=Circle   H=Hexagon   A=Applique   M=Miscellaneous

S=Square   R=Rectangle   D=Diamond   C=Circle   H=Hexagon   A=Applique   M=Miscellaneous

S=Square   R=Rectangle   D=Diamond   C=Circle   H=Hexagon   A=Applique   M=Miscellaneous

460/Index

S=Square   R=Rectangle   D=Diamond   C=Circle   H=Hexagon   A=Applique   M=Miscellaneous

S=Square   R=Rectangle   D=Diamond   C=Circle   H=Hexagon   A=Applique   M=Miscellaneous

S=Square   R=Rectangle   D=Diamond   C=Circle   H=Hexagon   A=Applique   M=Miscellaneous

S=Square   R=Rectangle   D=Diamond   C=Circle   H=Hexagon   A=Applique   M=Miscellaneous

S=Square   R=Rectangle   D=Diamond   C=Circle   H=Hexagon   A=Applique   M=Miscellaneous

S=Square   R=Rectangle   D=Diamond   C=Circle   H=Hexagon   A=Applique   M=Miscellaneous

S=Square   R=Rectangle   D=Diamond   C=Circle   H=Hexagon   A=Applique   M=Miscellaneous

S=Square   R=Rectangle   D=Diamond   C=Circle   H=Hexagon   A=Applique   M=Miscellaneous

S=Square   R=Rectangle   D=Diamond   C=Circle   H=Hexagon   A=Applique   M=Miscellaneous

S=Square   R=Rectangle   D=Diamond   C=Circle   H=Hexagon   A=Applique   M=Miscellaneous

S=Square   R=Rectangle   D=Diamond   C=Circle   H=Hexagon   A=Applique   M=Miscellaneous

S=Square   R=Rectangle   D=Diamond   C=Circle   H=Hexagon   A=Applique   M=Miscellaneous

S=Square   R=Rectangle   D=Diamond   C=Circle   H=Hexagon   A=Applique   M=Miscellaneous

S=Square   R=Rectangle   D=Diamond   C=Circle   H=Hexagon   A=Applique   M=Miscellaneous

S=Square   R=Rectangle   D=Diamond   C=Circle   H=Hexagon   A=Applique   M=Miscellaneous

S=Square   R=Rectangle   D=Diamond   C=Circle   H=Hexagon   A=Applique   M=Miscellaneous

S=Square   R=Rectangle   D=Diamond   C=Circle   H=Hexagon   A=Applique   M=Miscellaneous

S=Square   R=Rectangle   D=Diamond   C=Circle   H=Hexagon   A=Applique   M=Miscellaneous

S=Square   R=Rectangle   D=Diamond   C=Circle   H=Hexagon   A=Applique   M=Miscellaneous

S=Square   R=Rectangle   D=Diamond   C=Circle   H=Hexagon   A=Applique   M=Miscellaneous

S=Square   R=Rectangle   D=Diamond   C=Circle   H=Hexagon   A=Applique   M=Miscellaneous

S=Square   R=Rectangle   D=Diamond   C=Circle   H=Hexagon   A=Applique   M=Miscellaneous

S=Square   R=Rectangle   D=Diamond   C=Circle   H=Hexagon   A=Applique   M=Miscellaneous

S=Square   R=Rectangle   D=Diamond   C=Circle   H=Hexagon   A=Applique   M=Miscellaneous

S=Square   R=Rectangle   D=Diamond   C=Circle   H=Hexagon   A=Applique   M=Miscellaneous

S=Square   R=Rectangle   D=Diamond   C=Circle   H=Hexagon   A=Applique   M=Miscellaneous

S=Square   R=Rectangle   D=Diamond   C=Circle   H=Hexagon   A=Applique   M=Miscellaneous

S=Square   R=Rectangle   D=Diamond   C=Circle   H=Hexagon   A=Applique   M=Miscellaneous